THE LE
Guide to
MASONIC SYMBOLS

The Role of Freemasonry in
Understanding Human Symbolism

THE LEWIS
Guide to
MASONIC SYMBOLS

The Role of Freemasonry in
Understanding Human Symbolism

ROBERT LOMAS

www.robertlomas.com
www.bradford.ac.uk/webofhiram
@Dr_Robert_Lomas

Lewis Masonic

*Dedicated to
my Daughter and Son-in-Law*

First published 2013

ISBN 9780853184362

All rights reserved. No part of this book may be reproduced or transmitted in any form or by any means, electronic or mechanical, including photocopying, recording, scanning or by any information storage and retrieval system, on the internet or elsewhere, without permission from the Publisher in writing.

© Robert Lomas 2013

Illustrations ©Alex and Delyth Jamieson – All Rights Reserved

Published by Lewis Masonic

an imprint of Ian Allan Publishing Ltd, Hersham, Surrey KT12 4RG

Printed and bound by
CPI Group (UK) Ltd, Croydon, CR0 4YY

Visit the Lewis Masonic website at
www.lewismasonic.co.uk

Distributed in the United States of America and Canada by BookMasters Distribution Services.

Copyright
Illegal copying and selling of publications deprives authors, publishers and booksellers of income, without which there would be no investment in new publications. Unauthorised versions of publications are also likely to be inferior in quality and contain incorrect information. You can help by reporting copyright infringements and acts of piracy to the Publisher or the UK Copyright Service.

Contents

INTRODUCTION	The Hidden Influence of Ancient Symbols	9
PART ONE	**The Secret Influence of Symbols**	13
CHAPTER 1	Why Symbols Are More Powerful Than Words	15
	Symbols Made Us Human	15
	Symbols Began in Dark Caves	17
	The Heaven of Perfect Symbols	19
	How Humans Learned to Live with Symbols	21
	The Ancient Symbols Still Work	21
	Pictures Can Transfer Thoughts	24
	Symbols Taught Us How to Think	26
CHAPTER 2	How Symbols Turned Hunters into Farmers	28
	Symbols Let Us Communicate with the Dead	28
	Symbols Helped Hunters	30
	Symbols Taught Farming	32
	Ancient Symbols Found in a Birthing Chamber	35
CHAPTER 3	How Symbols Created Kingdoms	42
	The Importance of Counting	42
	The First Symbols	46
	The Symbol of Newgrange	46
	The Importance of Writing Symbols	47
	Fortune Favours the Symbol Writer	51
	A New Alphabet Appears	52
CHAPTER 4	The Power of Symbols on the Human Brain	54
	Humans Have Two Minds	54
	Symbols Have Sex Appeal	56
	The Influence of Stone Symbols	58
	Stone Symbols Have Sacred Power	59
CHAPTER 5	How Symbols Created Freemasonry	62
	Symbols and Myth Work Together	62
	Buildings Are Symbols	62
	How the True Cross Inspired the First Freemasons	64
	How Symbols Taught the First Freemasons	67
	The Emotional Power of Symbols	68
	How Symbolic Teaching Spread	72

Chapter 6	Symbols Can Penetrate the Mind of God	76
	A Symbol that Analyses Equality	76
	Masonic Slide Rules and Early Arithmetic	77
	Why Equations Are a Mystery	79
	The Great Architect	80
	Symbols Are the Key to the Mind of God	81
	The Heaven of Pure Symbols	83
Chapter 7	The Secret Symbol of Political Stability	87
	The Pillars that Inspired Republicanism	87
	The Pillars that Formed Freemasonry	90
	The Symbols that Taught George Washington	92
	The Masonic Meaning of the Two Pillars	93
	The Pillars that Established Ancient Egypt	95
	The Pillars and the Concubines	98
	The Pillars that Influenced the English Civil War	99
	The Pillars that Support the U.S. Presidents	100
	The Pillars that Reconciled Britain and America	100
Part Two	A Practical Introduction to Masonic Symbology	103
Chapter 8	Symbols of the First Degree	105
	The Square	105
	The Level	106
	The Plumb Rule	107
	The Altar	108
	The Volume of the Sacred Law	109
	The Compasses	110
	The Sun	111
	The Moon and Stars	112
	The North East Corner	113
	The Glory at the Centre	114
	The Left-Hand Pillar	115
	The Master of the Lodge	116
	The 24-inch Gauge	118
	The Common Gavel	119
	The Chisel	120
	The Form of the Lodge	121
	The Pillar of Wisdom	122
	The Pillar of Strength	123
	The Pillar of Beauty	124

	The Celestial Canopy 125
	Jacob's Ladder 126
	Faith 127
	Hope 128
	Charity 129
	The Mosaic Pavement 130
	The Blazing Star 131
	The Indented or Tessellated Border 132
	The Tracing Board 133
	The Rough Ashlar 134
	The Perfect Ashlar 135
	The Point Within a Circle 136
	Chalk, Charcoal, and Clay 137
	The Lewis 138
	The Square and Compasses, Both Points Covered 139
CHAPTER 9	SYMBOLS OF THE SECOND DEGREE 140
	The Square and Compasses, One Point Covered 140
	The Right-Hand Pillar 141
	The Two Pillars at the Entrance to King Solomon's Temple 142
	The Chapiters 143
	The Net-work 144
	The Lily-work 145
	The Pomegranates 146
	The Globes 147
	The Middle Chamber 148
	The Spiral Staircase 149
	The Wages 150
	An Ear of Corn near a Pool of Water 151
	The Five Noble Orders of Architecture 152
CHAPTER 10	SYMBOLS OF THE THIRD DEGREE 155
	The Square and Compasses, Both Points Revealed 155
	The Open Grave 156
	The Perfect Cube 157
	The Porch 158
	The Dormer 159
	The Square Pavement 160
	The Scurret 161
	The Pencil 162

	The Compasses	163
	The Sprig of Acacia	164
	The Emblems of Mortality	165
	The Bright Morning Star	166
CHAPTER 11	GENERAL SYMBOLS OF THE WIDER CRAFT	167
	The Equilateral Triangle	167
	The Double Triangle (The Seal of Solomon)	168
	The Triple Tau	169
	The Triangle within a Circle	170
	The Keystone	171
	The Vault	172
	The Uncompleted Temple	173
	The Pillars, Circle, and Centre	174
CHAPTER 12	THE TRACING BOARDS	175
	A Personal View of the First Degree Tracing Board	176
	A Personal View of the Second Degree Tracing Board	178
	A Personal View of the Third Degree Tracing Board	180
	A Personal View of the Royal Arch Tracing Board	183
	A View of the Centre	185
APPENDIX	THE STORY OF JOHN HOGG AND THE BIRTH OF THE LEWIS MASONIC IMPRINT	186
ACKNOWLEDGEMENTS		190
ABOUT THE AUTHOR		191
BIBLIOGRAPHY		192

Introduction

The Hidden Influence of Ancient Symbols

Ancient Masonic symbols shaped who we are today, and they can still powerfully affect our life. This book will lead you into that secret symbolic world.

Until recently only a select group of people were aware of the importance of symbols within the fabric of modern western society. This group had received extensive training in the use and power of symbols and been taught how to recognise the influence which could flow from the display of certain secret symbols of power in public places. They knew that the ability to understand symbols is an ancient skill in all humans but the influence of particular symbols on human actions is universal.

Recent popular literature has latched onto this idea and it has become a subject for extremely successful fictional thrillers. In particular, Dan Brown's The Lost Symbol has taken as its main theme the search for a great symbol of power. But is that symbol real? And do symbols really have that power that novelists attribute to them? One group in particular thinks they do and for them the study of symbols has become an important part of their life. It may be coincidence but many members of this group have become prominent figures in the history of humanity. They have helped invent modern science and forged the republics that brought freedom to the masses; they have been at the forefront of scientific development, and they have been influential writers, musicians, industrialists, astronauts, and politicians. But above all they have belonged to a secret Order which has spent the last six hundred years studying the way symbols interact with human beings to bring about progress or disaster. These people are Freemasons. Beginning in the late fifteenth century, Freemasonry described itself as "a peculiar system of morality, veiled by allegory and illuminated by symbols". The purpose of this book is to provide an authoritative guide to the secret symbology of Freemasonry. We will start with a biography of the symbols which have shaped western civilisation and then reveal little-known facts about the influence of these powerful symbols on human society.

Symbols speak to us at a level far deeper than writing. The fundamental ideas of Masonic teaching are deeply rooted in the use of symbols. Some of the symbols Freemasons use date back to the first attempts of the human race to carve symbols into stone. Shapes which Freemasons use in current ceremonies date back over 70,000 years. Some 200,000 years ago humans developed speech, then about 70,000 years ago they discovered a visual language of symbols. And 4,000 years ago those early symbols developed into alphabetic writing as a way to encode speech. It is through symbols that humans have expressed their most abstract ideas. As we will see, modern scientific studies reveal that all humans have deep-rooted emotional reactions to symbols in general, but it is Masonic symbols in particular that evoke the most positive emotional responses.

Symbolic thinking is deep rooted. It began over 70,000 years ago with the first known use of symbols by human beings. These symbols are still in use today and transcend any differences in human language. The first ritual use of symbols can be seen in the shamanistic symbols in the cave paintings of Northern Europe, which were created about 30,000 years ago. In the seventeenth century, symbolism branched out in two ways. One route was the use of loosely defined symbols to create images, emotions, and feelings within a ritual context, and the other was to help the human mind to reason. We call this later route mathematics and it has led to a deep understanding of the world.

There are three main types of symbols:

- Emotive Symbols encode feelings and aspirations. These are the oldest of all symbols and date back 70,000 years. They have been widely used to communicate emotion to illiterate people.
- Speech Symbols encode the sounds of language and enable humans to communicate through time and space. At one time these symbols were tightly restricted to an elite group, often linked to religions.
- Mathematical Symbols encode a means of understanding and predicting reality. Freemasons helped develop algebra and calculus, which in turn produced these counting symbols.

For well over two thousand years, since the time of Plato, many people have believed that a realm of perfect symbols exists. With careful training, an individual can be shown how to communicate with this realm and discover the true nature of these symbols. Plato developed this idea into a theory, which is deeply embedded in Masonic Symbology. It is this Masonic tradition that has preserved and developed the ancient emotive symbols and led to the discovery of mathematical symbols.

Using symbology, Freemasonry has been able to communicate its ideas by means of a unique and universal language. Once an idea has been formulated in symbols it can be transmitted without corruption. This guarantees a continuity of tradition. A modern Mason carries out his symbol work in exactly the same way a Mason of 500 years ago did. The Mason of today faces the same problems that a Mason living in the fifteenth century had to face, and the symbols provide the same answers.

Approximately sixty basic symbols are taught to aspiring Master Masons as they progress through the various degrees of Freemasonry. These symbols are introduced as a Candidate masters each of the successive degrees of the Craft, the Mark, and the Royal Arch. Eventually the symbols are combined into pictorial narratives called Tracing Boards, of which there are four main ones, each conveying different philosophical messages.

The Tracing Boards, which are displayed in British and other European Lodges, are used as visual aids to help with instruction, and also for meditation and reflection.

The importance of these visual summaries of Masonic symbols as an aid to individual understanding of the teachings of the Craft was established by a young Scottish publisher, John Hogg, whose story is told in the Appendix. Hogg published illustrations of the Tracing Boards alongside the words of the ritual to establish a whole new set of standards in Masonic publishing. He wrote under the pen name A Lewis and rather than using the name of his family's long-established publishing company, he used the imprint "Privately Printed for A Lewis".

Bro. Hogg is fondly remembered as the founder of Lewis Masonic, the longest established impendent Masonic Publisher in the world. But he was also the first publisher to realise the importance of illustrating books of Masonic ritual with the symbols and Tracing Boards which are a key part of the teaching of the Craft.

As a Mason himself, Bro. Hogg understood that Masonic symbols evoke emotions which cannot be conveyed by language alone. They also have an allegorical role, and surface on everyday items from bank notes to jewellery, and in the façades of state buildings. But the symbols studied by Freemasons have an even larger influence: the symbols of mathematics are used to manipulate conceptual abstractions. Two of the most influential mathematical thinkers, John Wallis (who invented algebra), and Isaac Newton (who invented calculus and physics), received Masonic instruction in the use of symbols.

Freemasonry's secret method of symbolic teaching, which it describes as "illumination by symbols", has exerted a powerful influence on key individuals in history. Why, for example, do U.S. presidents make a Masonic sign during their inauguration? It is because the first President of the U.S. was a Freemason and he deliberately introduced key items of Masonic symbolism into his inauguration. But the symbolic teaching of Freemasonry has been felt throughout history:

- Oliver Cromwell, first Lord Protector of the Republican Commonwealth of Great Britain, chose to have himself portrayed standing between the two porchway pillars of Freemasonry.
- The Masonically inspired French Revolution adopted the great tripartite motto of "Liberty, Equality, Fraternity", which is one of the sets of symbolic names given to three working pillars of the Masonic Lodge, portrayed symbolically as Doric, Ionic, and Corinthian.
- The great statement of intent "No taxation, without representation" was generated by the brethren of St. Andrews Lodge, Boston, and became the spark which kindled the greatest Masonic document of all times, the American Constitution. The idea for a written constitution came from the actions of Bro. Ben Franklin.

For over five hundred years the Symbology of Freemasonry has fostered a secret stream of radical ideas running just beneath the surface of popular culture. These ideas, illuminated by public symbols hidden in full view, have influenced and shaped the society we live in.

The earliest statement of Masonic aims and objectives was created as a crude set of symbols, known as the Kirkwall Scroll, drawn in the late fifteenth century. These symbols, which had been drawn and redrawn since men first discovered how to make marks on rocks, were painted on sailcloth and laid on the floor of the first Freemason's Lodges to teach the brethren. Since then, Freemasons have displayed and taught the hidden meaning of these symbols. Freemasons have long known that continual exposure to symbols changes the way people think.

The symbols have been used by three major republics, whose leaders were all inspired by the symbolic import of Brotherhood, Relief and Truth. The emotive power of these symbols remind people of basic truths about the human condition.

Despite these significant facts, no definitive guidebook to Masonic Symbology has been published, and the story of these symbols has remained mysterious. Until now.

In this book the heritage of A. Lewis has been applied to furthering the pioneering work of Bro. John Hogg and his illustrators to encourage daily steps in Masonic knowledge.

The book is divided into parts. Part One explains the history and origin of symbols and shows how they have interacted with humanity over the ages, while Part Two is a visual encyclopaedia of the Masonic teaching about symbols.

Part One

The Secret Influence of Symbols

For two thousand years, since the time of the philosopher Plato, people have understood that there is a source of pure symbols existing in a spiritual realm of perfection. Plato taught that, with careful training, an individual could be shown how to communicate with this realm and discover the true nature of these symbols. He developed a way to investigate the truth carried by shapes that is deeply embedded in Masonic symbology.

The first Freemasons were stoneworkers, employed to carve symbols of religious power into public places of worship. They recognised the power of symbols and realised that symbols were able to influence people's thoughts and actions. They studied the ancient symbols and learned how they had influenced the development of human thought.

The Masonic tradition preserved and developed the ancient emotive symbols and from its practice of symbolic reasoning created an environment which influenced the advancement of society. This book shares secret knowledge that has taken five hundred years to learn.

Chapter 1

Why Symbols Are More Powerful Than Words

Symbols Made Us Human

A symbol is a pictorial device which evokes a concept in its entirety. It bypasses the intellect and talks straight to the heart. Our intellect analyses but our heart synthesises. So a symbol evokes understanding without needing to convey verbal information.

Around 120,000 years ago, a new species of primate appeared in Africa. Its scientific name is Homo sapiens, but we know this creature as the modern human. When our species appeared there were other similar but more widespread species of humanoid apes around, such as the Neanderthals. Yet Homo sapiens were different. We were different because we could tap into a mystic power of understanding that is inherent in symbols. Symbols have helped us develop a unique form of consciousness that no other animal has.

All the races of humans are much more closely related than most of us realise. You might be even more surprised to know how closely we are related to our primate cousins, the African apes. Our genes are about 98 percent identical to those of an ape, and we share large chunks of our DNA sequence with all other life forms on Earth, even bacteria.[1] All humans are descended from a single female who lived in Africa less than 200,000 years ago. She is popularly called 'Mitochondrial Eve'.[2] As geneticist Bryan Sykes puts it:

'Mitochondrial Eve'... lies at the root of all the maternal ancestries of every one of the six billion people in the world. We are all her direct maternal descendants.[3]

Our common maternal ancestor lived only a few thousand generations ago. And her earliest descendants drew the first symbols and tapped into their power.

In the following chapters, you will learn about the power of these symbols, the history of their interaction with us, and how humanity's differential advantage came about because we

---

1 Dawkins, R. *The Ancestor's Tale*. London: Weidenfield and Nicolson. 2005 p. 25.
2 Cann R. et al "L Polymorphic sites and the mechanism of evolution in human mitochondrial DNA", *Genetics*, vol. 106, pp 479-99, 1984.
3 Sykes, B. *The Seven Daughters of Eve*. London: Bantam, 2001, p. 336.

evolved a type of brain which benefits from a direct relationship with them. This symbiotic relationship began during our early evolutionary history and continues to influence our development in ways most of us are often unaware of.

There is, however, a secret group of specialists who have spent the last 500 years working with these symbols. They learned how symbols can advance the human condition by enabling us to share understanding. This group is the Freemasons and their declared purpose is to study and understand symbols.

Ask any Freemason the question "What is Freemasonry?" and you will get the answer, "A peculiar system of morality, veiled in allegory, and illustrated by symbols." For 500 years, Freemasonry has used a system of allegorical ritual and exposure to the mystic power of symbols to sensitise its members to the life-changing power these symbols have. They continue to experience the deep understanding that symbols can inspire and their power to change the way humans develop.

When humans were first exposed to the mystic power of symbols, they changed us from brute animals into human beings in a way we still struggle to understand. James Shreeve, a well-known anthropologist, sums up the puzzle presented by this abrupt change.

Human beings – modern humans, *Homo sapiens* – are behaviourally far, far away from being 'just another animal.' The mystery is where, how, and why this change took place... An 'all-important transition' did occur, but it happened so close to the present moment that we are still reeling from it. Something happened that turned a passably precocious animal into a human being.[4]

Anthropology records how and when this change happened but offers no explanation. It is my contention that humanity came into contact with a powerful force outside itself, which has interacted with our collective mind ever since. This force is carried and communicated by symbols. In later chapters, we will discover that symbols are part of a great cosmic language which transmits deep understanding about the secrets of the universe.

In 1995, when James Shreeve wrote the statement above, it was thought that humanity's relationship with symbols began only 30,000 years ago in the deep dark caves of Northern Europe. Then much earlier evidence of the power of symbols came to light in a cave in southern Africa. *The Times* of London reported it:

A pair of decorated ornaments unearthed in a South African cave has been dated at more than 70,000 years old, proving that human beings could think abstractly and appreciate beauty much earlier than is generally accepted.

The engraved pieces of ochre, a type of iron ore, are by far the oldest examples of symbolic art – a standard benchmark for recognisably modern thought and behaviour. The earliest similar objects, from Europe, were made less than 35,000 years ago, and subtle intelligence is usually held to have begun at this time.

The find at Blombos Cave, 180 miles from Cape Town in the Western Cape, will therefore completely revise one of the first chapters of human history.

It indicates that not only did the first human beings evolve in Africa and spread throughout the world, but that they became mentally sophisticated by the time they did so.

This helps to explain the ease with which *Homo sapiens* supplanted other human relatives, such as the Neanderthals in Europe, and thus the development of the modern human race.

---

[4] Shreeve, James. *The Neanderthal Enigma*. William Morrow & Co, 1995.

All the anatomical features of *Homo sapiens* are known to have evolved in Africa between 150,000 and 130,000 years ago, but the question of when the species began to behave in modern fashion has remained more elusive.

The Blombos Cave, discovered by Professor Chris Henshilwood of the Iziko South African Museum in Cape Town, resolves the debate decisively.[5]

I am a Freemason and have been trained in the Masonic system of symbol sensitisation, and when I saw the image these long-dead humans had carved I recognised it immediately. Here is a sketch of the symbols.

I know them as the Masonic lozenge. It is an image I see every time I look at the floor of my Masonic Lodge, or at a Masonic Tracing Board.

---

[5] Henderson, M. "Scratches that trace the ascent of man", *The Times*, Friday Jan 11, 2002, p 5.

Symbols Began in Dark Caves

That ancient primeval lozenge symbol is alive and well today. If you look around you will see it built into the façades of buildings, in the logos embroidered into sports clothing, and mounted on the bonnets of cars. Why has it been drawn and redrawn for 70,000 years? Because simply looking at it creates emotions and insight, deep in our unconscious minds that we enjoy, so we respond to its power and feel good about it.

After this first symbol there are large gaps in the archaeological evidence of the interaction of symbols with humans until our ancestors starting drawing pictures on the walls of the caves of Europe some 40,000 years later. Those early humans kept their relationship with symbols a secret. They did not display the symbols on their buildings, clothing, and possessions, but they crawled miles underground into distant dark caves to experience the deep pleasure of seeing the symbols by the flickering flames of simple torches. We did not find evidence of the symbols our ancient ancestors painted on rock walls until 1879. The first to be recognised were images of bison on the walls of a cave at Altamira, in Spain. Then further symbols were found in caves at La Mouthe, and Tuc d'Audoubert in France.

These symbols were hidden deep underground, far along narrow tunnels thousands of metres long. Their purpose could never have been public display. They were difficult to reach and needed the use of unreliable rush lights and burning brands (the remains of which were found in the caves) to see them. The humans who drew them needed great courage to venture into those dark depths with only a flickering, feeble light to guide them. Yet they did struggle through these tunnels to draw a wide range of symbols. Historian of prehistoric art David Lewis-Williams describes them:

> [There are] animals, such as bison, horses, aurochs, woolly mammoths, deer and felines... There are also occasional anthropomorphic figures that may or may not represent human beings. Some of these are therianthropes (part-human, part-animal figures)... Then there is an image type that is exceptional in the way that it is made – handprints. Finally, there is a multiplicity of signs, geometric forms such as grids, dots, and chevrons.[6]

It is not the drawings of beasts or people which have had the most influence on humans. Those "geometric forms" are the symbols that really affect us, by driving our emotional responses and evoking an understanding of concepts that we struggle to put into words.

It is symbols of the type which first appeared at Blombos that show the continuing interaction between the evolving human mind and the evocative shapes of the symbols.

Analytical psychologist Carl Gustav Jung confirms that symbols speak to us of "things beyond the range of human understanding". They tap into a source of knowledge that is not normally accessible to our conscious minds. Jung defined such symbols as:

> [A] term, a name or an image that may be familiar in daily life, yet it possesses specific connotations in addition to its conventional meanings. It implies something vague, unknown or hidden from us... Thus a word or an image is symbolic when it implies something more than its obvious and immediate meaning. It has a wider 'unconscious' aspect that is never precisely defined or fully explained. Nor can one hope to define or explain it. As the mind explores the symbol it is led to ideas that lie beyond the grasp of reason... Because there are innumerable things beyond the range of human understanding, we constantly use symbolic terms to represent concepts that we cannot define or fully comprehend.[7]

He goes on to expand this idea, saying:

> There are unconscious aspects of our perception of reality... even when our senses react to real phenomena, sights,

---

6 Lewis-Williams, D. *The Mind in the Cave*. London: Thames & Hudson, p. 29.

7 Jung, C. G. *Man and His Symbols*. London: Aldus, 1964.

and sounds, they are somehow translated from the realm of reality into that of the mind. Within the mind they become psychic events, whose ultimate nature is unknowable (for the psyche cannot know its own psychical substance). Thus every experience contains an indefinite number of unknown factors, not to speak of the fact that every concrete object is always unknown in certain respects, because we cannot know the ultimate nature of matter itself.[8]

But what is this knowledge and where does it come from? This is a question which has haunted the human race for at least 2,500 years. The Greek philosopher Plato (427-347 BCE) thought symbols came from a transcendental world of perfect and beautiful forms that can be reached only by the human soul. He believed that the most important human knowledge is recalled by the soul from the time before it was born. He said that if we consider our knowledge of equality we have no difficulty in deciding whether or not two people are equal in height. But they are never exactly the same height. It is always be possible to discover some difference — however minute — with a more careful, precise measurement. All the examples of equality we recognise in ordinary life only approach, but never quite attain, perfect equality. But since we realise truth from our experience, we must somehow know for sure what true equality is, even though we can never see it.[9] This kind of thinking led to the discovery of the symbols of geometry and mathematics, which opened up human understanding of reality.

The Heaven of Perfect Symbols

All the symbols we can see around us are imperfect instances, but we have an inner knowledge of abstract things like truth, goodness, and beauty, as well as equality. These are the Platonic Forms, abstract entities that exist independently of the physical world. Plato said that ordinary objects are imperfect and changeable, but they faintly echo the perfect and immutable forms of their symbols. Later, you will see how many of the key symbols that have influenced human developments are found among these Platonic Forms. Although we can never draw a perfect square, a perfect equilateral triangle or a perfect lozenge, we know what they are because our soul knows their symbolic, perfect form.

Plato argued we cannot possibly have knowledge of these perfect forms through any bodily experience, so our knowledge must be a memory that our souls carry from the transcendental place where the symbols exist in perfect form. Plato, whose ideas inspired part of the Masonic teachings, believed that the world is essentially intelligible, but it is our intellect, not our senses, that have the ultimate "vision" of true being. We understand the

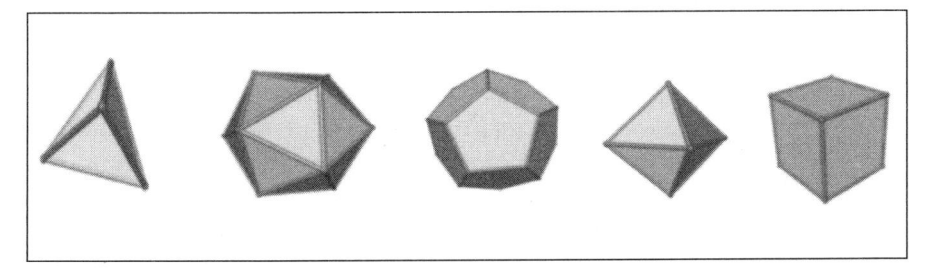

8 *Ibid*   9 Plato, *Phaedo* 75b

world by the deep knowledge that is conveyed into our heart by symbols.

Both Plato and Jung tell of a reality that lies beyond normal human consciousness and which can only be reached through symbols. This symbolic knowledge has a spiritual or transcendental dimension, which has been the subject of Masonic study and teaching over the centuries. Aniela Jaffé, a student of Jung's, confirms that the early cave symbols have a spiritual power:

> Animal pictures go back to the last Ice Age (between 60,000 and 10,000 B.C.E). They were discovered on the walls of caves in France and Spain at the end of the last century, but it was not until early in the present century that archaeologists began to realise their extreme importance and to inquire into their meaning. These inquiries revealed an infinitely remote prehistoric culture whose existence had never even been suspected. Even today, a strange music seems to haunt the caves that contain the rock engravings and paintings. According to the German art historian Herbert Kuhn, inhabitants of the areas in Africa, Spain, France, and Scandinavia where such paintings are found could not be induced to go near the caves. A kind of religious awe, or perhaps a fear of spirits hovering among the rocks and the paintings, held them back. Passing nomads still lay their votive offerings before the old rock paintings in North Africa. In the 15th century, Pope Calixtus II prohibited religious ceremonies in the "cave with the horse pictures". This goes to prove that the caves and rocks with the animal paintings have always been instinctively felt to be what they originally were – religious places. The spiritual power of the place has outlived the centuries.[10]

Jaffé confirms that those symbols were intended to be looked at in secret, to create a sense of awe, and inspire action on the part of the observers. As she explains:

> In a number of caves the modern visitor must travel through low, dark, and damp passages till he reaches the point where the great painted 'chambers' suddenly open out. This arduous approach may express the desire of the primitive men to safeguard from common sight all that was contained and went on in the caves, and to protect their mystery. The sudden and unexpected sight of the paintings in the chambers, coming after the difficult and awe-inspiring approach, must have made an overwhelming impression on primitive man.[11]

Symbols appeared first as secret devices drawn in the hidden confines of caves to be viewed only by those brave enough to venture into their depths. But over the next 25,000 years symbols would come out of the darkness and into the light.

---

10 Jung, C. G (ed). *Man and His Symbols*. London: Aldus, 1964.

11 Jung, C. G (ed). *Man and His Symbols*. London: Aldus, 1964.

How Humans Learned to Live with Symbols

By the early Neolithic age (about 12,000 years ago) symbols were being carved into all sorts of portable artefacts. The late Professor Marija Gimbutas of UCLA made these early portable symbols her lifelong study. She said the most frequently occurring symbols developed an independent life of their own. Wherever humans moved they would engrave certain types of symbols around them, on rocks and on artefacts such as pots or sticks. These symbols were rooted within the consciousness of the people who drew them and, as I show, remain there to this day. Gimbutas said:

> The old European sacred images and symbols are too deeply implanted in the psyche to be uprooted.[12]

These symbols track humanity's evolution from simple hunter-gatherers to sophisticated farmers, and Gimbutas believed it possible to decipher their impact and meaning. She said:

> Symbols are seldom abstract in any genuine sense; their ties with nature persist, to be discovered through the study of context and association. In this way we can hope to decipher the mythical thought which is the *raison d'être* of this art and basis of its form. My primary presupposition is that they can best be understood on their own planes of reference, grouped according to their inner coherence. They constitute a complex system in which every unit is interlocked with every other in what appear to be specific categories. No symbol can be treated in isolation; understanding the parts leads to understanding the whole, which in turn leads to identifying more of the parts.[13]

Gimbutas was right. It is possible to

---

12 Gimbutas, M. *The Language of the Goddess*. London: Thames & Hudson, 2001.
13 *Ibid*

decipher the meanings and import of these enduring symbols. They have a hidden power that they exert on humanity. I discovered this by testing if the deep powers of the ancient symbols still affect modern human minds.

The Ancient Symbols Still Work

To test how deeply these ancient symbols were "implanted" in the psyche of modern humans, I conducted a series of tests on volunteer students to see how they responded to them. I used a technique called Galvanic Skin Response (GSR). GSR measures the degree of emotional arousal which a symbol causes and is founded on the idea that you have no control over what makes you sweat. This made it possible for me to monitor what was happening in parts of the students' brains that they were not consciously aware of. When they felt strong emotions their brains forced them to sweat. Sweat is a good conductor of electricity, so the more they sweated, the easier it became to pass an electric current across the surface of their skin. They weren't consciously aware it was happening, but I was able to measure it.

GSR is one of the key tests that has been used as a lie detector for many years but recently a group of scientists at Wellcome Department of Cognitive Neurology used functional magnetic resonance to scan subject's brains to see exactly which parts of their brain caused these GSR measurable sweats. The areas involved are the left medial prefrontal cortex, bilateral extrastriate visual cortices, and cerebellum. These are parts of the brain that create emotions. So symbols are not evoking understanding in our "heart" but in our left medial prefrontal cortex. But the heart is a more romantic metaphor.

The sweat response happens when our attention activates these emotional parts of our brain. It is an evolutionary response which ensures that even if we are concentrating on something else our attention can be draw to important events outside our bodies. It works by causing us to feel an "inexplicable" (meaning it is not something our consciousness can control) emotional response to some stimuli which we may not be consciously aware of. The key areas contributing to this response are in the limbic system of the brain, an area below our normal level of consciousness. But our consciousness certainly feels the emotions it produces. This is how symbols evoke understanding in our hearts.

The fact our brains have this built-in indicator of the emotional impact of symbols has allowed me to study how people from different backgrounds respond to symbols. I work at an international business school and had access to volunteers from around the world. I was able to test people who had been brought up in British, African, Asian, American, European and Chinese cultures, and had been taught to read in different writing systems, using different methods of recording words, and speaking different mother tongues. I tested equal numbers of females and males in each culture/alphabet group. I repeated this test over a number of years and my results have been consistent.

I took a set of twelve shapes. Six were taken from modern contemporary jewellery and six were ancient symbols; one of the symbols was from Blombos and the rest were of the type that has been associated with the spread of farming societies. I chose modern jewellery as its decorative motifs are designed to appeal to people.

I set up a GSR meter between the thumb and forefinger of the right hands for each volunteer. Once their baseline reading stabilised I showed them a card with an image on it. I allowed them to look at the image for at least a minute, until their GSR settled again. Then I noted the reading, before showing them another image. When I analysed the results, I found that all the ancient symbols caused a consistent change in galvanic skin response. The implication of this test was that the ancient symbols caused an emotional response in my test subjects. The responses to the modern jewellery shapes were less consistent. But I was unable to tell from this data if the response to the ancient symbols was positive or negative. Did the subjects like these symbols or did they find them disturbing? As their response was subconscious I soon found that there was little point in asking them how they felt about the images because they struggled to articulate their feelings. The only sure way to find out was to conduct a follow-up survey with the same subjects, but asking different questions about the symbols that caused their emotional response. I asked them to rank the same set of images in terms of attractiveness.

I placed the twelve images I had used for the GSR test on a table in front of each subject and asked them to examine them. The actual images used are shown below.

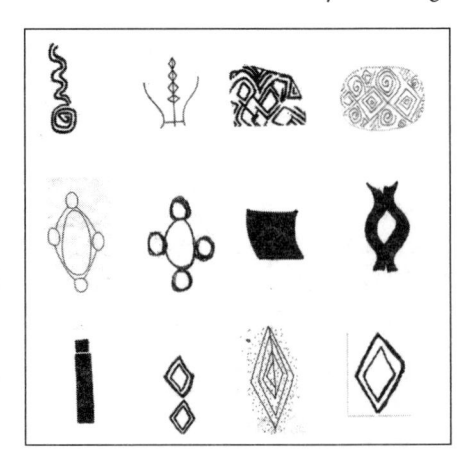

Next I asked them to hand me the image they found most attractive. I recorded their choice and placed the card out of sight. I then asked them to pick the most attractive of the remaining images. This process continued until there was only one image left. In this way I created a ranking system for the images. Each image had a possible rank value of twelve down to one. When I had completed the full sample I calculated an average attractiveness score for each image.

All the top scoring images were those that caused a significant GSR response. The sweating I had measured was the glow of pleasure not a cold sweat of fear.

Here are the top five symbols, scored according to their attractiveness to my students. And notice that a Blombos symbol was found to be significantly attractive, even after 70,000 years.

The most significantly popular symbol is one which Gimbutas had recorded in many similar forms between Anatolia and Orkney. It is an elaboration of the 70,000-year-old Blombos lozenge, and has been paired with a spiral. Gimbutas says that the spiral became particularly popular as a pottery symbol in southeast Europe around 6300 BCE and spread west.

There was no statistically significant difference between the different ethnic groups, but no matter which nationality my volunteers were, or what mother tongue they had learned to speak, read and write,

Overall Results- All Subjects

Score 9.28

Score 8.47

Score 7.77

Score 7.7

Score 6.72

Female Ranking

Score 9.57

Score 9.24

Score 8.11

Score 7.59

Score 7.52

Score 7.02

Male Ranking

Score 8.98

Score 8.95

Score 7.93

Score 7.73

Score 7.29

Score 6.82

there was a significant difference between the male and female responses. Here is how they differ:

The females found the spirals more attractive, whilst the males were drawn to variations on the lozenge and V shapes. Both male and females found the ancient symbols of the lozenge and the spiral consistently more attractive than the shapes taken from modern contemporary jewellery.

These symbols would not have persisted for so long simply because they are pretty; human taste in beauty changes. It appears that some transcendental evolutionary force burned them into our brains. Now I could see that human brains are hard-wired to like particular symbols, so there must be an evolutionary pay-off. But I still had to uncover it.

Pictures Can Transfer Thoughts

Betty Edwards, a Professor of Art at California State University, noticed how certain persistent symbols interact with humans. She found that her students could see consistent meaning in some drawings.

Students suddenly see that drawings (and other works of art) have meaning. I am not, of course, referring only to drawings of things—portraits, landscapes, still-life subjects. That kind of meaning can be summed up in a few words. But meaning is also expressed in the parallel visual language of a drawing, whether it represents recognisable objects or is completely non-objective. This different kind of meaning requires a different kind of comprehension. A drawing, to be comprehended for meaning, must be read by means of the language used by the artist, and that meaning, once comprehended, may be beyond the power of words to express. Yet in its parts and as a whole, it can be read.[14]

We have parts of our brains which look at abstract shapes and relate to the emotions and thoughts that were in the mind of the person who drew that shape or symbol.[15] This is the same emotional response I found in my volunteers.

Sensitivity to the emotive message of symbols is innate but can be trained and enhanced.

Edwards describes this process in terms of drawing:

In its simplicity, drawing is the silent twin to reading. Both reading and drawing can be done at any age from early childhood to the final day of a lifetime, if the eyes last that long. Both can be done in almost any environment, at any time of the day or night, by any person of any age who has minimal physical and mental health. Prehistoric human drawings predate written language by about ten thousand years. It seems possible that a language of drawing may derive from innate brain structures, just as verbal language apparently derives from innate structure. The fact that you know (part of) the parallel visual language already — though you perhaps don't know that you know it, indicates at least a possible innate brain structure for visual language. How, then, to tap into your natural ability to use — and understand the expressive power of this visual language? Clearly, by drawing — and by learning how to draw — just as we tap into the power of verbal language by learning how to read and write.[16]

Images allow people to express ideas or feelings that are too complicated or imprecise to fit into the straitjacket of written words. Edwards says "drawings can show relationships that are grasped immediately as a single image, where words are necessarily locked into a sequential order".[17]

Words have to be processed by marching into your mind in single file, while ideas encoded in pictorial symbols flood into your heart in a parallel wave.

When humans discovered how to make long lasting-marks, the first thing we met was a visual language of symbols which did not encode words but conveyed emotion. This secret language of symbols is still open to us. Freemasonry teaches that different symbols work on our minds in different ways and some symbols are more powerful than others.

Betty Edwards developed a technique she called Analog Drawing where she set exercises whose goal was to "dredge up that inner life of the mind by using an alternative, visual language [analogue drawings] to give it tangible form — in short, to make inner thought visible".[18] The images her students drew of "femininity" immediately attracted my attention as they were similar to the early emotive geometric shapes my volunteers liked.[19]

In particular one of her analog drawings of femininity showed what looked like an image of the ancient Blombos lozenge.[20] Yet

---

14   Edwards, B. *Drawing on the Right Side of the Brain*. London: Fontana/Collins, 1987.
15   Ibid.
16   Edwards, B. *Drawing on the Artist Within*. London: Collins, 1987.
17   Ibid.
18   Ibid.
19   Ibid.
20   Ibid.

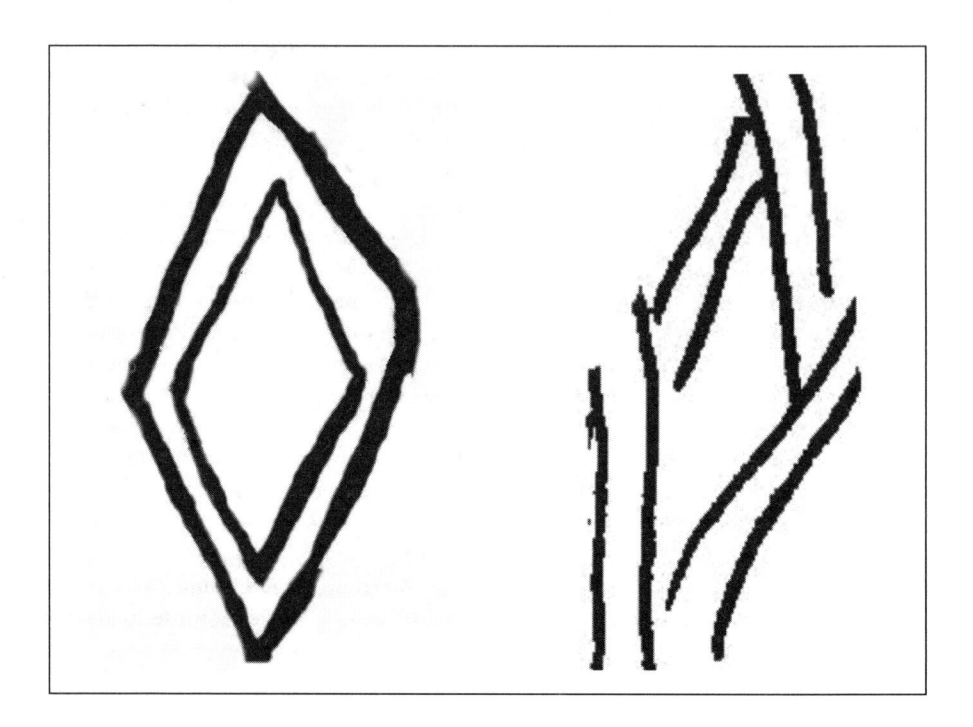

Edwards could not have been aware of the Blombos symbol as it was not found until twenty years after she recorded this image. (Shown above to right of Blombos symbol)

It appears to be a universal symbol of femininity, and that is a subject which always interests young males. Was this why my male students rated it so highly?

Edwards says that teaching her students to become sensitive to symbols made them better thinkers. This is a lesson Freemasonry has been teaching for hundreds of years.

I asked a number of artist friends to use Edwards' analog method to draw their own symbols of femininity, without explaining why I was interested or giving any indication of what I expected. The images are shown below and have similar features to Edwards' findings.

Symbols Taught Us How to Think

Symbols and language evolved together and are a key part of what defines us as human. The cave paintings in Lascaux, Chauvet, and Altamira show that symbols were used to influence reality 30,000 years ago, to increase success in hunting, and increase fertility among the people. Professor of Prehistory Steven Mithen describes the sudden surge in modern behaviour that symbol exposure caused.

> There was a cultural explosion 60,000–30,000 years ago...*H. sapiens sapiens*... adopted certain forms of behaviour never previously seen...notably the origins of Art.[21]

The "art" Prof. Mithen is talking about are the symbols of animals, people and Platonic Forms which were drawn deep inside the underground cave systems.

The oldest symbols drawn by modern humans date from 70,000 BCE and were geometric. By 35,000 BCE a mixture of pictorial and geometric symbols were widespread across Eurasia and North Africa.

21 Mithen, S. *The Prehistory of the Mind*. London: Phoenix, 1996.

In the following chapters, we will see how three major types of symbols, previously mentioned in the Introduction, drove the development of human civilisation.

- Emotive Symbols encode feelings and aspirations. These are the oldest of all symbols and date back over 70,000 years. They have been widely used to communicate emotion to illiterate people.
- Speech Symbols encode the sounds of language and enable humans to communicate across time and space. At one time these symbols were tightly restricted to an elite group, often linked with religion and a ruling class.
- Counting Symbols encode techniques of measuring, recording and keeping track of how many possessions you have and eventually gave birth to the cosmic language of Mathematical Symbols.

At each evolutionary appearance of a new group of symbols, the way they interacted with humanity was different but always brought about changes in the organisation of society. Symbols make humans different from other animals. It was Freemasonry's study of these ancient, transcendental symbols which led to the greatest breakthroughs in human achievement

Chapter 2

How Symbols Turned Hunters into Farmers

Symbols Let Us Communicate with the Dead

The first symbols, discovered over 70,000 years ago, still retain the power to influence us today. Symbols made us human and, as we developed them, they taught us new skills. The appearance of one particular type of symbol changed human society by teaching us how to co-operate in the hunt.

Carl Jung said that symbols arise in "our unconscious psyche". This is the inarticulate part of our mind which keeps a vigilant watch on our surroundings. If we did not have such a built-in survival feature we would have died out long ago. Our ancestors would have been surprised and eaten by lions while they admired the smoothness of a pebble, unaware of what was going on around them. But if we were not able to ignore our surroundings and concentrate on detail, we would never have learned how to hunt in tribes, farm our food, or build cities.

Jung believed our unconscious psyche, that interacts with symbols, played an important role in the development of the human mind. He did not put forward any theory of how symbols work, but he showed that archetypal symbols have an enormous impact on an individual, shaping their emotions, their ethical and mental outlook, their relationships with others, and affecting their whole destiny. Von Franz, one of Jung's students, sums up this idea:

The archetypes, or archetypal symbols, act as creative or destructive forces in our mind: creative when they inspire new ideas, destructive when these same ideas stiffen into conscious prejudices that inhibit further discoveries. To Jung, his concepts were... heuristic hypotheses that might help us to explore the vast new area of reality opened up by the discovery... If all men have common inherited patterns of emotional and mental behaviour [which Jung called the archetypes or archetypal symbols], it is only to be expected that we shall find their products [the results of acting under the influence of these shared archetypal symbols] in practically every field of human activity.[1]

Professor Gerald Edelman, the Director of the Neuroscience Research Institute and winner of the Nobel Prize for Physiology in 1972, has studied how ancient emotive symbols interact with human minds. I had the good fortune to meet Dr. Edelman, and discuss his views on the evolution of human consciousness, when he visited my own university to deliver a keynote speech at our Darwin Centenary Conference in September 2009.

Edelman identified two important evolutionary drivers that developed the human mind. These are distinct modes of thought called "logic" and "selectionism". He sums this up:

There are two main modes of thought — logic and selectionism (or pattern recognition). Both are powerful, but it is pattern recognition that can lead to creation, for example, in the choice of axioms in mathematics. If selectionism is the mistress of our thoughts, logic is their housekeeper.[2]

Symbols are much longer lived than any human. We can look at the symbols drawn by our ancient ancestors 70,000 years ago and feel the same emotional response to them as they did. My GSR tests prove this. Symbols enable human thoughts and aspirations to transcend the limits of our short lifespans.

1   Jung, C. G (ed) *Man and His Symbols*. London: Aldus, 1964.
2   Edelman, G. M. *Wider Than the Sky: A Revolutionary View of Consciousness*. London: Penguin, 2004.

Evolutionary theory says that change is driven by the interaction of competing forces. The appearance of emotive symbols was only the beginning, not the end, of the story of their interaction with humans. A symbol's ability to transmit emotional and creative ideas across time and space confers enormous advantage on any human who becomes sensitive to their power.

Emotive symbols are of two types: geometric and realistic. The geometric emotive symbols were the first to appear but initially they did not have a great impact on human progress. The symbols which gave humanity that initial push were realistic symbols associated with hunting and gathering. They were eventually surpassed by the more powerful geometric emotional symbols. These realistic symbols still play a role in the Masonic symbolic repertoire.

Symbols Helped Hunters

The creative explosion of human thought in Western Europe 30,000 years ago was driven by realistic emotive symbols. Professor David Lewis-Williams, an academic expert in prehistoric art, describes what happened:

> To seek a driving mechanism for the West European Creative Explosion... we need to consider the divisive functions of image-making. In doing so, we distance ourselves from earlier functionalist explanations, such as art for art's sake, sympathetic magic, binary mythograms, and information exchange, all of which see art as contributing to social stability. The most striking feature of the west European Upper Palaeolithic is a sharp increase in the rate of change... greater diversity in the kinds of raw materials used for artifact manufacture, the appearance of new tool types, the development of regional tool styles, socially and cognitively more sophisticated hunting strategies, organised settlement patterns, and extensive trade in 'special' items. Even more striking is the explosion of body decoration, elaborate burials with grave goods, and, of course, portable and parietal images [images drawn deep in caves]. It is clear that all these areas of change were interdependent—they interlocked. They were not a scatter of disparate 'inventions' made by especially intelligent individuals; rather, they were part of the very fabric of a dynamic society.[3]

Symbols were being woven into the thinking processes of humanity. They were creating and spreading ideas by forcing everyone who viewed them to identify with the emotional state of the person who drew the symbol. In this way they drove the co-operative tribal effort to hunt effectively and feed the growing group.

The impact of hunting symbols on human development provides dramatic support for Edelman's theory. He says that the mental imagery provoked by seeing and recalling symbols, helps humans thrive in the real world. He calls this the evolution of "higher level consciousness".

The symbols of hunting made it possible for groups of humans to share their "mental representations". This was the cause of humanity's dramatic progress. Williams draws on Edelman's research to help explain this evolutionary mechanism:

> Higher-order consciousness involves the ability to construct a socially based self-hood, to model the world in terms of the past and the future, and to be directly aware. Without a symbolic memory, these

---

3   Lewis-Williams, D. *The Mind in the Cave*. London: Thames & Hudson, 2004.

abilities cannot develop... Long-term storage of symbolic relations, acquired through interactions with other individuals of the same species, is critical to self-concept... Edelman explains the evolution of higher-order consciousness in neurobiological terms, but we need not consider all the details here... The difference between primary consciousness and higher-order consciousness is that members of the species *Homo sapiens*, the only species that has it, can remember better and use memory to fashion their own individual identities and mental 'scenes' of past, present, and future events. This is the key point... The pattern of modern human behaviour that higher-order consciousness made possible was put together piecemeal and intermittently in Africa... It seems likely that fully modern language and higher-order consciousness were, as Edelman argues, linked: It is impossible to have one without the other.[4]

This is the key to understanding the realistic symbols of hunting scenes, animals, and hunters, secretly drawn deep within the dark caves.

Our brains had reached an evolutionary stage where we were ready for a wider access to the transcendental eternal Platonic heaven of symbols. This developing relationship with symbols made us different from our Neanderthal cousins. The symbols were shaping the inner structure of our evolving brains.

Williams explains how these cave symbols were used:

We saw that a crucial threshold in human evolution was between two kinds of consciousness, not merely between moderate and advanced intelligence. Neanderthals were able to borrow only certain activities from their new *Homo sapiens* neighbours not because they were hopelessly bemired in animality and stupidity but because they lacked a particular kind of consciousness. They could entertain a mental picture of the present and, by learning processes, sense the presence of danger or reward. But they were locked into what Gerald Edelman calls 'the remembered present': Without developed memory and the kind of fully modern language that must attend it, they were unable to enter into long-term planning [or] initiate complex kinship and political systems.[5]

This is why the symbols of hunting were hidden deep in caves. They conferred power on those who could access their representations of hunts and chases, noble beasts, and brave hunters. Those who were invited to view them saw birds and bison, deer and horses all flowing along the walls with rampant and successful hunters in pursuit. They felt the emotive power of the symbols and carried that inspiration out with them, to enhance their own hunting skills and became motivated to lead the hunt.

Williams says the purpose of the images was to enable the tribal leaders of the hunting bands to engage with the spirits of the animals they hunted. This would ensure that the group could find and kill enough prey animals to survive. Images of these leaders appear in the cave, often shown as "therianthropes" (part-human and part-animal symbols), implying that they can think like a hunter and like a prey animal, and so lead the human band to the food it needed.

---

4   *Ibid*

5   *Ibid*.

subsistence farming. After some three and a half million years of living a successful nomadic lifestyle, humans gave up the idyll of hunter-gathering and chose the hard work, uncertain harvests and winter worry of farming. It was the spiritual power of these symbols that caused humans to exchange the thrill of the chase for the muddy squalor of the farmyard.

When *Homo sapiens* first evolved as a species, they lived in small, economically self-sufficient family-based groups. They found their own food and made their own weapons, tools, and anything else they needed. Only when some of these primitive groups settled down, learned how to grow crops, raise livestock, and build houses, did villages emerge. From these villages came new disciplines, such as division of labour, large building projects, and intricate social organisations which laid down the foundations of civilisation. The true secret of why farming began was hidden in the symbols these early farmers carried with them.

Geneticist Jim Wilson carried out a survey of the native Orcadian population and identified the maternal heritage that had the largest effect on the population of the west of Britain came from the area we now call Turkey. They came from Anatolia, where a city known as Çatalhöyük had thrived. But Çatalhöyük did not prosper by farming. Its citizens made their living by making stone knives and trading them for food with passing hunter-gatherers. But it was from Çatalhöyük that the first farming settlements rippled out to spread over the whole world. And it was in Çatalhöyük that the new symbols of farming emerged. Wilson's analysis showed that farming was spread by women, and as I show, the symbol of farming began as a symbol of womanhood not unlike this goddess from Çatalhöyük.

There is a consensus view from neurologists, art-historians, psychologists, philosophers and physicists that humanity's close encounter with realistic emotional symbols created a new dimension of human possibility. Without the interaction of symbolic representation, there could be no gods and no god-like aspirations.

Over time, symbols emerged from the depths of the caves into the light and mutated into powerful symbols of gods and goddesses. These symbols, and the beliefs they transmitted, made the next step possible: The change from hunter-gathering to farming.

Symbols Taught Farming

Hunter-gathers had an easier lifestyle, lived longer, and worked less than early farmers. Yet humanity decided to opt for the hard slog of

This farming symbol had been noticed by the late Professor Marija Gimbutas. She documented a whole range of ancient symbols for the last 30,000 years and said:

> Symbols... constitute a complex system in which every unit is interlocked with every other in what appears to be specific categories... The religion of the early agricultural period of Europe and Anatolia is richly documented. Tombs, temples, frescoes, reliefs, sculptures, figurines, pictorial paintings, and other sources.[6]

One particular symbol, which was associated with the earliest farming settlements, had consistently appealed to my volunteers. Here it is:

6   Gimbutas, M. *The Language of the Goddess*. London: Thames and Hudson, 2001.

She knew how the symbol stamp was used because it was found alongside the token clay model of an embossed sacred loaf.[8] The clay-token of a loaf of bread (shown below), impressed with these sacred symbols, is around 9,500 years old.

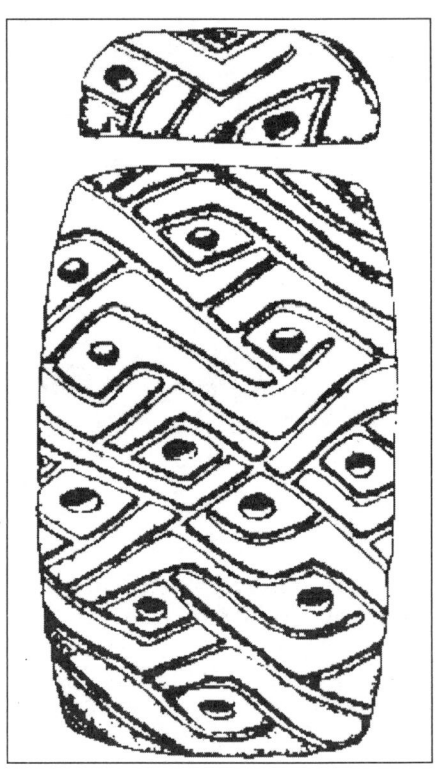

It combines lozenge and spiral symbols. It is about 7,000 years old and Gimbutus found it in eastern Yugoslavia. She described it as a "loaf-shaped clay object which was probably a model of sacred bread made as an offering to the Pregnant Goddess".[7] Early farmers made bread with symbols on them, rather like the hot-cross buns which modern-day Christians make to celebrate Easter, and they also made miniature clay tokens of their loaves.

Here is the oldest version of the combined symbol that Gimbutas recorded:

By 6500 BCE, these symbols had spread westwards into Europe.[9] The map below shows the dates of the growth of farms from Anatolia to the west coast of Europe.[10] Recognisable versions of the lozenge and spiral symbols spread alongside the farming villages, as the diagram shows. The oldest symbols are in the East and the most recent in the West.

8   Ibid.
9   Renfrew, C and Bahn, P. *Archaeology: Theories, Methods and Practice*. London: Thames & Hudson, 1998.
10 Renfrew, C.(Contrib) *Bronze Age Migrations in the Aegean*. London: Birchall, 1973.

7   Ibid.

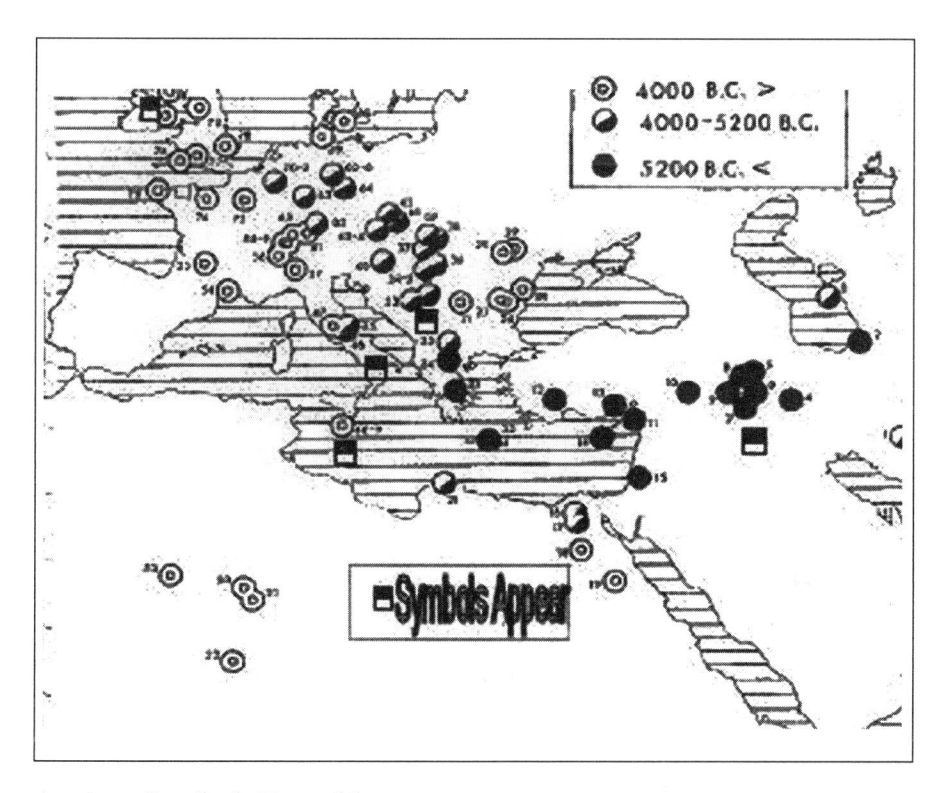

Ancient Symbols Found in a Birthing Chamber

The dates of the appearance of the lozenge and spiral symbol match the sequence of the change-over from hunter-gathering to farming. The symbols travelled with the farmers, helping and inspiring them in the difficult times of establishing a farm in the trackless wilderness. At first I was puzzled as to the import of the symbols, but Gimbutas's collection held an important clue. She had recorded a realistic statue of a woman's torso, overlaid with the emotive geometric lozenge and spiral symbols. It was a Rosetta stone linking realistic womanhood symbols with emotive geometric farming symbols.

Gimbutas also discovered that the lozenge and spiral symbol was used in rituals of birth and farming at Çatalhöyük. As she explains:

In the early Neolithic, peoples constructed...birthing shrines. At Çatalhöyük... excavations revealed a room where inhabitants apparently performed rituals connected with birthing. They painted the room red, reminding us that red, the colour of blood, was the colour of life. Stylized figures on the walls illustrate women giving birth, while circular forms and wavy lines painted nearby may symbolise the cervix, umbilical cord and amniotic fluid. A low plaster platform could have been used for actual birthing. The colour and symbolism in the room suggest that people regarded this as a religious event and that they accompanied it with ritual.[11]

11 Gimbutas, M. *The Living Goddesses*. Los Angeles: University of California Press, 1999.

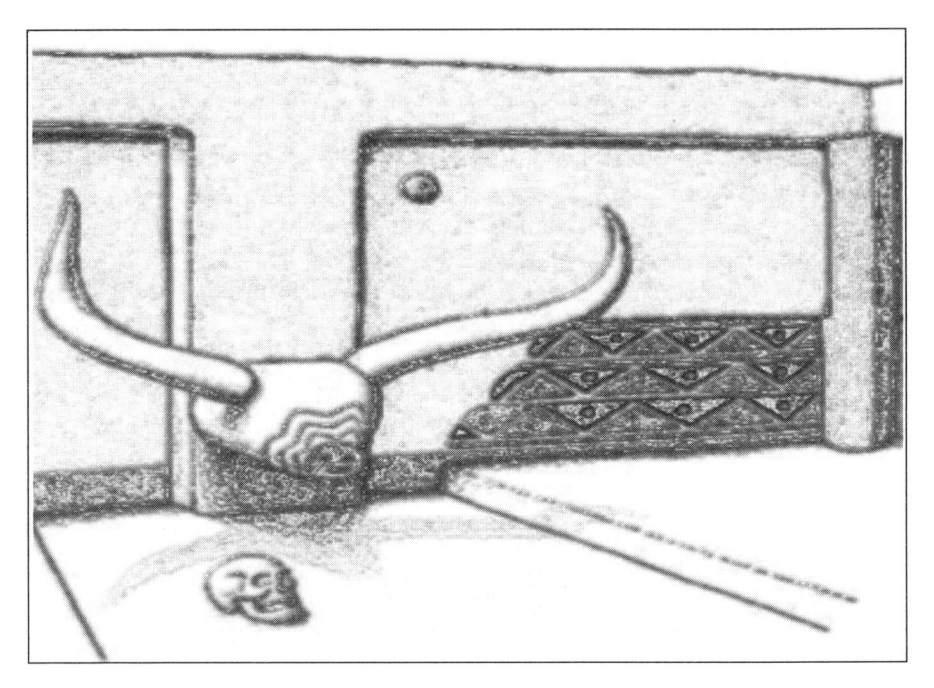

The circular forms and wavy lines were the lozenge and spiral shape also found on the token-model of the symbol-impressed loaf. She pointed out that symbols of a pregnant Earth mother were:

> ... frequently unearthed near bread ovens. She [the pregnant Earth mother] personified the analogy between human and animal pregnancy and the annual cycle of plant germination, growth, and harvest.[12]

Archaeologist James Mellaart excavated altars within birthing shrines at Çatalhöyük and found offerings of deposits of grain preserved between layers of red clay on symbolic altars.[13] More recently, similar "votive deposits" including carbonised barley seeds have been found covered over in post-cavities.[14] Gimbutas found that a ritual of adding grain seeds into symbolic clay figures spread along with the practice of farming. As she explains:

> The early Cucuteni (Tripolye) culture, which dated from circa 4800-3500 B.C., provides us with the clearest insight into Neolithic rituals honoring the pregnant vegetation goddess... figurines showed traces grain, and some sixty figurines bore evidence of grain impressions on the surface... When technicians x-rayed these very porous clay figurines, they found three grain types (wheat, barley, and millet) stuffed inside... Here we have powerful evidence for a ritual associating grain, flour, and baking, performed for the goddess in order to assure abundant bread.[15]

---

12 Ibid.

13 Mellaart, J. Çatalhöyük. London: Thames & Hudson, 1967.

14 http://www.catalhoyuk.com/archive_reports/1997/ar97_03.html

15 Gimbutas, M, The Living Goddesses. Los Angeles: University of California Press, 1999.

How Symbols Turned Hunters into Farmers

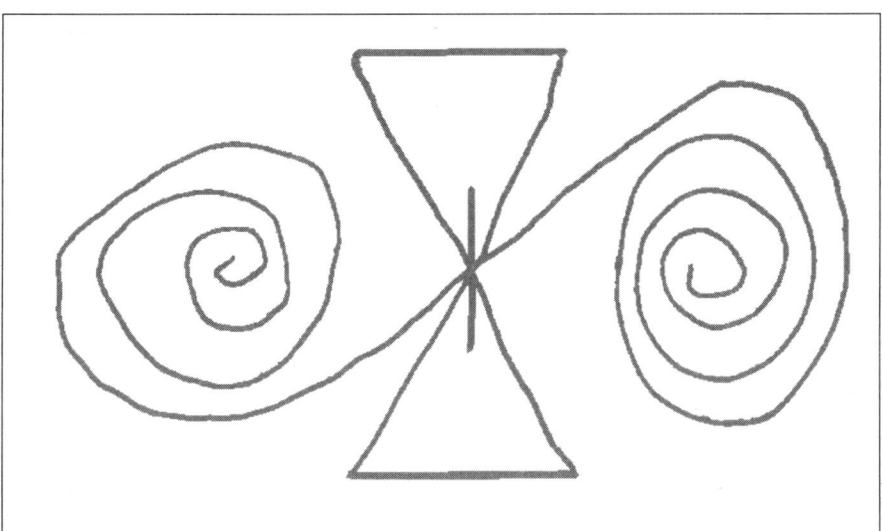

The ritual importance of placing seeds within the layered clay was the clue to understanding the symbolic goddess figures and the symbols carved on the female torso. It reveals a context for the combined realistic and geometric figure, which dates from around 5000 BCE.[16]

Drawing the symbols flattened out, instead of wrapped around the torso, reveals a familiar symbol. Gimbutas found that the egg-shaped buttocks are decorated with energy symbols, whorls and concentric circles, which naturally occurring patterns are created by the shadow of the noon-day sun.[17]

16 *Ibid.*

17 Lomas, R and Knight, C. *Uriel's Machine*. Massachusetts: Fair Winds Press, 1999.

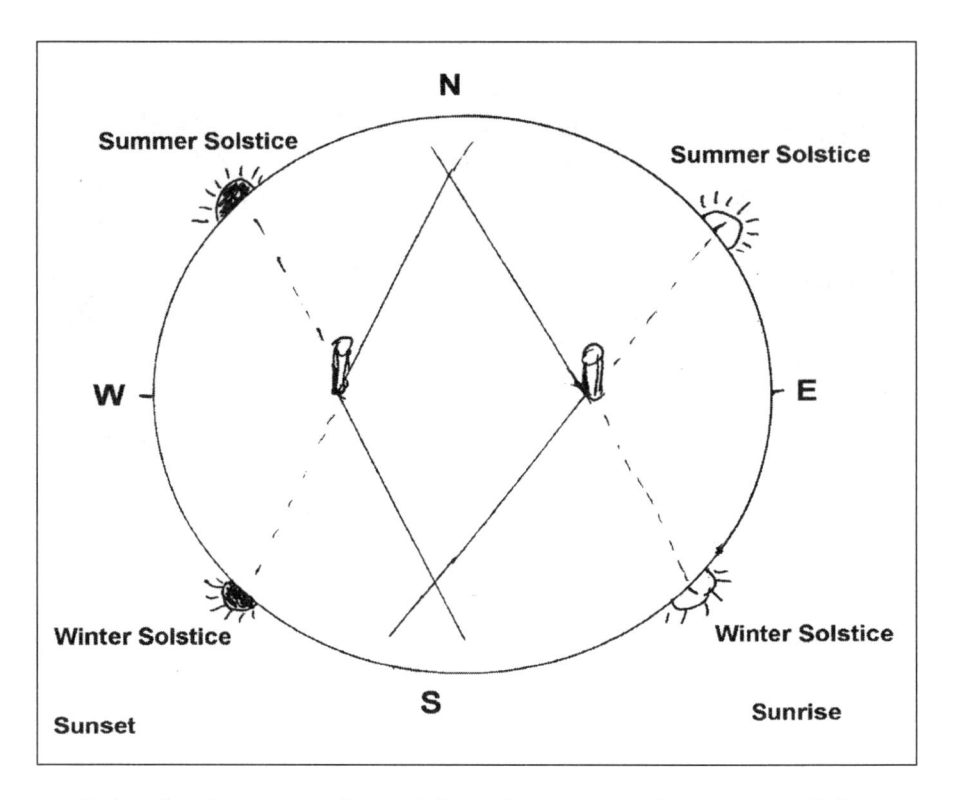

[Diagram: Circle with compass directions N (top), S (bottom), E (right), W (left). Summer Solstice marked at upper-left and upper-right; Winter Solstice marked at lower-left (Sunset) and lower-right (Sunrise). Two crossing lines form an X through the centre with two small standing-stone figures.]

Gimbutas's collection is evidence of the long-term use of the lozenge and spiral symbol which I showed still retains the power to fascinate my students. Gimbutas placed the symbol in a ritual religious context.

Innumerable Neolithic figurines preserved in their original settings the intimate richness of Old European spirituality... Their makers incised them with symbols, such as two or three lines, spirals or meanders, a chevron or a lozenge... artisans could create schematic figurines easily, and, like the Christian cross, in religious practice these figures communicated the same symbolic concepts as the more representational art. These simplified images... express a sacred message.[18]

The geometrical emotive symbols were embossed onto semi-realistic images of the fertile female form before becoming free-standing symbols. The symbolic import of the various parts of the female torso relate to the symbols. The downward pointing triangle is a symbol of the vulva and womb "sprouting life and giving birth".[19] The upward pointing triangle, in figures A and B, formed by the spread of the woman's legs, symbolised death and the womb as tomb. This use can be seen in the structures of "horn-mouthed tombs" which were built at this time as symbolic wombs to house the dead.[20] Gimbutas says that "the caves, crevices, and caverns of the earth are natural manifestations of the primordial womb of the Mother. Burial in the womb of the earth

18 Gimbutas, M, *The Living Goddesses*. Los Angeles: University of California Press, 1999.

19 Ibid.
20 Ibid.

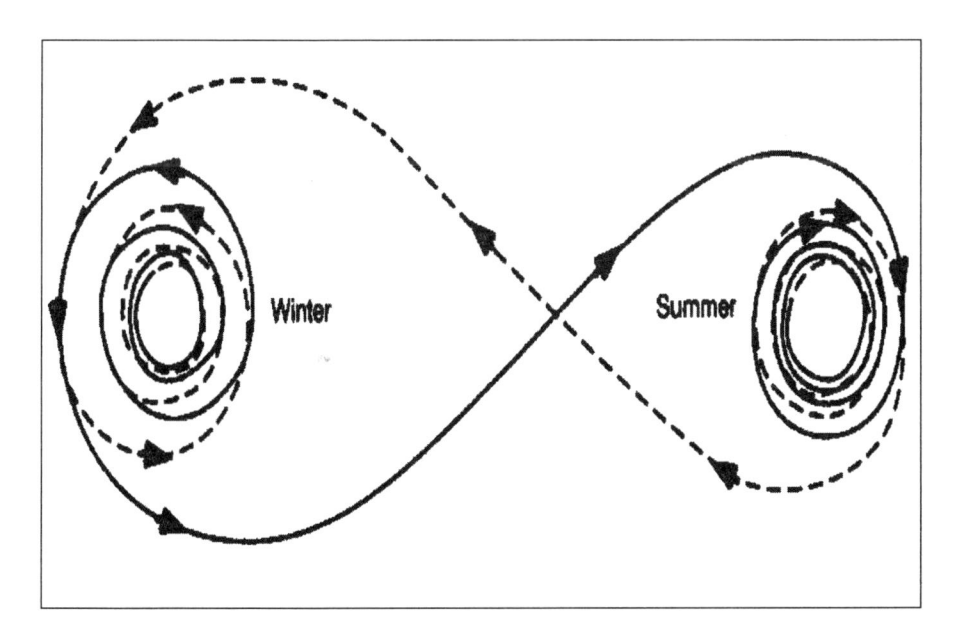

is analogous to planting a seed, so it is a simple step to expect new life to emerge from the old."[21]

Now the emotive power of the combined symbol becomes easy to explain. The upward pointing triangle represents death and the act of planting a seed in the womb. The downward pointing triangle represents the new life that will come in the spring. Their points meet at the vulva of the goddess and at the intersection of the double symbol of fertility, which is the goddess's exaggerated and fertile buttocks.

The "V" or chevron, when topped off to form a lozenge, or diamond shape, is a pattern which is created by the shadows cast on the land by the rising and setting sun as it moves through the seasons. See below:

The further north, the taller and thinner the lozenge shape becomes. In latitudes near the equator the lozenge becomes short and fat.[22] I have used this observation to check the shape of many lozenges, including the earliest ones ever found (70,000 BCE at Blombos Cave) and found them to be consistent in locating the latitude of the site where they were engraved.[23] Likewise the shape of the two spirals, which was superimposed on the buttocks of the goddess, can be created by marking out the path of the sun's shadow during the seasons, with each spiral taking a quarter of a year to appear. This observational symbolism is carried out by plotting the fall of the tip of the shadow of the free-standing pole at midday.[24] The symbol traced out by the natural movement of the sun draws out the pattern which appears on the woman's buttocks above.

As farmers became more successful, and more settled, they began to build not just villages but large communal structures. These structures were used for religious rituals, and the farmers carved their religious symbols on the walls of their places of worship to inspire them to continue to labour on their land.

---

21   Ibid.
22   Lomas, R and Knight, C. *op. cit.*
23   Lomas, R. *Turning the Hiram Key*. London, Lewis Masonic, 2005.
24   Lomas, R and Knight, C. *op. cit.*

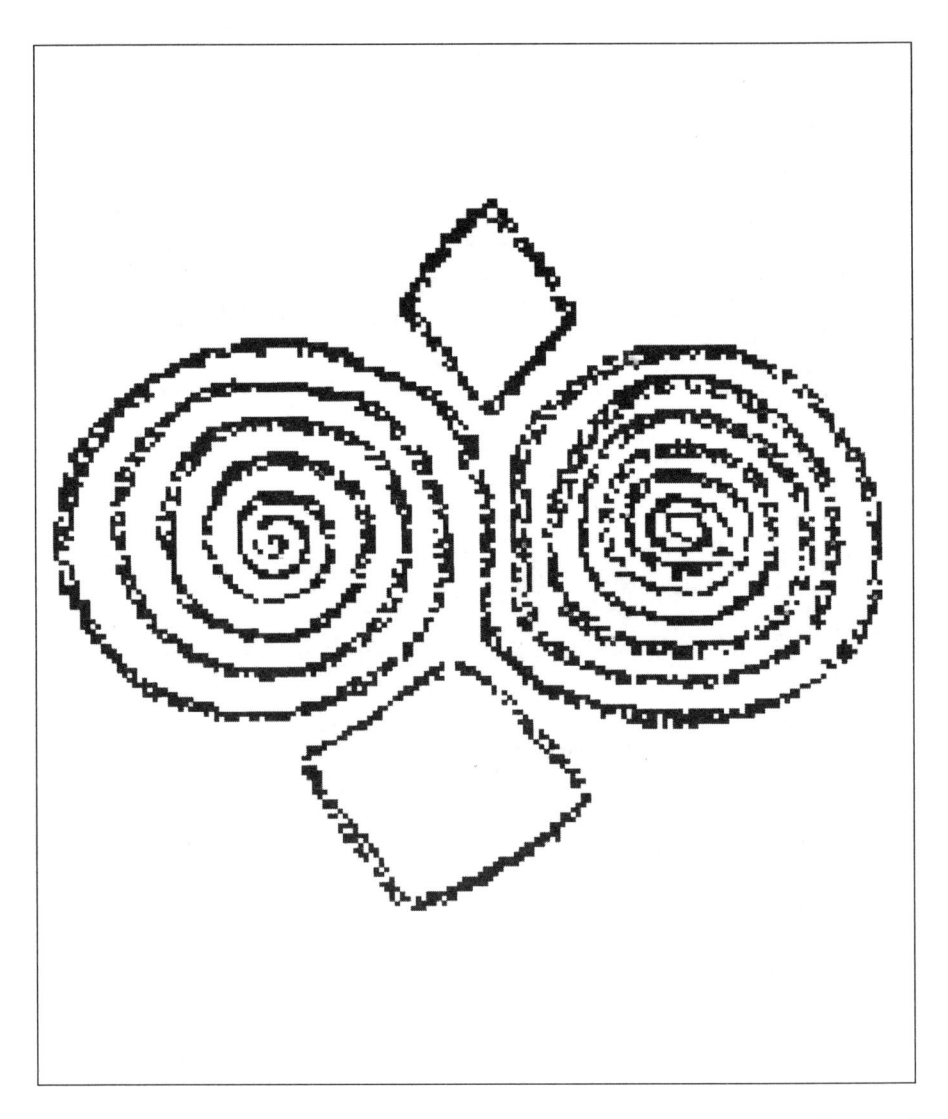

Above is an image of the farming symbol displayed on the wall of a massive tunnel mound at Newgrange in Ireland. It dates from about 5,000 years ago.

The two lozenge shapes are taken from the extreme latitudes of the British Isles, and they intercept, in the symbol of a downward pointing triangle pointed to an upward pointing triangle, at the place where the spring spiral of the sun's path meets the spiral of the beginning of summer. This season is known as spring or the vernal equinox. It is the time to plant your seeds for an autumn harvest. The mundane meaning of the symbol is "Plant your dead seed in the womb of mother earth at the vernal equinox and by the end of summer it will be reborn as abundant grain to give you bread through the winter." Not only is it a powerful geometrical emotive symbol, it can be read as a textbook on how and where to grow grain.

Both elements of this symbol are to be found in the Masonic teaching about symbols. The spiral and lozenge are key elements in the Second Degree Tracing Board.

As humans became more settled, a new form of symbol appeared which was able to transmit more precise information than these early emotive symbols. Individuals with knowledge of this new symbol would create the first empires. Symbols were about to change the human race again. They would facilitate a concept of wealth, and the power that wealth can bring.

Chapter 3

How Symbols Created Kingdoms

The Importance of Counting

About 9,000 years ago in Mesopotamia, in a land then called Sumer, a group of symbols appeared which made it possible for humans to count objects and also to keep records of what they owned. These symbols began in the small farming villages that were starting to appear, and enabled farmers to keep track of their produce. They marked the beginning of wealth but they also contained the seeds of power and domination.

Before humans farmed there were no domesticated pack animals to carry things. If you wanted to keep something, you had to carry it in your hands, or on your back. This limited what you could own, both in size and weight. Hunters had no wealth and little incentive to count their few bits and pieces. But when they stopped hunting, gathering, and following the meandering herds of prey animals and began to farm, they accumulated goods.

As farming settlements became more widely established so did the number, value, and weight of an individual's personal goods. For the first time it became possible to own buildings where you could live for the rest of your life. With the domestication of animals, ownership extended to flocks and herds of semi-tame beasts. But if you were to survive through winter, without hunting, then you had to keep track of your reserves of food and domesticated beasts. This was when a new form of symbol revealed just how useful it could be.

"Counting" symbols began on farms. The clay-token loaves we saw in the previous chapter were not toys they were a way of keeping track of the number of loaves baked. Archaeologist Denise Schmandt-Besserat, professor of Middle Eastern Studies at the University of Texas, studied and classified over 8,000 of these symbolic counting tokens that had been excavated from all over Sumer. She says:

> A system of tokens... small clay objects of many shapes — cones, spheres, disks, cylinders, and so on — served as counters in the prehistoric Near East and can be traced to the Neolithic period, starting about 8000 B.C. They evolved to... keep track of the products of farming, then... [as more cities grew] to keep track of goods manufactured in workshops. The

development of tokens was tied to the rise of social structures, emerging with rank leadership and coming to a climax with state formation.¹

The tokens began as miniature clay models of the actual goods they symbolised. Grain was stored in conical clay storage vessels so a measure of grain was represented by a small cone. Oil was kept in ovoid jars and so a measure of oil was symbolised by a small clay ovoid. For two measures of oil you kept two ovoids. You had tokens for various animals and various types of food. For each object that you needed a record of quantity, a token was made to symbolise the individual item. Now the purpose of making clay symbols of embossed loaves makes sense. If you made a number of loaves, ready to trade at a forthcoming festival, you would need to keep a token for each loaf to know how many you had in stock.

Two new functions of symbols were beginning to emerge. Schmandt-Besserat explains what was happening in the ongoing interaction between humanity and the power of symbols:

The earliest evidence of signs, in the form of notched tallies, date from the Middle Paleolithic... Symbolism was used both in rituals and, at the same time, for the compilation of concrete information. From its beginnings in about 30,000 B.C., the evolution of symbolic information processing in the prehistoric Near East proceeded in major phases, dealing with data of increasing specificity. First, during the Middle and late Upper Paleolithic, ca. 30,000-12,000 B.C., tallies referred to one unit of an unspecified item. Second, in the early Neolithic, ca. 8000 B.C., the tokens indicated a precise unit of a particular good... the name of the sponsor/recipient of the merhandise [was] indicated by seals.²

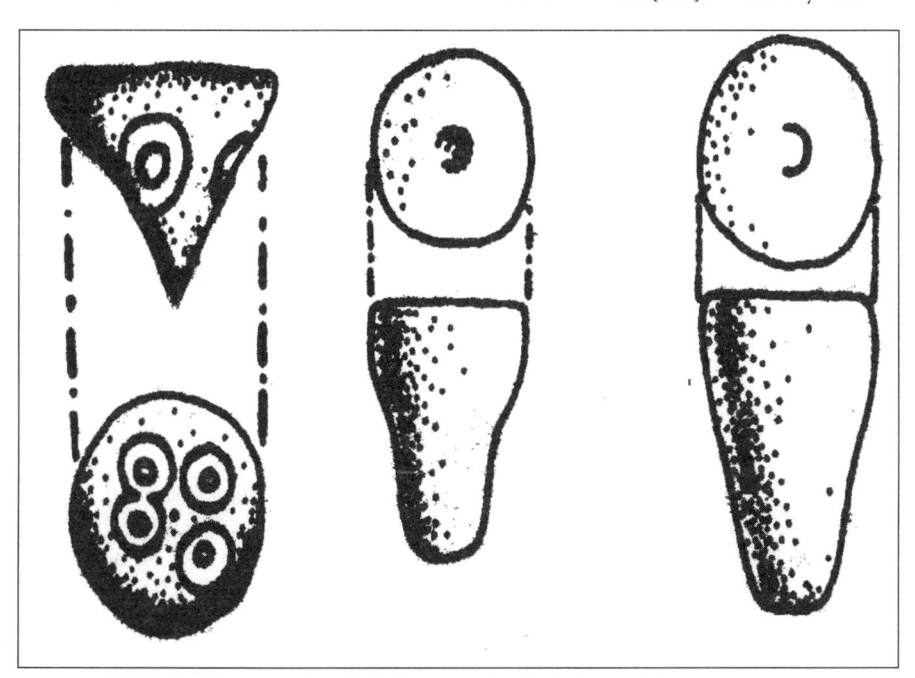

1 Schmandt-Besserat, D. *How Writing Came About.* Houston: University of Texas Press, 1996.

2 *Ibid*

The Lewis Guide to Masonic Symbols

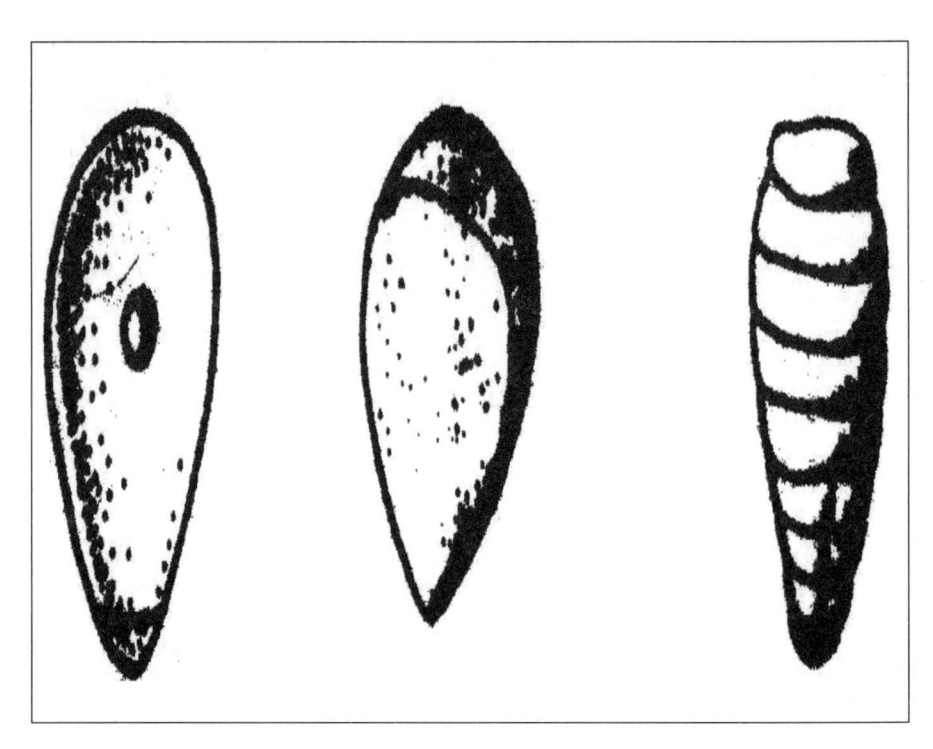

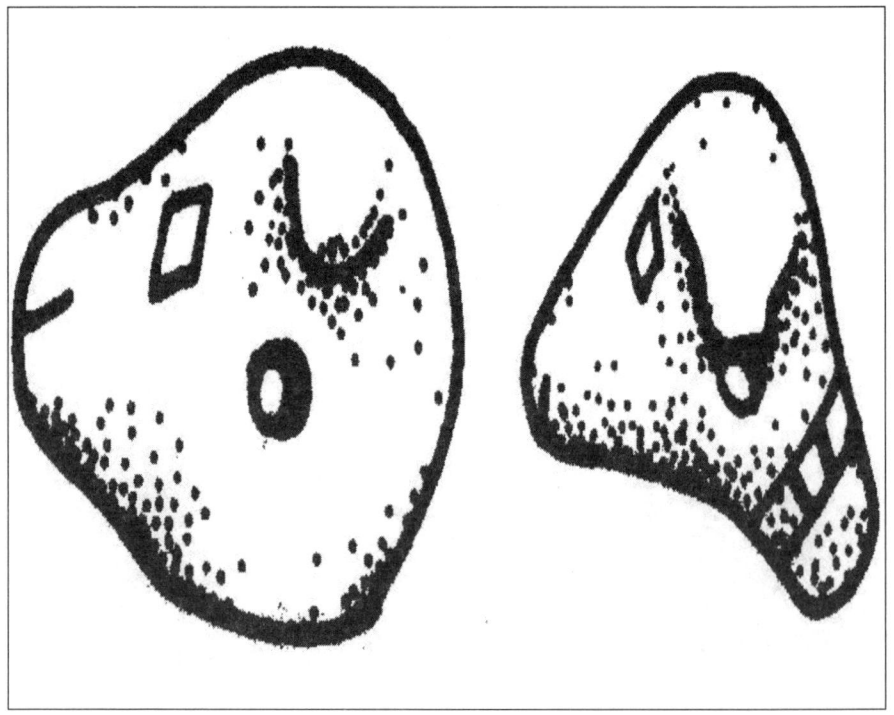

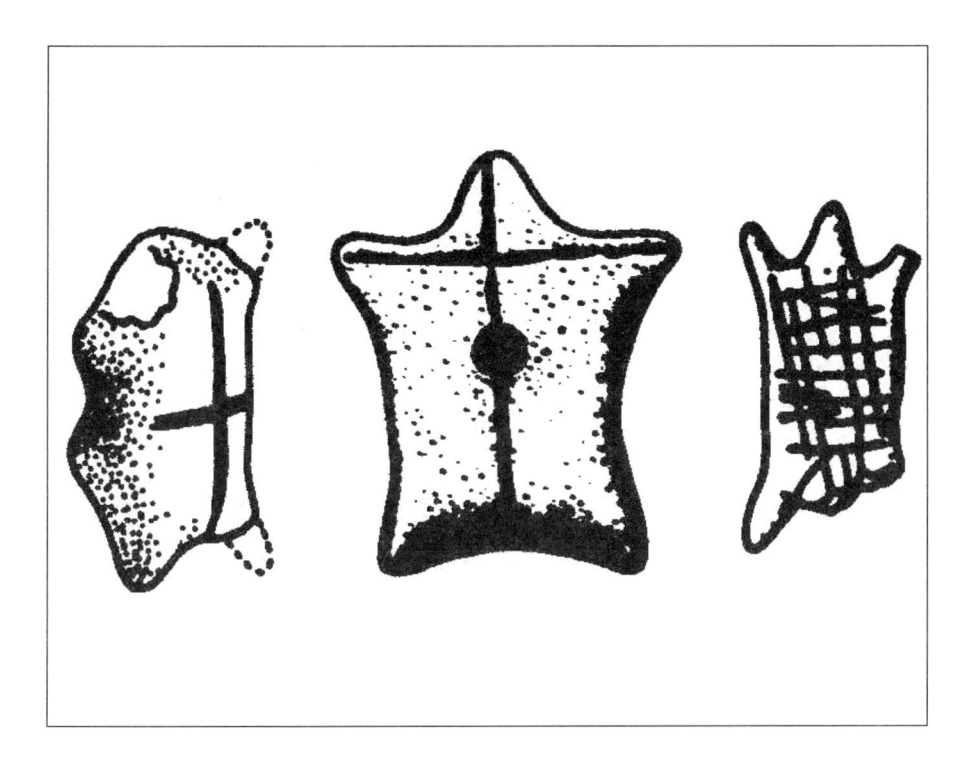

A group of individuals soon saw a chance to prosper by seizing a share of everyone else's goods. Today we call this process taxation. But before you can tax somebody you need to be able to measure what they have. The symbols of counting spawned the accountant and the taxman.

Here are examples of those early symbols. Below are cone tokens, used to indicate measures of grain (after Schmandt-Besserat).

These are ovoid symbols used to indicate measures of oil (after Schmandt-Besserat).

Here are some animal head symbols. Used to indicate how many of each animal was owned (after Schmandt-Besserat).

Finally, here are some animal skin symbols (after Schmandt-Besserat).

Some of the tokens had holes in them to allow them to be strung on a cord and kept together. Others did not. Symbols without thread-holes were sealed inside clay containers which acted as envelopes when people needed to carry their symbols about.

The hunter-gatherers had not needed long-range communication. They lived in small self-contained bands and their main concern was successful hunting. They followed the herds and harvested wild food. They traded for tools, such as stone axes or obsidian knives, swapping food or captured-live-animals with communities such as Çatalhöyük.[3] The farmers were different. They also needed stone tools, unless they lived by an outcrop of obsidian or flint, in which case they could make implements like the people of Çatalhöyük. Successful farms could exist only on fertile land, so farmers stayed in one place. They could trade tools from passing bands of hunters, but only if they could keep track of what they owned and what was available to trade. Farmers needed symbols of counting.

---

3   Jacobs, J. *The Economy of Cities*. London: Pelican, 1968.

The First Symbols

Ancient symbolic tokens have been found throughout Israel, Iran, Iraq, Turkey, and Syria. They were fired to harden them and make them last. Schmandt-Besserat realised that they were part of a larger symbolic system when she found small and large cones, thin and thick discs, small and large spheres, and even fractions of spheres, such as half and three-quarter spheres.

The way these symbols act became clear when Leo Oppenheim, an archaeologist from the University of Chicago found a container in Nuzi, northern Iraq, dating from about 2000 BCE. It was sealed and intact. On the outside was writing and inside a selection of the symbolic tokens that Schmandt-Besserat had seen proliferating across the farmers' lands. It was the key to decoding their purpose. The inscription on the container was a list of the forty-nine different animals owned by a shepherd named Ziqarru. Inside the container were groups of seven different symbol tokens. By linking the twenty-one "ewes-that-lamb", described on the outside, with the twenty-one identical symbol tokens inside, the first steps were made to link symbol-shapes with objects.[4]

The farmers became wealthy, and measured their wealth by assigning a symbol to each object. Then they began to produce more food than they could eat. Soon a hierarchy emerged, which realised it was possible to live off this food surplus without working to produce it. The new potential overlords joined forces and used sacred emotional symbols to impress on the farmers the need to placate their gods.

The token symbols established a mode of "concrete" counting, an idea that appeared long before the discovery of the abstract numbers of mathematics.

Soon, one of the most powerful symbol groups would come into being, and these would be the precursors to writing. Schmandt-Besserat sums it up:

> The consequences of this discovery are significant. Writing resulted not only from new bureaucratic demands but from the invention of abstract counting....counting was not subservient to writing; on the contrary, writing emerged from counting.[5]

These symbols enabled humanity to think and plan for the future, instead of just responding to everyday needs. As the realistic tokens of the clay ovoids of oil jars became geometric symbols of a measure of oil, so humanity came to rely on these symbols to help it organise itself.

The token-symbols first manifested as mundane counters or realistic images and helped humanity keep track of its foodstuff and basics of daily life. Symbol users could manage goods and build an economy because they had access to instruments of power. They had emotive — geometric or realistic — symbols which manipulated people's feelings and they had counting token-symbols which enabled them to manage food production. These two types of symbols created new social patterns and enabled data to be manipulated for the first time.

The Symbol of Newgrange

Around 3500 BCE, a pre-literate elite on Orkney — a group of islands off the north coast of Scotland — was able to persuade, or force, the local population to build three massive stone ring structures, a village with a large meeting hall, and an enormous tunnel mound. (The Ring of Brodgar, the Stones of Stenness, the Ring of Bookan, the

---

4   Schmandt-Besserat, *op. cit.*

5   *Ibid.*

neolithic settlement of Barnhouse, and the mound of Maeshowe respectively.) The Ring of Brodgar itself took over thirty years to complete, at a time when the average lifespan was about twenty-four years. The Barnhouse Great Hall and village cost an additional £3 million (expressing the work in modern cost terms) and took at least another ten years to build, while the massive mound of Maeshowe cost nearly £50 million and took a further fifty years. The reason for building those sites was religious, as the sacred symbol of the double lozenge and interlaced spirals were used at the sites. Here is the symbol as displayed by the Orkney farmers/builders.

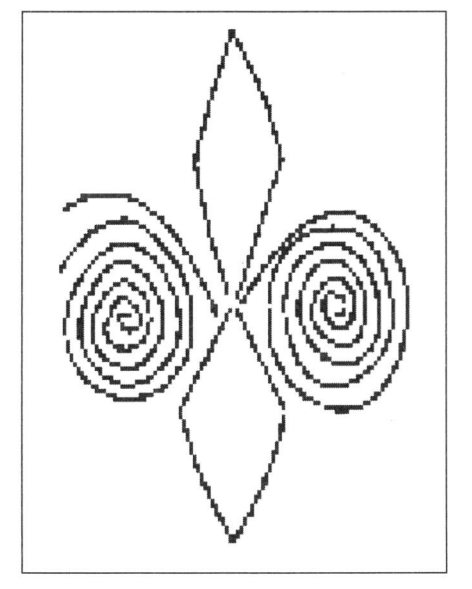

A group of three even more spectacular temples to pre-literate geometric emotive symbols were built in the Boyne Valley of Ireland, around 3200 BCE. Three massive tunnel mounds were built and their interiors covered in geometric emotive symbols. The most striking is a large engraving of the sacred farming symbol on the rear footstone of the mound of Newgrange. Here is that symbol:

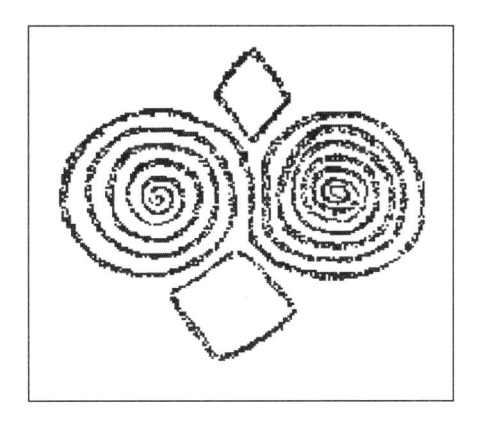

The symbols of counting and record-keeping would soon evolve and change humanity fundamentally. A new group of alphabetic symbols was about to join forces with the basic sounds of speech and greatly extend the range of language.

The Importance of Writing Symbols

Writing is a special form of symbolic magic. It enables me to converse with a friend in a distant country and understand her reply, instantly. It lets my dead mother tell me about the trauma of her childhood which she would never talk about when she was alive, and it lets the ancient inhabitants of the first cities of Sumer, in Mesopotamia, recite to me the stories of their first king, Gilgamesh.

The symbols of writing do much more than encode the spoken word; they make it permanent, and so give it greater authority. And they allow it to be carried to distant regions without corruption.

It is no coincidence that the symbols of writing appeared at the time of the rapid growth of the cities of Sumer. Dense populations of city dwellers needed more complex social organisations than isolated farm families or hunting groups. City people had more wealth to steal so they built defensive walls to increase security. They lived together for social reasons and built meeting places, monumental temples, and palaces. They protected their wealth from roving thieves by using counting symbols to provide effective economic records.

Archaeologist W John Hackwell studied the emergence of alphabetic symbols of writing and drew attention to the role of the custodians of religious symbols, the priests:

> Since life in Mesopotamia centred around the temples, such economic record keeping was probably the function of the priests. Indeed, some archaeologists have suggested that the invention of writing was the result of a demand for more efficient recording than the clay tokens offered. Perhaps it was the priests who invented the idea.[6]

But priests did not simply decide to invent writing in order to make the Sumerian city-state work more efficiently. There had been 5,000 years of opportunity for interpreters of sacred geometric symbols to extend their influence by inventing writing. But nobody had. All that happened was that small, isolated communities (such as Malta, Orkney, and Ireland for example) were persuaded to work long and hard hours to build structures to display the sacred symbols, presumably with the pay-off of making them feel good inside. The overlords realised that they could hold ceremonies and rituals to exploit this human response. They lived in luxury without the need to take part in the daily farming toil which fed their community.

The symbols of writing did not come about because of social change. They caused that social change. They were an untapped source of influence on humanity and their

---

[6] Hackwell, W John. *Signs, Letters, Words*: Archaeology Discovers Writing. New York: Charles Scribner's Sons, 1987.

emergence made the growth of city-states and empires inevitable. The cities of Sumer and the later empires of Assyria, Egypt, and Babylon all grew out of the mystic power of writing symbols.

At first, every item to be recorded had to have a special realistic token-symbol made to represent it. You needed different token-symbols to count quantities of grain (cones) or quantities of oil (ovoids). But "concrete" symbols for counting particular things were a turning point in information processing. They inherited from their Palaeolithic ancestors a way of abstracting data from reality and preserving it in symbols. The new symbols of writing made long-distance communication possible.

They also brought about a higher-order consciousness, as Schmandt-Besserat explains:

> Corresponding to the increase in bureaucracy, methods of storing tokens in archives were devised. One of these storage methods employed clay envelopes, simple hollow clay balls in which the tokens were placed and sealed. A drawback of the envelopes was that they hid the enclosed tokens. Accountants eventually resolved the problem by imprinting the shapes of the tokens on the surface of the envelopes prior to enclosing them. The number of units of goods was still expressed by a corresponding number of markings. An envelope containing seven ovoids, for example, bore seven oval markings. The substitution of signs for tokens was a first step toward writing. Fourth-millennium accountants soon realised that the tokens within the envelopes were made unnecessary by the presence of markings on the outer surface. As a result, tablets — solid clay balls bearing markings — replaced the hollow envelopes filled with tokens. These markings became a system of their own which developed to include

not only impressed markings but more legible signs traced with a pointed stylus. Both of these types of symbols, which derived from tokens, were picture signs or "pictographs". They were not, however ... pictures of the items they represented but, rather, pictures of the tokens used as counters in the previous accounting system.[7]

An example of this can be seen in the shape of one of the first symbols used by the Sumerians in a type of writing called cuneiform. It is the symbol for barley, which is simply a drawing of a plant stem with symbolic seed heads branching off it. The seed heads are shown using the traditional downward pointing V, or chevron, which Gimbutas told us was a long-established symbol of the mother goddess of farming.

Here is the cuneiform symbol for barley. Notice the series of V's or chevron symbols placed on the stem.

The chevron symbols have a separate religious significance. Gimbutas explains:

> Chevrons, V's, zig-zags, M's, meanders, streams, nets, and tri-lines are frequent and repetitious in Old European symbols... We shall begin our journey with the Goddess's hieroglyphs, the V and chevron...graphically, a pubic triangle is most directly rendered as a V. This expression and its recognition are universal and immediate. It is, nevertheless, amazing how early this bit of "shorthand" crystallised to become for countless ages the designating mark of the Goddess.[8]

The use of a series of downward pointing V's in the first writing symbol for barley symbolises the divine origin of farming. I have already mentioned how farming started as a series of irrational symbolic religious acts of spring planting by women devotees of a farming goddess. This apparently irrational religious symbolism rapidly conferred evolutionary advantage on its followers and contributed to the success of farming.[9]

The chevron symbol made the leap from inscriptions on realistic figurines of the goddess, to freestanding religious symbol around 18,000 BCE. Gimbutas explains:

> [We see] Little figurines [of the Goddess]... their divine generative function emphasized by a large pubic triangle. Some of them are decorated by a series of panels, each with a somewhat different chevron design—chevrons in columns, opposed, or inverted. These figurines, tentatively dated to circa 18,000-15,000 B.C., are of inestimable value for the insight they

---

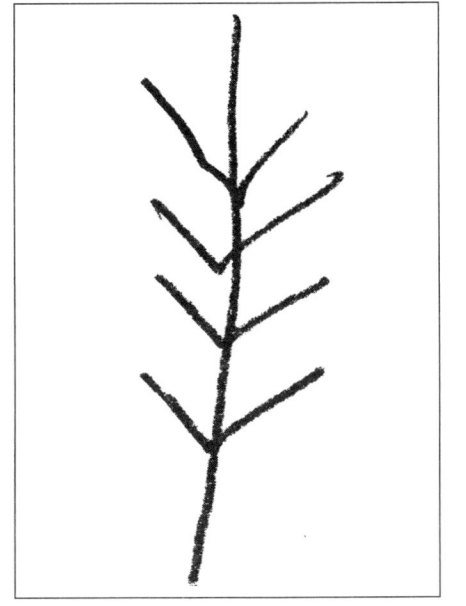

7   Schmandt-Besserat, D *op cit*.

8   Gimbutas, M. The Language of the Goddess. London: Thames & Hudson, 2001.

9   Lomas, R. Turning the Templar Key. London: Lewis Masonic, 2007.

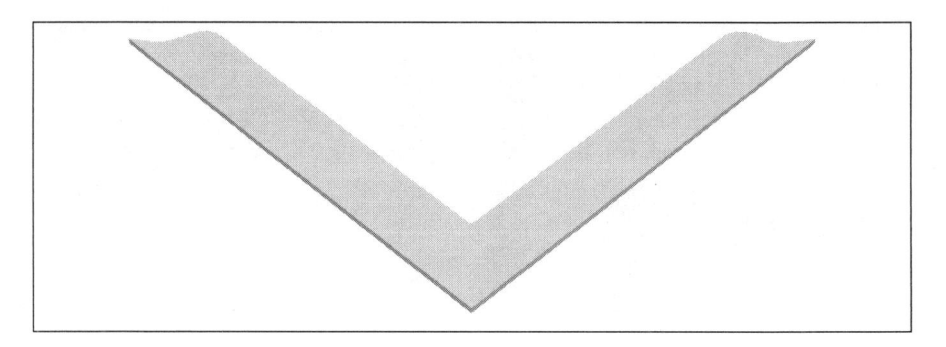

afford into the antiquity of the V in connection with an anthropomorphic goddess.[10]

As I show in a later chapter, Freemasonry preserves the symbol of the chevron in the shape of the Master's Square.

The first writing symbols of cuneiform were more closely linked to their counting-token ancestors than to the sounds of spoken language. They were representations of the word for an object so each word had to have its own symbol. This is called a logogram and every word you want to use needs a distinct symbol. Every writer and every reader must learn every one of those logograms if they are to read and write. This required tremendous effort to learn and so its use was restricted to a limited number of skilled people.

The system of privilege which drove the expansion of Sumer was linked to the power of the newly discovered writing symbols. Schmandt-Besserat explains:

> During the period from 3500 to 2500 B.C., Sumer had a redistribution economy involving three main components: (1) a temple which conferred meaning and pomp on the act of giving; (2) an elite who administered the communal property; and (3) commoners who produced surplus goods and surrendered them to the temple. This redistributive economy relied upon a system of record keeping and, indeed, could not have succeeded without it. This function was fulfilled in the third millennium B.C. by cuneiform writing and, going further back in time, by tokens.[11]

As cuneiform exploited the writing symbols they evolved to represent the sound of a syllable of speech instead of a word. This meant a smaller set of standardised symbols could be memorised and it simplified the task of writing and reading. Here is a later cuneiform symbol for the word "barley" from around 600 BCE.

10 Gimbutas, M. op. cit.

11 Schmandt-Besserat, D. op. cit.

The little triangle shapes were made by pressing a stylus into soft clay, but as a system of encoding speech it was still complex and used over 2,000 symbols, each of which had to be memorised.

Writing symbols mutated into a different set of logograms in Egypt where they were called hieroglyphs. Each hieroglyph is one of four types. It can be an alphabetic sign which represents a single sound, although the Egyptians took most vowels for granted and did not write them down. It can be a syllabic sign which represents a combination of consonants. It can be a stylised picture of the object it describes (rather like the barley symbol shown above), in which case it is followed by an upright stroke, to indicate that the word is complete with the one sign. Or it can be a determinative, which is a picture of an object to help the reader understand an abstract idea. The Egyptians only used the alphabetic hieroglyphs to sound out imported words, and so failed to discover the real power inherent in the alphabetic symbols of writing.

Above is my first name, which I have written in alphabetic hieroglyphs:

As you can see, it is not an easy script to write. To become a good writer, I would need to practise a lot more. Nevertheless this group of writing symbols helped the Ancient Egyptians become wealthy and successful. But the symbols of writing had another trick to play on humanity.

Fortune Favours the Symbol Writer

The Canaanites or Phoenicians were a mixture of desert dwellers and sea traders. They lived in a series of little city-states along the western seaboard of the land of Canaan. The alphabet they adopted later spread to a struggling little kingdom called Israel, and the Jews used its symbols to write the Bible. The Phoenicians were manufacturers of, and traders in, glass and high-quality purple dye. But most important of all, they were skilled seamen who ranged far and wide to trade. They had little time for the complex and clumsy symbols of cuneiform or hieroglyph but discovered that a small set of symbols could stand for all the possible sounds of a complete spoken language.

Alphabetic symbols empower a small group of geometric images (usually thirty or fewer) to represent every sound which a speaker can utter.

These symbols quickly became the dominant type of writing symbol among the Phoenician traders. As Hackwell points out:

> The Sumerian writing system became abstract and linear. Archaeologists and experts in ancient Semitic languages expected to find evidence that the users of cuneiform took the next logical step—that of using signs to represent clusters of

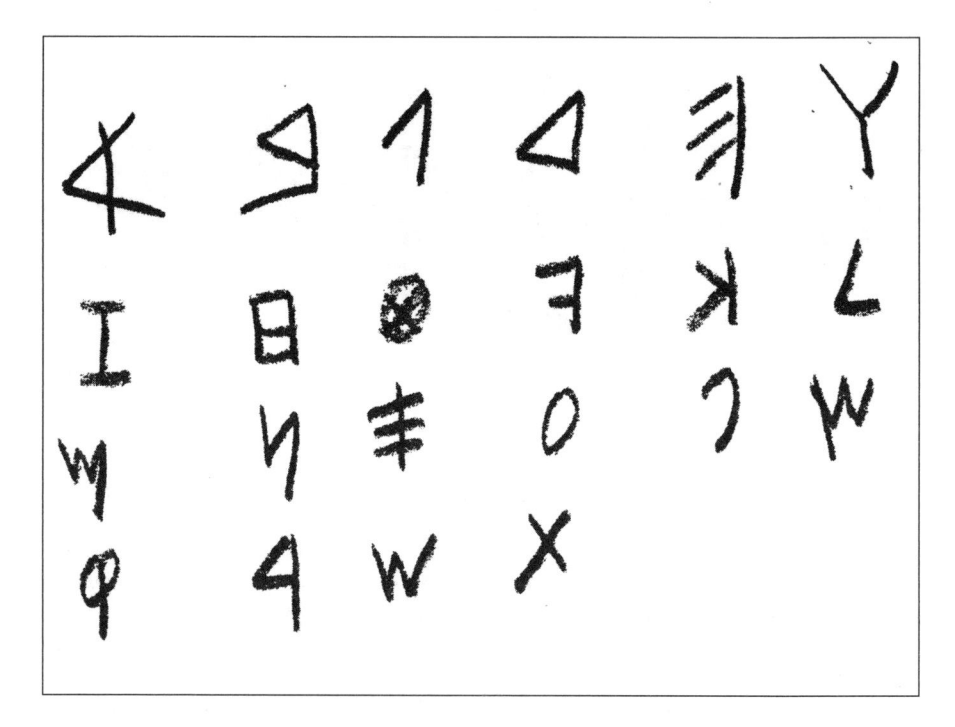

sounds, called syllables. But such is not the case. The Canaanites appear to have bypassed that concept when they discovered the alphabet, for they recognised that speech consisted of basic sounds that could be represented with a very few signs.[12]

Between 1200 and 900 BCE, a Canaanite symbolic alphabet appeared which could preserve and transmit any thought which could be put into words in Hebrew, Phoenician, or Aramaic. Above are the symbols of that alphabet.

The following page shows my name written in Phoenician symbols (I have written it from left to right, not right to left, as the Phoenicians used):

When David became king of the Jews, the Phoenicians were using an alphabet of just twenty-two geometric symbols which could store and transmit any word that a Phoenician could say. These were the writing symbols that carried a message from King Solomon to King Hiram of Tyre seeking help to build the iconic Temple of Jerusalem. The symbol of that famous temple, and the role it played in creating a system to understand Masonic Symbology, is something which I will discuss later in this book.

The symbols of writing quickly spread to Greece, powering the explosion of classical knowledge and preserving the words of Socrates and Plato, and the works of Euclid, for us to read today. The Greek alphabetic symbols spread to Rome and gave birth to the Latin alphabet.

A New Alphabet Appears

So far, we have seen four waves of symbols which have driven the progress of humanity. The first symbols were geometric

---

12   Hackwell, W John, .op. cit.

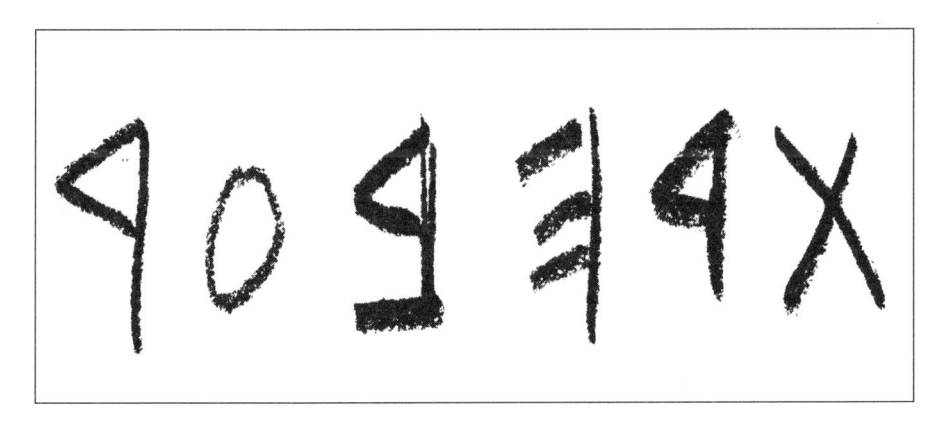

emotive symbols. As farming became established, the geometric emotive symbols reappeared and became more powerful. At first they were drawn on top of the realistic images, such as loaves of bread and images of fertile women, but eventually they became separate, purely geometric, images. Initially they were engraved onto portable objects, such as figurines and tokens of sacred bread, but as the cult of farming became more successful they were used to adorn permanent buildings (such as the Newgrange complex).

As settled communities grew and become more prosperous, humans started to own more objects and a set of symbols emerged to help them count things. The cumbersome way of counting with a token for each animal, or jar of oil, gave way to a new set of abstract number symbols which could count anything real or imaginary and even count themselves. These new symbols had no limit. They could count anything no matter how large. They could count the stars in the universe or the grains of sand on a beach. This was something new, and far beyond the capability of concrete symbol counting.

Initially used as a means of administering and controlling the actions of people, this new class of symbols proved to have the power of storing and increasing knowledge. (And notably, Freemasonry came to distrust written language, as it can easily become a tool of repression. Freemasons insisted on teaching using emotive symbols and poetic verbal metaphor.)

The power of symbols within writing is limited by their failure to be unambiguous. This is not a problem for emotive symbols as they create unambiguous empathic feelings.

The power of symbols has created a complex society very different from the groups of hunter-gatherers who first scratched the simple lozenge symbol on scraps of red ochre. But the early symbols have never gone away. It is just that we humans pay more attention to the newer language symbols, because they speak to our minds in words. The older symbols work in different, more subtle, less obvious ways, so we feel them in our "hearts" and cannot explain why we feel as we do.

Over 500 years ago, Freemasonry recognised that some parts of our brains have a strange, yet powerful, relationship with particular symbols. As a Freemason I am aware of symbols and their import.

To understand how and what symbols do to our minds we need to look inside our heads. There is something in the human brain that gives symbols their sacred power.

Chapter 4

The Power of Symbols on the Human Brain

Humans Have Two Minds

The human mind has evolved to recognise and respond to symbols, but this is a part of our mind which feels rather than speaks. This makes it almost impossible for us to put into words the effect symbols have on us. Yet the emotions symbols can trigger between humans have changed the way society has developed. To understand why humans are the only species which has this ongoing relationship with symbols, we need to look inside our heads.

In your brain, there are two complete working halves. The left and right hemispheres of the human brain are both individually capable of keeping you alive and functioning even if the other side of your head was destroyed. There is a more subtle purpose. You have an evolutionary advantage in having two cerebral hemispheres. If this was not so, then humans would have evolved a less complex, and less biologically demanding, unified brain. Current brain research shows that it is this twin-brained evolutionary development which has facilitated how we interact with symbols.[1]

Your two hemispheres communicate via a structure called a corpus callosum, which is a massive connecting cable made up of about 800 million neurons linking your hemispheres. During the latter half of the twentieth century, one radical treatment for epilepsy involved cutting this link and creating an individual with two disconnected brains. Roger Sperry studied these patients and discovered that the two hemispheres are different and have evolved for different purposes.[2] He found that the right hemisphere loves symbols and metaphor, while the left hemisphere likes words. Many vertebrates and all birds have also evolved split brains.

Consciousness fulfils two conflicting functions, best understood in terms of how our attention works. To carry out delicate tasks, your brain needs to focus attention narrowly

---

[1] McGilchrist, I. The Master and His Emissary. Connecticut: Yale University Press, 2009.
[2] Sperry, R. The Eye and the Brain. San Francisco: Freeman 1956

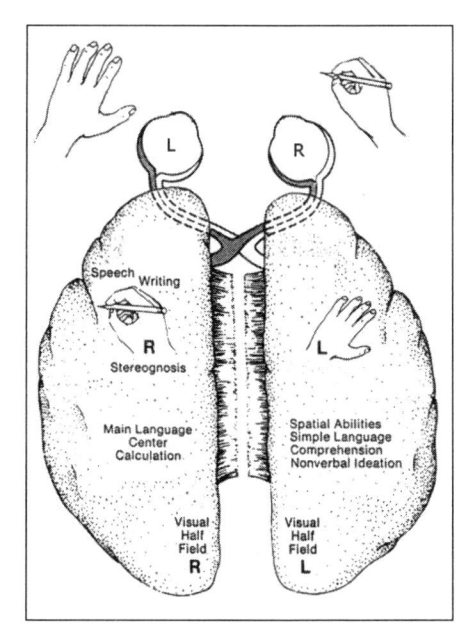

(say to pick up a grain of corn instead of the piece of stone that lies next to it), but at the same time it has to maintain a wide open field of attention so it remains aware of predators. If you cannot concentrate you starve, and if you do not remain alert you get killed and eaten. The evolutionary answer was to evolve two brains, a right brain taking a wide overview, using symbols to compress information about the nature of surrounding reality, and a left brain able to concentrate on more detailed tasks. These two different ways of paying attention have made us susceptible to the influence of symbols.

The result of this evolutionary survival quirk has given humans two thinking systems, one that is articulate, and one that responds to symbols. Your intellect analyses but your "heart" synthesises. A symbol evokes understanding without needing to convey information.

The human left brain is unable to understand metaphor, narrative or the import of emotive symbols. We listen to stories,

visualise symbols and react emotionally to images with our inarticulate right hemisphere.[3]

Your left hemisphere concentrates its narrow focused attention while your right hemisphere stays alert to what is happening around you. But each hemisphere understands the world in a different way. The right hemisphere recognises meaning in symbols and sees connections. The left sees bits of the world which it often cannot link together. The emotional response to ancient symbols happens in our right hemispheres. The way our brains work helps us concentrate on a topic of interest and ignore anything outside.[4] It gives us our hidden sense of the meaning of symbols, which we struggle to put into words.

Our right hemisphere has evolved to detect threats. It is good at spotting emotional changes and alerting us to potential problems. To some extent we process language in both hemispheres, but the way in which each hemisphere interprets what it reads or hears is different. The left hemisphere is good with words, including syntax and grammar, but it is the right hemisphere that understands context and metaphor. And it is the right hemisphere which perceives visual symbols, although it is unable to explain them in words. At this point it is worth noting that the function of the corpus callosum, the wiring that connects the two hemispheres, is not to communicate information between the hemispheres, it is to inhibit one or other of the hemispheres from acting. Our brain's evolutionary advantage stems from this fact: if the right hemisphere perceives a threat, it can turn off the focused attention of the left and force you to become alert to

---

3   McGilchrist, I. op. cit.

4   Arnheim, R. Visual Thinking. California: University of California Press, Berkeley, 1969.

your surroundings. This is essential to avoid being eaten by predators. Likewise, the left hemisphere can stop the right hemisphere from prattling on, indulging its curiosity about everything around it, and get you to focus attention on tasks that are necessary to stay alive. But this means that when we try to use words to explain symbols we encourage our left hemisphere to inhibit the right. This was why my students were not able to explain how the symbols affected them, although they were consistent in spotting ones with a powerful emotional message.

Symbols Have Sex Appeal

A surprising side effect of the interaction between symbols and the right hemispheres of human brains is that some symbols have an unexpected ability to be sexually attractive.

The ancient symbols of farming were associated with sacred temples devoted to various goddess figures. These symbols, as my survey showed, appeal to a basic instinct in both young men and young women. Further tests showed that both men and women produced a strong galvanic skin response when looking at these traditional shapes; in other words the symbols made them sweat. When I followed up with additional tests, I found that their emotional response was one of attraction. I got a further clue when many students said that those ancient geometric symbols are sexy. They seem to tap into a deep emotional level of the human spirit.

Then I found something even more interesting. My daughter, who is a jeweller, turned some of these goddess images into pendants and bracelets. The feedback she got from the women who wore the pieces was that the symbols were extremely sexy.

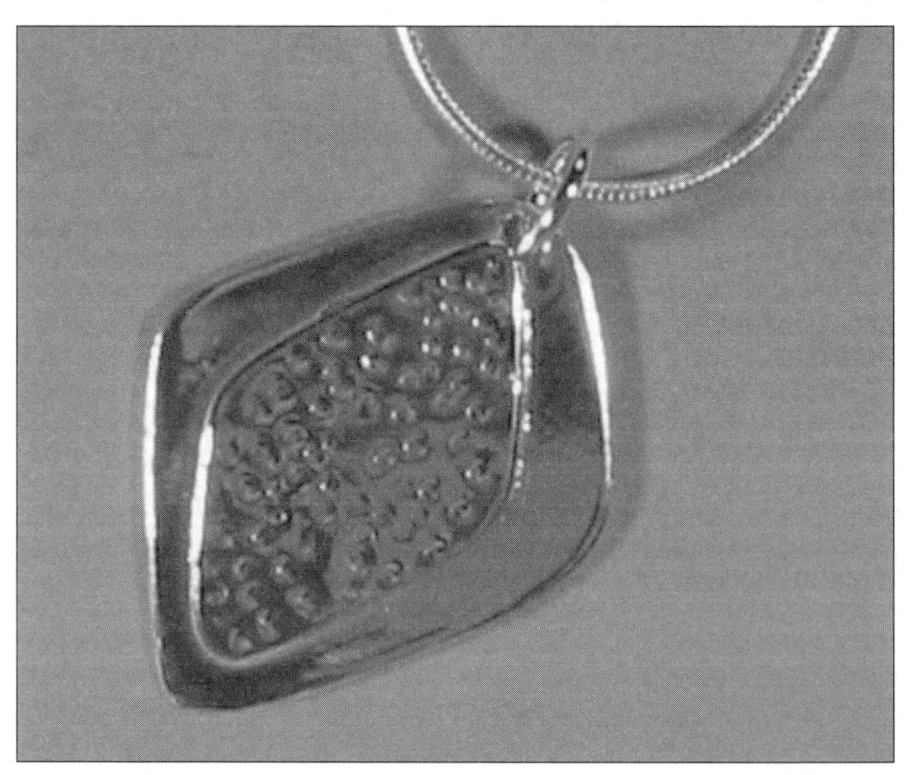

My tests show that both men and women have a strong galvanic skin response when they look at these traditional symbols. Ancient goddess symbols are sexy because they tap into the human sense of smell.

Professor Martha McClintock, of the University of Chicago, published a groundbreaking study thirty years ago showing that the menstrual cycles of women living together tended to synchronise. Subsequent brain scan research has shown that compounds known as pheromones, found in male and female sweat, trigger activity in the brains of the opposite sex. These subjectively odourless chemicals are sensed by two small pits, the vomeronasal organ (VNO), high inside each nostril. They are known to trigger mating and other behaviour in rodents. And they play a similar, if less frenetic, role in humans. Humans are sexually attracted to the scent of fresh sweat in the opposite sex. And these ancient symbols trigger fresh sweat.

We have all seen the effect of pheromones on animals. A dog that urinates on a post is leaving pheromones behind to claim territory. A female dog in heat releases pheromones that will attract male dogs from miles around. Ants leave behind pheromones to mark a fast trail to unsuspecting picnickers. Humans look at ancient symbols and sweat pheromones.

Pheromones are responsible for the physical chemistry that is the "love at first sight" we sometimes experience. They deliver messages about a person's sexual state and play a role in helping us choose a mate whose genetic resistance to disease complements our own. This serves the evolutionary purpose of helping couples who are likely to have healthy children recognise each other. This is why symbols which trigger the emission of human pheromones remain popular. They are inherently sexy.

But a word of warning. You cannot simply rely on wearing the right symbols to make you sexy. Not all male pheromones are equally attractive. The male pheromone androstenone is not the same as androstenol. Androstenol is the scent produced by fresh male sweat and is attractive to females. Androstenone is produced by male sweat after exposure to oxygen — i.e. when less fresh — and is perceived as highly unpleasant by females. So, men who believe that macho, sweaty body odour is attractive to women are deluding themselves. They need to constantly produce fresh sweat or change their clothes every twenty minutes to remove any trace of the oxidized sweat. Generally, the female-repelling androstenone is the more prominent male body odour, as the fresh-sweat odour of androstenol disappears quickly, unless constantly replenished. And that replenishment is something that sexy symbols can help with.

This is why my volunteers found these ancient symbols sexy. When males or females see one of these symbols they exude fresh sweat which is sexually attractive to the right person. Claus Wedekind, a scientist at the University of Bern, did a series of tests to find out how humans use body odour to select mates. He asked a group of women to sniff T-shirts that had been worn by a group of unknown — and unwashed — men. All they had to do was say which shirts smelled best. The experiment was designed to find out if humans, like mice, use body odour to identify genetically appropriate mates. Female volunteers, like their rodent counterparts, were attracted to genetically suitable men.

The ancient farming symbols which males and females both find attractive, stimulate them to give off fresh, sexually attractive sweat.

No wonder these erotically charged symbols were venerated as sacred. But the sexual attraction of these symbols has a firm biological basis both in the way our brains are wired and the way in which they stimulate us to emit sexual odorants.

The Influence of Stone Symbols

This "sweat" response to particular symbols is more than simple recognition. A "shape" can generate emotions to make us act quickly. Simple organisms may identify a shape without needing to understand fully its true character. They just feel the fear. A good example of this can be seen in young birds, which have similar split brains to humans. A newly hatched chick can distinguish between the shape of a hawk and the shape of a goose by the shadow they cast from the sky. The chick will try to hide from the hawk's silhouette and ignore the goose's.

Emotions are triggered without any thought on our part. Fear is triggered by seeing a snake, long before the left hemisphere thinks the word "snake". Symbolic shapes and smells trigger emotions without any need for judgement. Emotions are like smoke alarms. They go off because they detect particles in the air. So when we are in danger we have a psychological mechanism in place that reacts to dangers and triggers bodily responses, just as there is a mechanism in a smoke alarm that sounds an alarm when it detect smoke particles. And that mechanism responds to symbols.

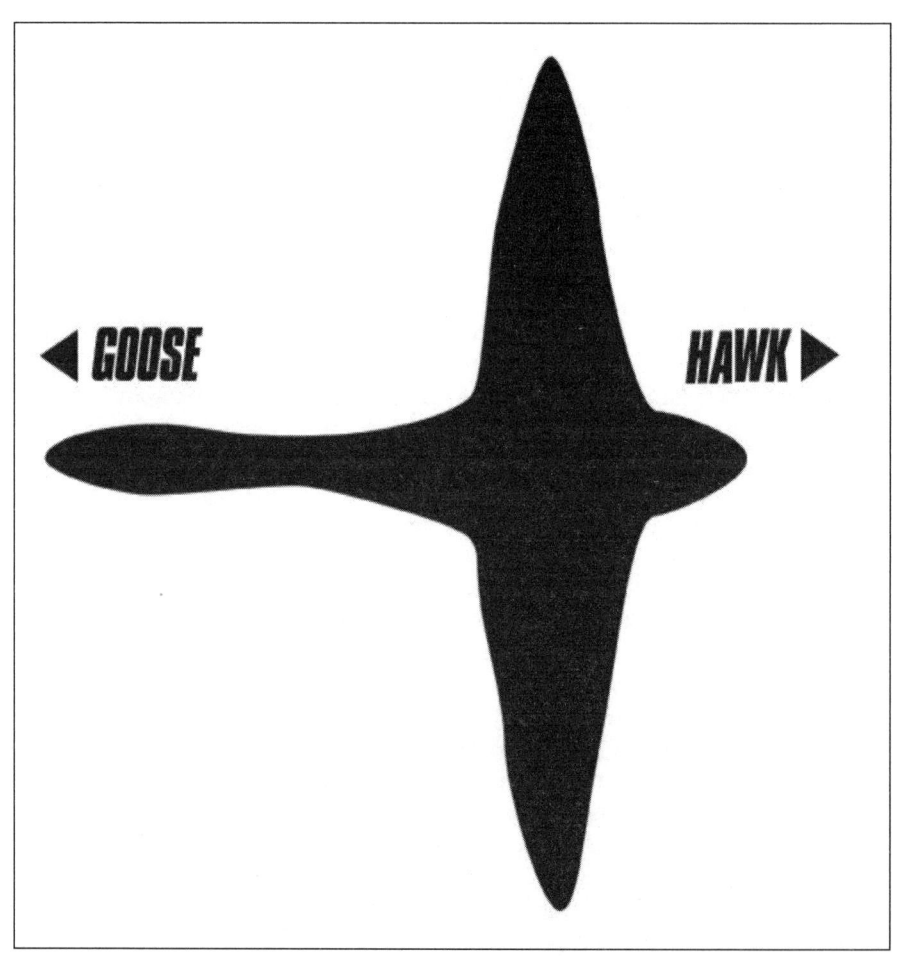

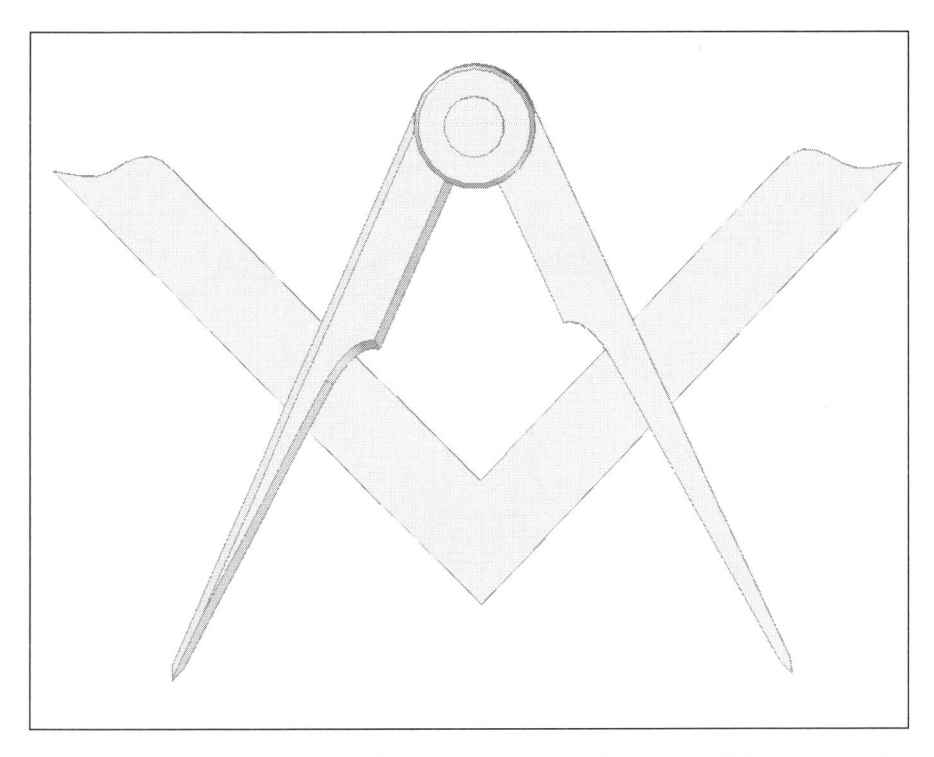

Freemasonry recognised this effect 500 years ago and set about sensitising its members to the import of certain symbols. It did this by distracting the verbal left hemisphere as it performs ritual actions, and so left the right hemisphere free to enjoy the emotional warmth of the symbol. It is no coincidence that the badge of Freemasonry echoes the oldest lozenge symbol ever drawn, the sexy chevron.

Stone Symbols Have Sacred Power

As humans settled down to farm and built towns and cities, symbols appeared on buildings. Stones were used as markers, or for building large structures, and symbols were carved into them. During the late Neolithic period, before the symbols of writing appeared, the emotive symbols of farming can be found carved into the stone walls of chambers all over what is now Europe. Perhaps some of the best examples of these stone-carved symbols can be seen in the Boyne Valley of Ireland at the three mounds of Newgrange, Knowth, and Dowth. These are massive man-made hills with rock-lined chambers constructed inside them. The rocks both inside the mounds and on the kerbstones surrounding them are completely covered with examples of the sexy farming symbols which still excite modern men and women.

A traditional lozenge and spiral symbol of farming is carved on the kerbstone at Newgrange. Archaeologist George Eogan says:

> We do not know the nature of the ceremonies, but the various features, such as stone settings, must have served a related purpose... It may be assumed that part of the ritual involved exotic items, notable amongst which would have been the conical stone objects [counting

The Lewis Guide to Masonic Symbols

The Power of Symbols on the Human Brain

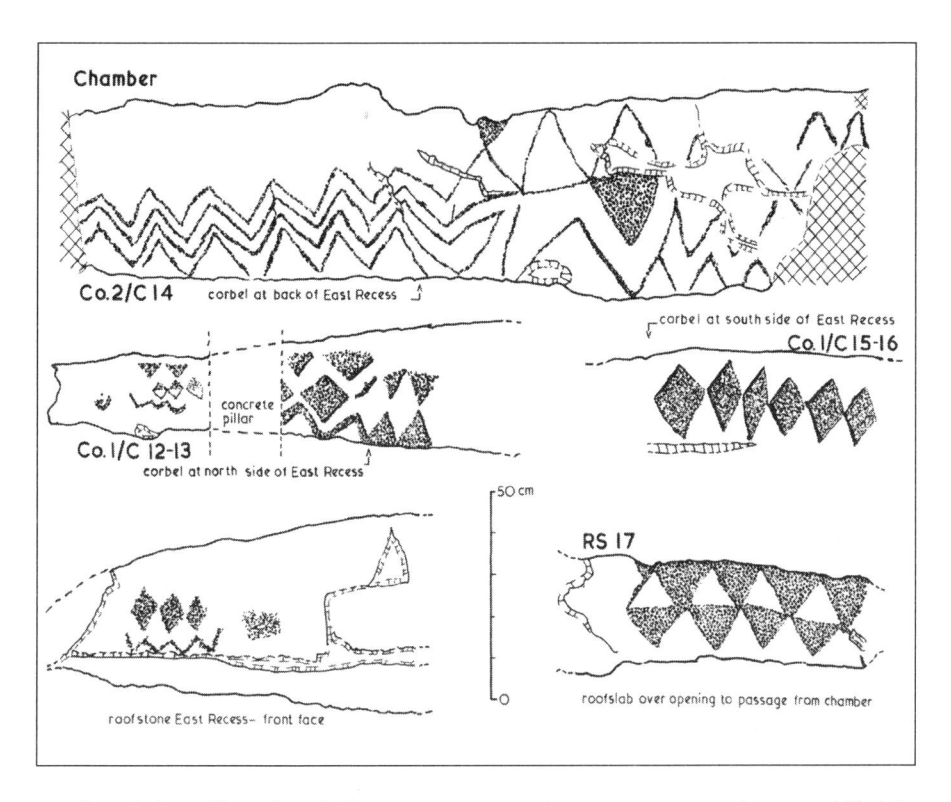

tokens?] from Knowth and Newgrange... the rites could in part have concerned fertility, emphasising the continuity of society.[5]

With the rise of cities, more and more symbols came to be carved into places of worship and a particular class of stoneworkers, men known as masons, became skilled in shaping stones and carving these symbols. It is no coincidence that a group of medieval stone-Masons realised that stone symbols could influence human minds. They set out to study the symbols and the way people responded to them.

---

5 Eogan, G. Knowth and the Passage Tombs of Ireland. London: Thames & Hudson, 1986.

Chapter 5:

How Symbols Created Freemasonry

Symbols and Myth Work Together

During the mid-fifteenth century, in Scotland, the aid of powerful emotive symbols was enlisted by an elite group of kings, priests, and would-be kings, as tools to sustain political support. There were two important aspects to this means of manipulation. Emotive geometric symbols were carved into the stonework of prestigious buildings, where the people regularly assembled, and popular myths were recited about the import of these symbols.

At that time a rich Scottish noble, William Sinclair, accumulated more land than the king and wanted to seize the crown of Scotland. The Stuart kings had the Abbey of the Holy Rood that housed the powerful symbol of the True Cross, but Sinclair had no symbolic building or venerated symbol to prove his right to rule. So he hired an architect, deeply versed in the power of myth and symbolism, and commissioned him to build an ornate symbol-carved building to rival the Holy Rood and the abbey that housed it.

A group of stoneworkers became embroiled in this battle and saw firsthand the power that symbols had. When Sinclair's bid for power failed, these stoneworkers were put out of work, but a group of them came together in Aberdeen to study the power of symbols and develop ways to sensitise individuals to their import. This group are the first Freemasons, and they were men deeply skilled in the ancient tradition of carving symbols into stone and creating places of public assembly. The symbols they studied created modern Freemasonry.

Buildings Are Symbols

We saw in a previous chapter that around five or six thousand years ago, before the arrival of the symbols of writing, humans built stone structures to hold religious assemblies. We can see from the ruins of those crude temples that their architects had discovered they could heighten the sense of excitement experienced by their followers if they carved emotive geometric symbols into the stone walls of the temples.

The new skill in shaping stones into emotive symbolic structures blossomed in Ancient Egypt. There the symbol of the triangle, which we saw so copiously carved into the walls of

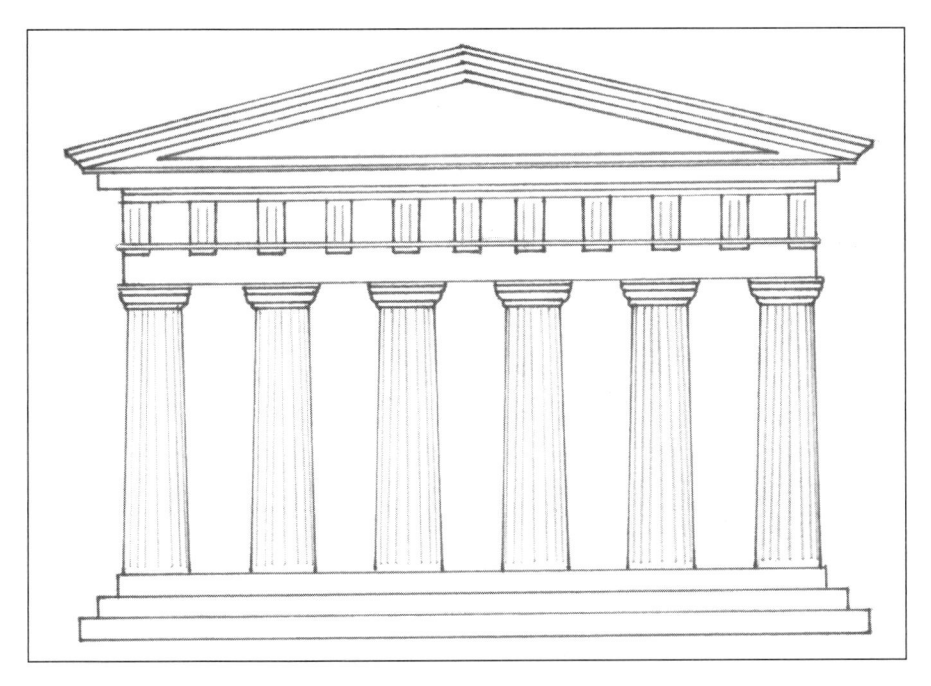

Newgrange, was writ large in the shape of the pyramid. Who can fail to be awestruck when they stand at the base of such a structure?

New skills in the working, moving, and shaping of stone were developed to create these massive chevron symbols. The Egyptians quarried stone, shaped it, lifted it into place, and bound it together.

They invented the trade we now call masonry, but it was the Greeks who discovered a new group of symbols which would be used by future architects. For symbolic temples to stand firm, they had to be built according to certain rules of structure. These rules were revealed to humans by the symbols of geometry. Geometric symbols came into their own during the classical Greek period.

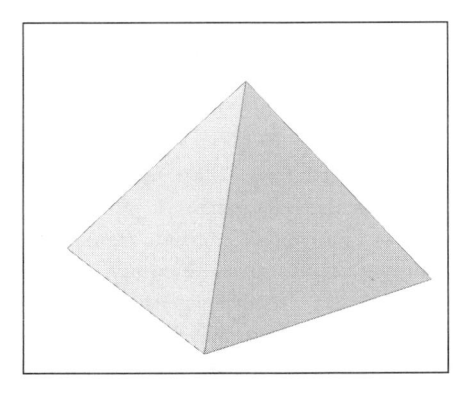

Knowledge of the nature of the symbols of geometry was needed by every builder in stone, and over time bigger and more magnificent temples were built.

By the Middle Ages in Britain this custom of constructing inspirational religious buildings had evolved into the tradition of cathedral building. And at Canterbury you can see the symbol of the triangle built into the façades. The stonemasons who built these magnificent buildings were highly skilled craftsmen who used the symbols of geometry. The buildings that stonemasons spent their whole lives constructing were more than symbolic structures; they incorporated emotive symbols into their façades. The Neolithic tradition of using emotive geometric symbols to inspire worshippers was manifest in their creation. In particular the men who founded Freemasonry, and established its study of symbology, witnessed the power of one particular emotive geometric symbol: the Cross. The evolution of this symbol had a great influence on the origins of Freemasonry.

How the True Cross Inspired the First Freemasons

Without writing symbols, the Roman Empire could not have spread so far or lasted so long. Yet even after this great success, reading and writing were far from being universal. Only a few administrators, leaders, and priests within the Roman Empire were able to use these symbols.

The later Roman emperors, when they proclaimed themselves gods, created stone statues and busts to distribute throughout their empire. The realistic symbol of the god-emperor was intended to carry a religious idea and create an emotional state of mind in vast numbers of illiterate individuals. This knowledge was not lost when Christianity became the official religion of the Roman Empire. The success of the Latin cross provides a powerful example of how a symbol is capable of conveying an entire religious philosophy.

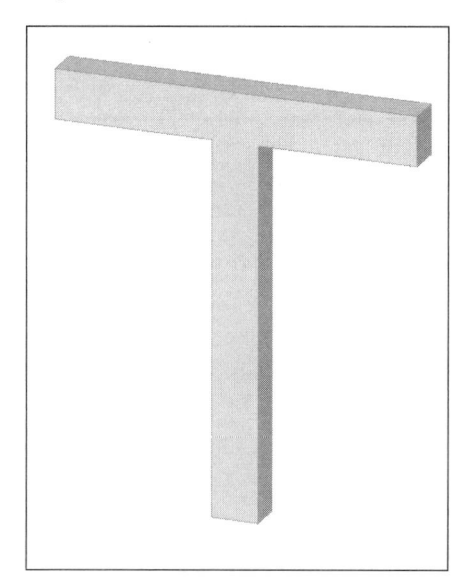

The cross of crucifixion, on which Jesus was put to death, was not an inspirational emotive symbol. It was a practical machine to cause pain. It did not have an upper section but was a simple T-shape, carefully crafted by the Romans to inflict a tremendous amount of pain with little effort. The individual to be punished would have his arms either tied or nailed to the cross piece (called the patibulum) which he would then be forced to carry to a previously erected upright post. The cross piece would be lifted onto the upright (called the stipe), leaving him with his weight suspended by his arms. His heels would then be nailed to the upright with his legs bent. The arms are fixed outward onto the cross piece, but left slightly bent. The victim will suffocate quickly, because he cannot move his lungs to breathe. His body is suspended on just three points of searing pain. Blood loss is minimal, and the victim remains fully conscious. He is in terrible pain.

The victim's body weight works against him, causing him to sag downwards, producing traumatic tension in the muscles of his arms, shoulders, and chest wall. The pain is indescribable as the ribcage is drawn upwards so that his chest is held in a position preventing exhalation. In order to avoid asphyxiation, the victim has no alternative but to push down on the wounds of his nailed feet to raise his body, so that his lungs can blow out and gasp in another chestful of air. The panic of not breathing is exchanged momentarily for the massive pain of standing upon impaled flesh. The overall effect of repeating this vile dilemma is increased anoxia (shortage of oxygen), leading to agonising cramps and a dramatically raised metabolic rate. Eventually the legs will cramp and fail and the victim will no longer be able to breathe. This could take days to occur and the trauma would be tremendous for the victim, just as it was intended to be. This Roman tool of torture had no symbolic dimension and its shape was never inspirational, unlike the powerful symbol of the True Cross.

The symbol of the Latin cross is different from the Roman torture device. It is not the shape of the tool used by the Romans to punish individuals but a symbol which echoes a man with his arms outstretched to God and his head held high.

This powerful symbol of the Latin cross evolved into a badge of kingly power in the Middle Ages. It was exposure to this potent symbol and its accompanying myth which inspired the first Freemasons to begin a systematic study of the power of symbols.

An early queen of Scotland, St. Margaret, who married King Malcolm in 1069, had brought a piece of the True Cross with her as her dowry. Malcolm's descendants built a magnificent symbolic building, the Abbey of the Holy Rood, to house the True Cross. Today the abbey stands behind Holyrood Palace and is a ruin.

The myth which became attached to the symbol of the Holy Rood (as the fragment was known) is that King David was attacked by a stag whilst out hunting and the Holy Rood materialised between him and the raging animal and saved his life. A symbol of a stag with a Latin cross intertwined in hits antlers was carved in stone at the entrance to the abbey. The same symbol now forms part of the entrance to Holyrood Palace, home of the Kings of Scots, which was built beside the ruins of the abbey. In the abbey's prime, pilgrims went there to venerate the fragment, listen to the recital of the myth, and give thanks to God for saving their king's life.

For many generations of Scottish kings up to James II, the symbol of the Holy Rood supported their God-given right to rule. However, in the middle of the fifteenth century that rich noble with designs on the crown, Sir William Sinclair, hired the architect Gilbert Haye, a man who was deeply versed in the power of symbol and myth, to construct a building to rival the Abbey of the Holy Rood.

The end result was an ornate building called Rosslyn Chapel, which is steeped in symbolism and marinated in myth.[1] And the men who were to become the first Freemasons worked on its construction.

When Sinclair's bid for the crown of Scotland failed, his estates were broken up, his inspirational chapel fell into disrepair, and the stonemasons who had carved the symbol-packed building were put out of work. A sizeable group of them moved to Aberdeen, to work together on a large church dedicated to St. Nicholas.[2] These men realised that they had stumbled upon a great truth and set about trying to understand what they had learned about symbols and myth. They had been shown symbols, which they then carved. They had also been told poetic myths, which made sense of the emotions the symbols evoked in their hearts. They developed ways of passing on this knowledge to their apprentice masons. These men created the "peculiar system of morality, veiled in allegory and illustrated by symbols" that has become Freemasonry. The evidence for this can be seen in a piece of symbolic representation which they created. The first Masonic Tracing Board.

1 Lomas, R. Turning the Templar Key. London: Lewis Masonic, 2007.
2 Ibid.

How Symbols Taught the First Freemasons

The activity of the first members of the Lodge of Aberdeen only came to light when an early artefact of Masonic Symbolism, known as the Kirkwall Scroll, was carbon dated on 21 July 2000. The Kirkwall Scroll is a hanging cloth made up of three pieces of sailcloth sewn together and hand-painted.

The carbon dating was reported in an article by Orkney journalist Kath Gourlay, which appeared in *The Times* and the *Daily Telegraph*. It said:

> The results of radiocarbon dating carried out on a rare wall hanging have shocked members of a Masonic Lodge in the Orkney Islands, who have been told that their document is a medieval treasure worth several million pounds...radiocarbon dating of the scroll points to the huge 18-ft sailcloth hanging as being fifteenth-century.[3]

But the issue of the age of the symbol-covered cloth was not straightforward. There were two radiocarbon dates for the scroll. An old one for the centre section and a much later date for both outer sections.

The cloth was thought to be an early Masonic floor-cloth (something rather like a carpet which is painted with symbols to be laid on the floor for a Masonic ritual to take place on it) from an eighteenth-century London Masonic Lodge. It had been given to the Lodge by a Mason named William Graham. He joined Lodge Kirkwall Kilwinning on 27 December 1785, and presented the scroll to the Lodge a month later on January 27th, 1786. For many years it was generally believed that William Graham had painted the floor-cloth himself as a gift to the Lodge he was joining.

But the carbon dating ruled out this possibility for the centre section.

The 280-year difference between the age of the central strip and the two side strips made the claim that William Graham painted the whole cloth impossible. The outer strips have been cut from a single strip of material before being sewn to the outer edges of the centre. Graham would have had to obtain two strips of cloth, one new and the other 280 years old; then he would have had to cut the new cloth in two and sew the two half-strips to the outside of the older cloth before starting to paint. Why bother? If he wanted a wider strip of canvas he could just have sewn the new strip alongside the old to obtain the greater width. The radiocarbon evidence indicates he added the outer strips to preserve the inner cloth. I showed in *Turning the Hiram Key* that Graham disguised the older central section because it contained symbols which the Kirk of Scotland considered pagan. Many of them are ancient emotive symbols of farming.[4]

All the Masonic symbols that form the subject matter of the modern degrees of Freemasonry can be found on the scroll. Before its carbon dating the accepted view was that Freemasonry developed rituals, based on old craft guild mystery plays, and then later added symbols to illustrate its rituals. The discovery of a complete set of ancient emotive symbols on a floor-cloth dating to the earliest known Masonic Lodge reveals a different explanation.

The poetic rituals and myths were attached to the symbols to help Freemasons understand the symbols' meanings and to help them become sensitive to the emotive power the symbols project. Early on, Masons become aware of the import and power of these symbols.

---

3   Gourlay, K. Daily Telegraph, July 2000.

4   Lomas, R. Turning the Hiram Key. London: Lewis Masonic, 2005.

The Emotional Power of Symbols

When the estates of William Sinclair were broken up in 1480, Gilbert Haye's workforce was disbanded and some of them went to work in Aberdeen. The Burgh Council Minutes of 1483 contain the earliest written reference to a Masonic Lodge anywhere in the world. The Lodge of Aberdeen was attached to the burgh church of St. Nicholas, which was being rebuilt at the time. In that Lodge were a number of Masons who had worked on the powerful symbolism of Rosslyn Chapel. They took with them to Aberdeen a partial understanding of the innate power of symbols and set up a system of Lodge governance to help teach this.[5]

It was the practice of all early Masonic Lodges to draw symbols on the floor of the Lodge-room, and the Kirkwall Scroll shows that this concept went right back to the birth of Freemasonry.

Bro. W L Wilmshurst, a founder master of my own Lodge, wrote about the use of floor-cloths. The symbols of the degree to be conferred would be drawn on the floor of the Lodge and later erased by the candidate. This is what Wilmshurst said, in a private paper:

> In earlier days, when the Craft was not a popular social institution but a serious discipline in a philosophic and sacred science, instruction was not treated casually. The Tracing Board was not, as now, a product of the Masonic furnisher's factory; it was the most revered symbol in the Lodge; it was a diagram which every Brother was taught to draw for himself, so that both his hand and his understanding might be trained in Masonic work. The literary records show that at each Lodge meeting the Tracing Board of the Degree about to be worked was actually drawn from memory with chalk and charcoal on the floor of the Lodge by the Master, who from previous practice was able to do this quickly and accurately. In advancing from West to East during the Ceremony, the Candidate took the steps of the Degree over the diagram. The diagram was explained to him as an integral part of the Ceremony, and, before being restored to his personal comforts, he was required to expunge it with a mop and pail of water, so that uninitiated eyes might not see it and that he might learn a first lesson in humility and secrecy.

The central strip of the Kirkwall Scroll shows seven panels, each describing a step leading from the west to the east of the Lodge, as it was unrolled from bottom to top. The lessons begin with the basic symbols of the Craft; the central, pivotal step shows a tomb, symbolising the death of the ego; and the sequence progresses to an idyllic vision of the ecstatic bliss of the centre, displayed using realistic hunting-type symbols. A continuity of vision is maintained, from the sun, the moon and stars and the vision of the rising of a lozenge-shaped all-seeing eye in the first step, to an ordered arrangement of the heavens with the repeated symbols showing the stars rearranged as pillars around the moon as the centre. This well-structured sky stands above a final scene of oneness with nature. Each scene in this floor-cloth fits one of the seven spiritual steps to awareness that are still taught in esoteric Freemasonry.

The early Scottish Freemasons used just two simple ceremonies: a ritual of Initiation, and a procedure for becoming a Fellow of the Craft which entitled them to become a Master of the Lodge. Their records talk of them "having the Mason Word". They looked at symbols and tried to understand them and recited ritual poetry whilst they walked along the floor-cloth looking at the symbols.

5   Ibid.

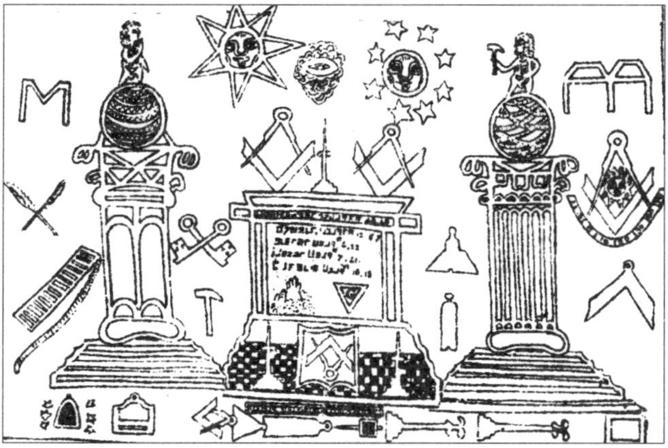

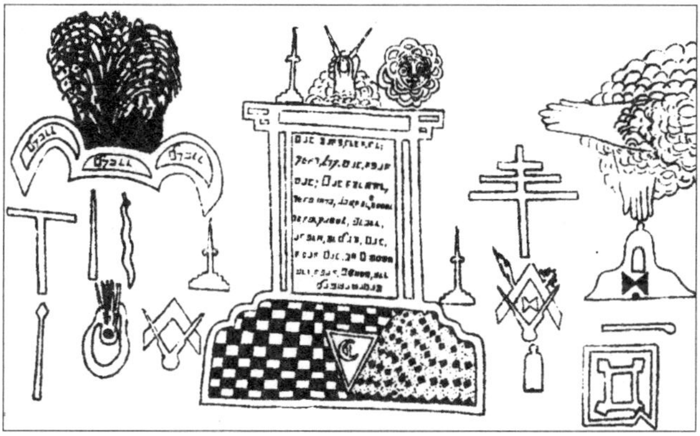

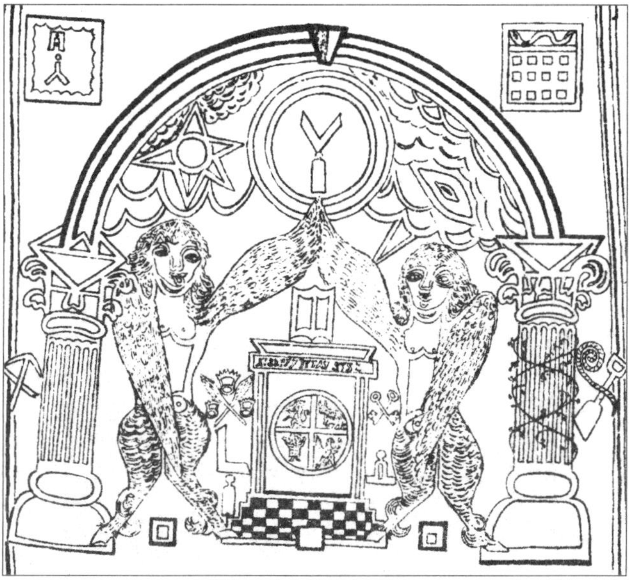

The Lewis Guide to Masonic Symbols

How Symbols Created Freemasonry

The Kirkwall Scroll with its symbols would have been unrolled during these ceremonies and the newly made Masons exposed to the symbols' wordless emotive messages as the members of the Lodge recited their mythical stories.

Over time many additional rituals have been added to the canon of Freemasonry and each helps a Masonic Candidate to learn more about a particular symbol and its power. The first Masons chose well, as the panels they created show the main symbols which have since had enormous impact on the development of many societies.

The only group of people to have studied those symbols over many generations is the Freemasons. Over the last 500 years Masons have developed ways of sensitising individuals to the import of these symbols. Our way of teaching is odd. It involves reciting ritual; it involves "the art of memorie" because our rituals must be completely committed to memory and not read from books. (Freemasonry distrusts the written word as a potential tool of tyranny.) It involves acting out myths, and telling and listening to heroic tales. And all these actions take place in full view of the symbols which are being studied and talked about. Yet the symbols are never straightforwardly explained. Because it is impossible to capture their full import in words, the Craft has learned not to try. Instead it uses metaphor and poetry to quiet the left hemisphere so that the right hemisphere can impart its understanding of the symbols.

Those first Masons must have realised that certain groups of symbols work well together and, as Wilmshurst says, "symbols always comprise so much more than can be verbally explained".

With the first Freemasons came the first attempts to understand the power of symbols, to sensitise individuals to their messages and to try to harness their power for the good of society.

How Symbolic Teaching Spread

The first Aberdeen Lodge of Freemasons had been given a practical demonstration of the enhanced force created by combining myth and symbol by the architect of Rosslyn Chapel, Sir Gilbert Haye.[6] He took the story of the building of Solomon's Temple as a way of teaching the import of ancient symbols such as St. Matthew's staff. Those first Freemasons created a system of teaching which has continued to expand to the present day. When a Candidate stands before the First Degree Tracing Board and listens to the rolling poetry of the traditional explanation of its landmarks, which is delivered from memory by a Past Master, he is immersed in the import of the symbol and feels its meaning in a way no rational explanation can hope to emulate. During the ritual the Freemason lives the symbol.

The import of the symbols is one of the secrets of Masonry which cannot be stolen or given away.

You can see the continuity of teaching as Freemasonry spread southwards from Scotland, first to York and much later to London. The oldest known Tracing Boards in Yorkshire date back to the early eighteenth century and are painted on wooden panels. They have not been carbon dated so their exact age is unknown. But from their documented history they are at least 300 years old. Their images are similar to those of the Kirkwall Scroll and were used for the same purposes.

---

6   Lomas, R. Turning the Templar Key. London: Lewis Masonic, 2007.

How Symbols Created Freemasonry

73

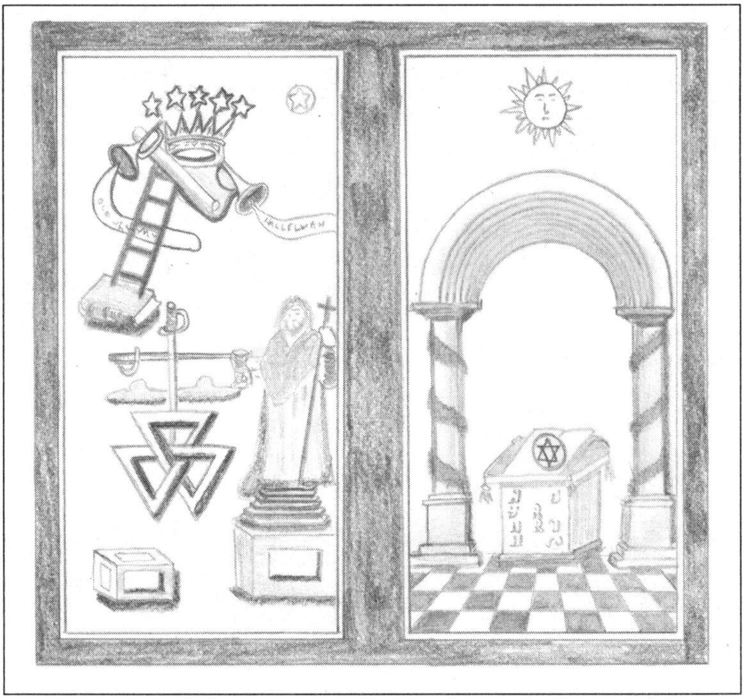

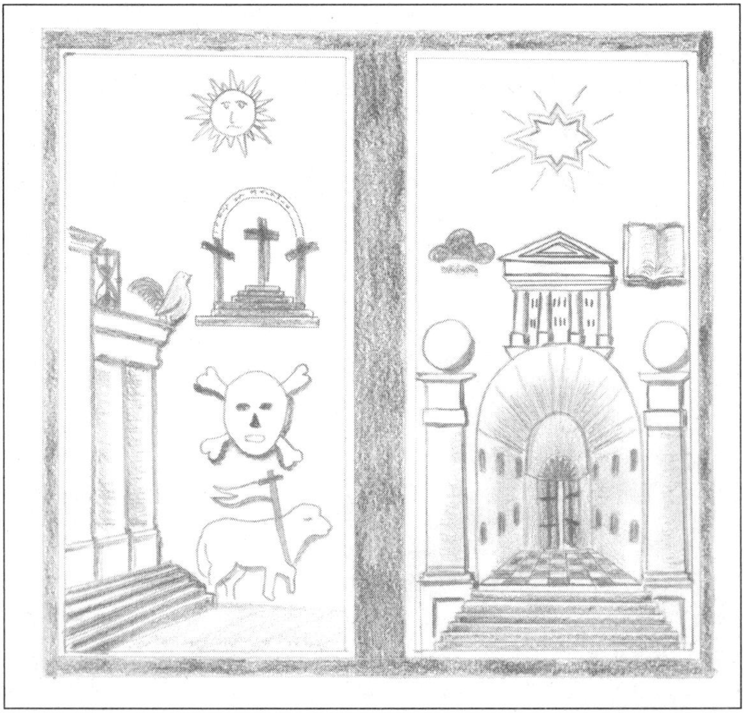

Next, let us take a look at a much later tracing table cloth. This is a silk cloth which could be laid on a camp table to hold a Lodge within a military company in the field, which dates from around the time of the American Revolution. We see the same symbols still being taught:

Freemasonry had discovered a way to organise groups of men so that they could pass on ways of self-improvement and learn the import of the messages carried by symbols.

Chapter 6

Symbols Can Penetrate the Mind of God

A Symbol that Analyses Equality

Immediately after the Restoration of the British Monarchy in 1660, a group of Freemasons, sensitised to the import of symbols by their ritual training, tapped into a completely new set of symbols. These unleashed a power that has completely changed the world. They made it possible to predict exactly the time and extent of many natural events. They made it possible to destroy the world. These symbols are nothing less than the words of a great cosmic language which lays bare the secrets of how the universe works.

England suffered a devastating civil war in the seventeenth century. It began as an argument about the importance of the Stuart kings compared to their Parliaments, and ended with King Charles I beheaded in public. During this turbulent period, symbolic science began. Somehow, in the midst of the bitter battles between King and Parliament, the symbols of modern, mathematical science appeared among humanity. A superstitious country, which burnt alive at least 100 elderly women a year on suspicion that they were causing disease by casting the "evil eye", suddenly developed a critical mass of discerning mathematical scientists who quickly became adept in the application of the symbols of science. This did not happen by chance. A symbol that was used by Masons to stand for Equality and Balance was rotated through "an angle of ninety degrees or the fourth part of a circle" to reveal a whole new meaning. Today, we find it on every computer keyboard and we call it the equal sign "=".

The chain of events which led to the recognition of this new symbol and the exploration of its power began on 28 November 1660, at Gresham College, London. This was the first meeting of the Royal Society, held after a public lecture by Christopher Wren. At this meeting, Freemason Bro. Sir Robert Moray brought together a group of men who were already trained to be alert to the import of symbols and who were inspired by the philosophical teaching of Freemasonry to study "the hidden mysteries of nature and science".[1]

---

1 Lomas, R. The Invisible College. London: Transworld, 2009.

The survivors of a civil war were not the most likely people to found modern science. After the death of Oliver Cromwell, Britain tottered on the brink of fresh conflict, until the controversial decision was taken to invite the King to return. Meanwhile, Sir Robert Moray brought together the founding members of the new Royal Society who had recently fought on opposite sides of the brutal civil war. His aim was to get them to solve the problems of geometry and military building and strengthen King Charles II's weak navy. Moray offered his Brother Masons a chance to study interesting problems and an opportunity to earn the favour of the newly restored king. But the symbols of mathematics opened up a much wider prospect.

Inspired by Masonic discussion about how the "hidden mysteries of nature and science" could help you "better know your Maker"; the founders of the Royal Society did more than simply solve a few military problems. They questioned the basic premises of religion and theology. Then they made contact with a group of symbols which enabled them to read and understand the plans of the Great Architect of the Universe.

John Wallis, who became the prophet of this new family of symbols, wrote about his links to the Craft and its role in the early meeting of the Royal Society. This Masonic environment was open to all symbols, and helped him recognise and understand the power which was latent in the symbols of mathematics.

Masonic Slide Rules and Early Arithmetic

John Wallis, who became Savilian Professor of Geometry at Oxford in 1649, recognised that certain symbols could be utilised to stand in for real things, and could then be manipulated to explain (or as scientists say "model") what was happening in the real world. When he passed this knowledge onto his brethren in the Royal Society, it opened up a whole new range of possibilities.

In 1678 he wrote a pamphlet about the meetings which led to the formation of the Royal Society:[2]

About the year 1645, while I lived in London (at a time when, by our civil wars, academic studies were much interrupted in both our Universities), beside the conversation of divers eminent divines as to matters theological, I had the opportunity of being acquainted with divers worthy persons, inquisitive into natural philosophy, and other parts of human learning; particularly into what hath been called New Philosophy or Experimental Philosophy. We did by agreements, divers of us, meet weekly in London on a certain day and hour, under a certain penalty, and a weekly contribution for the charge of experiments, with certain rules agreed amongst us to treat and discourse of such affairs... These meetings we held sometimes at Dr. Goddard's lodgings in Wood Street (or some other convenient place near), on occasion of his keeping an operator in his house for grinding glasses for telescopes and microscopes; sometimes at a convenient place (The Bulls Head) in Cheapside, and (in term time) at Gresham College at Mr. Foster's lectures (then the Astronomer Professor there) and, after the lecture ended repaired, sometimes to Mr. Fosters lodgings, sometimes to some other place not far distant.

2   Ibid

Our business was (precluding matters of theology and state affairs) to discourse and consider of Philosophical Enquiries...About the year 1648/9 some of our company being removed to Oxford (first Dr. Wilkins on his appointment by the Protector as Warden of Wadham College, then I and soon after Dr. Goddard) our company divided. Those in London continued to meet there as before (and we with them, when we had occasion to be there) and those of us at Oxford...continued such meetings in Oxford and brought these studies into fashion there.[3]

The "Philosophical Enquiries" Wallis mentions are the formal Masonic interest in the secret science of symbols and how they give insight into the hidden mysteries of nature. He was about to release what had formerly been a totally hidden power. He had got into the habit of discussing his ideas at Masonic meetings whose purpose was to sensitise the brethren to the import of symbols. There was no better venue or audience for his ideas at that time. This sensitisation prepared Wallis for a great step forward by opening his mind to a new family of symbols. These were more powerful than either the symbols of counting or the symbols of writing, although they draw on properties inherent in both. These are the symbols of mathematical equality, or as we know them today, the symbols of algebraic equations.

As a boy, Wallis had been fascinated by the symbols of counting. This was how he was first introduced to the idea that symbols could potentially manipulate reality. In later life, he said about the experience:

Mathematics, at that time with us, were scarce looked on as academical studies, but rather mechanical — as the business of traders, merchants, seamen, carpenters, surveyors of lands and the like.[4]

His first encounter with representative symbols was at the hands of a Freemason. Wallis was taught as a private pupil by Freemason and astrologer William Oughtred, the man who invented the slide rule. (The slide rule reduced multiplication and division to a simple mechanical manipulation of symbolic number positions, making it much easier to calculate the positions of the stars when casting a horoscope.) Wallis lived in Oughtred's house in Albury and received instruction in arithmetic. As a young man, Wallis moved to Cambridge where he became a Fellow of Queen's College. When he married Susanna Glyde in 1645, he gave up his fellowship and moved to London to become Secretary to the clergy of Westminster Abbey. There he renewed his friendship with his old tutor and was introduced to Oughtred's fellow Freemasons. He must have been pleased to find that there were men who shared the same interest, and who were able to guide him towards the deeper import of many symbols.

William Oughtred was a member of an early Lodge of speculative Freemasons but he was also the author of a book on arithmetic, *Clavis Mathematicae*. Oughtred introduced Wallis to the Masonic way of studying symbols. Wallis writes in his autobiography that he was so inspired by the inherent logic of Oughtred's book that he mastered its ideas within a couple of weeks. Before Wallis, nobody had realised the great power inherent in the symbol of equality and the Masonic philosophy of balance and harmony which it symbolised.

---

3   Wallis, J. A Defence of the Royal Society. London: Private Pamphlet, 1678.

4   http://www-history.mcs.st-andrews.ac.uk/Biographies/Wallis.html

Why Equations Are a Mystery

There is an incredible mystery hidden within the simple equations that we all learn at school.

Albert Einstein was so impressed by the knowledge that the symbolic theory of equations opened up that he wrote:

> We are in the position of a little child entering a huge library filled with books in many languages. The child knows someone must have written those books. It does not know how. It does not understand the languages in which they are written. The child dimly suspects a mysterious order in the arrangements of the books, but doesn't know what it is… We see a universe marvellously arranging and obeying certain laws, but only dimly understand these laws. Our limited minds cannot grasp the mysterious force that moves the constellations.[5]

The symbolic power of equations comes from two key factors:

- A symbol can be used to represent something which is real, like the speed a stone falls to the ground or the number of gulps of trapped air a man can take in a diving bell without running out of oxygen (these are actual problems considered by members of the early Royal Society).
- The equality described by an equation is total, absolute, and uncompromising.

The equals sign "=" first appeared in a book written by a Welshman from Tenby, Robert Recorde, who became a fellow of All Souls College, Oxford, in 1510.[6]

Recorde was a dedicated educationalist who wrote school textbooks about arithmetic and geometry in English, which was unusual for the time. He first used a symbol to stand in for the words "is equal to" in his 1557 book, *The* Whetstone of Witte. This is how he described the symbol "=":

> To avoid the tedious repetition of these woordes: is equalle to: I will settle as I doe often in woorke use, a paire of paralleles, or gemowe lines of one lengthe: =, bicause noe .2. thynges, can be moare equalle.[7]

When John Wallis began to discover the full power of the "=" symbol, he had the benefit of Masonic training to sensitise him to the two parts of Recorde's revelation. Freemasonic sensitisation suggests that the "=" symbol looks like the two pillars "☒" laid horizontally and meaning "is equal to". The Masonic ritual, Wallis would have learned, says this about the Level:

> The Level is to lay levels, and prove horizontals.
>
> The Level demonstrates that we are all sprung from the same stock, partakers of the same nature, and sharers in the same hope; and although distinctions among men are necessary to preserve subordination, yet ought no eminence of situation make us forget that we are Brothers; for he who is placed on the lowest spoke of fortune's wheel is equally entitled to our regard; as a time will come and the wisest of us knows not how soon when all distinctions, save those of goodness and virtue, shall cease, and Death, the grand leveller of all human greatness, reduces us to the same state.
>
> The Level being an emblem of equality, points out the equal measures the Senior Warden is bound to pursue in conjunction

---

5   Jammer, M. Einstein and Religion: Physics and Theology. New Jersey: Princeton University Press, 2004.
6   http://www.maths.ox.ac.uk/about/history
7   http://www.archive.org/details/TheWhetstoneOfWitte

with the Master in the well ruling and governing of the Lodge.

The Level teaches equality.

When moving from the degree of an Apprentice to that of Fellowcraft, he would first have to acknowledge the power of another symbol. The ritual describes it thus:

> First the Master asks the Junior Warden: "Bro. Junior Warden, are you a Fellowcraft Freemason?"
> He replies, "I am Worshipful Master. Try me and prove me."
> The Master responds. "By what instrument in architecture will you be proved?"
> The Junior Warden replies, "The Square."
> The Master counters, "What is a Square?"
> And the Junior Warden replies, "An angle of ninety degrees or the fourth part of a circle."

At the time Wallis began to study the symbols of algebra, the "=" sign was hardly known and little used. He would have recognised both the level and the rotations of the fourth part of a circle, and juxtaposition of these symbols gave him a great insight.

In 1656, Wallis wrote a book called *Arithmetica infinitorum* where he drew on this relationship between the Level and the Square to work out the value of π (a number that relates the diameter of a circle to its circumference). The challenge of figuring out this transcendental property of a circle from a series of counting symbols laid out in a logical order intrigued him.

In his *Treatise of Algebra*, Wallis explained how symbols can reveal matters which are otherwise inaccessible to human understanding. He said that a symbolic equation had the power to uncover the mechanisms of nature. The name he chose for accessing this hidden power was "algebra". He took the word from the Arabic, and it means "to bring together." He had read how the word was used by Muhammad ibn Musa al-Khwarizmi, around the year 830 CE in a book titled *The Science of Bringing Together and Opposing*. Al-Khwarizmi's book was about Wallis's first love, the symbols of counting. As a native of what is now Iraq and had once been Sumer, al-Khwarizmi was a son of the land whose rulers had grown rich on the influence of counting symbols. He explained how symbols of counting could be used to deduce facts. For example, if you start with ten tons of grain, eat half a ton a month for six months, then you will have seven tons left in your storehouse. Wallis took this simple idea of counting imaginary practical events and discovered it could be used to manipulate any type of number symbol.

In his *Treatise of Algebra*, Wallis discovered ways to evaluate equations which would later be used by Newton in his fundamental work on physics.

The Great Architect

The newly formed Royal Society was a potent package. It brought together a lively group of thinkers, pre-sensitised to symbols, and gave them money, encouragement, and a journal to share knowledge. Without this freedom to study the works of the Great Architect of The Universe (the symbolic term Freemasons use for the power which governs the Cosmos) Newton's ideas would never have been published. Less than a generation earlier, Galileo had been persecuted for daring to suggest the Earth might revolve around the sun. Yet only fifty years later, Newton was able to write about knowing the Mind of God through the symbolic equations which the Great Architect used to control the movements of the heavens.

Today, all Freemasons recite a formal statement of the Galileo heresy as part of the ritual of being admitted to the Fellowcraft Degree. To become a Fellowcraft Freemason you have to admit in front of the whole Lodge that the earth goes round the sun. This is a permanent memorial to the work of Bro. Sir Robert Moray who put into practice his Masonic Oath to "study the hidden secrets of Nature and Science in Order to better know his Maker". By doing so, he encouraged the study of symbols as an extension of human reasoning. The tools Newton discovered grew from an alliance between the Masonic symbols of geometry and the newly discovered analytic symbols of algebra.

Newton said of this insight into the mind of God:

Have we any idea of the substance of God? We know him only by his most wise and excellent contrivances of things, and final causes; we admire him for his perfections; but we reverence and adore him on account of his dominion; for we adore him as his servants; and a god without dominion, providence, and final causes is nothing else but Fate and Nature. Blind metaphysical necessity, which is certainly the same always and everywhere, could produce no variety of things. All that diversity of natural things which we find suited to different times and places could arise from nothing but the ideas and will of a Being necessarily existing. Thus, the diligent student of science, the earnest seeker of truth, is led, as through the courts of a sacred Temple, wherein, at each step, new wonders meet the eye, till, as a crowning grace, they stand before a Holy of Holies, and learn that all science and all truth are one which hath its beginning and its end in the knowledge of Him whose glory the heavens declare, and whose handiwork the firmament showeth forth.[8]

This comment by Newton shows that he feels the symbols of mathematics, which enabled him to understand the movements of the heavens, are thoughts that come directly from the Great Architect of the Universe, not something invented. The Royal Society's study of "the hidden mysteries" led to the success of physics and widespread application of its laws.

But we should never forget it was Masonic training that sensitised Wallis to a deeper meaning within the symbol of the two pillars and made it possible for him to see within Recorde's rotated symbol of equality a new symbol that would give him a route into the mind of God. But what is less well known is that certain symbolic teaching Newton received from other Freemasons guided him as well.

Symbols Are the Key to the Mind of God

Sir Isaac Newton was an alchemist, a keen student of the mystical architecture of King Solomon's Temple, and the man who discovered the system of scientific symbol manipulation which has dominated technological thinking for the last 400 years. Not everyone is aware of his alchemical, hermetic, and esoteric interests, or how these helped him reveal the full power of the new symbolism he saw emerging from the writings of John Wallis.

When Newton first went to Cambridge University as an undergraduate he seemed odd to his fellow students. He had no interest in socialising and spent all his time thinking and making notes about algebraic symbols. When the Black Death swept

---

8 http://www.isaacnewton.ca/gen_scholium/scholium.htm

through Cambridge, his degree studies were interrupted and he spent a year at his home in Lincolnshire to avoid catching the plague, sitting and thinking in solitary isolation.

Newton's notebooks show that during his first term at Cambridge he bought a copy of Freemason William Lilly's book *Christian Astrology*. He struggled to understand it because it involved two branches of symbolic reasoning known as geometry and trigonometry. This pushed him to study the writings of Lilly's fellow Mason, John Wallis. Newton's student notes show that Wallis became an early inspiration:

> About the beginning of my mathematical studies, the works of our celebrated countryman, Dr. Wallis, fell into my hands...[9]

Wallis inspired Newton's interest in arithmetic, alchemy, astrology, and methods of arithmetic calculation. After reading Wallis, Newton felt inspired to look at the works of Euclid. (The Propositions of Euclid form part of the ritual explanations about certain symbols which Freemasonry teaches, and myths about Euclid form a key part of the Masonic canon.) Reading Wallis also inspired Newton to read and absorb the symbolic ideas in Oughtred's *Clavis Mathematicae*.

Many people think that Newton became a Freemason when he joined The Royal Society in 1671. It seems likely, as it was an organisation dominated by speculative Freemasons. However, I have been unable to find any record of an Initiation, even though Newton's notebooks show that his interest in symbolic thinking grew rapidly after mixing with men from the Royal Society.

Newton first met with the Royal Society in 1664 while he was still a student. From then on he took a special interest in Solomon's Temple, writing more unpublished notes about this than he did about mathematics or science.[10] Solomon's Temple is a subject of special interest to Freemasons, because it is the underlying myth used in the Masonic method of sensitising members to the hidden meaning of symbols and the power of symbolic buildings. Masonic myth says Solomon's Temple was inspired by God, whom in this ritual instance Freemasons call the Grand Geometrician of the Universe.

Newton became a fellow of Trinity College, Cambridge, in 1667, and Lucasian Professor of Mathematics two years later. Between 1673 and 1683, he gave a series of lectures on algebra and the theory of equations, but much of his spare time was taken up studying in Solomon's Temple as he tried to understand the method of thinking used by the Grand Geometrician.[11] His work on equations extended Wallis's use of the equals "=" symbol, but was not published until 1707 in a book called The Universal Arithmetic.

During 1692, he corresponded with John Wallis and discussed ideas about a form of symbolic representation which he turned into his greatest work on the reality of nature.[12] The method of symbolic manipulation he discovered is now known as the calculus, but then was called the method fluxions. It combined the symbolic visualisation system of Euclid with Wallis's representation of physical quantities as algebraic symbols. Newton drew on the

---

9 http://202.38.126.65/navigate/math/history/Mathematicians/Wallis.html

10 http://www.newton.ac.uk/newtlife.html

11 http://www.maths.tcd.ie/pub/HistMath/People/Newton/RouseBall/RB_Newton.html

12 http://www.maths.tcd.ie/pub/HistMath/People/Newton/RouseBall/RB_Newton.html

Masonic idea of God as the Grand Geometrician of the Universe to bring Euclid's system of graphic symbols together with the mathematical analysis made possible by algebraic symbols. He published this work during 1687 as Principia Mathematica. It was a landmark step towards understanding the universe. As the Stanford Encyclopedia of Philosophy explains:

> No work was more seminal in the development of modern physics and astronomy than Newton's Principia. Its conclusion that the force retaining the planets in their orbits is one in kind with terrestrial gravity ended forever the view dating back at least to Aristotle that the celestial realm calls for one science and the sublunar realm, another... The ultimate success of Newton's theory of gravity made the identification of the fundamental forces of nature and their characterization in laws the primary pursuit of physics. [13]

Newton's discovery of the hidden secrets of the symbol of equality gave a totally new view of how the universe is controlled and ordered. The French mathematician Lagrange described the Principia as the greatest production of the human mind, and said he felt dazed at such an illustration of what man's intellect might be capable. In describing the effect of his own writings and those of Laplace it was a favourite remark of his that Newton was not only the greatest genius that had ever existed, but he was also the most fortunate, for as there is but one universe, it can happen but to one man in the world's history to be the interpreter of its laws.[14]

Newton's understanding came from his study of Masonic Symbolism. The innate power of the symbols to influence human minds can be seen by the way this Masonic knowledge affected the thought processes of others as Newton shared it. In particular there was a dispute between the German philosopher Gottfried Leibniz and Newton about who discovered calculus.

What is less well known is that both Newton and Leibniz were exposed to the same symbolic teaching by Freemasons of the Royal Society: Newton through his association with John Wallis, and his reading of Lilly and Oughtred; Leibniz through a protracted correspondence with Bro. Sir Robert Moray, the Freemason who founded the Society.

The symbolic mix of geometric insight and algebraic analysis which is the calculus appeared simultaneously to two men as if it had been fully formed in another place and was just waiting for a chance to manifest in human minds.

Masonic teaching offers a means of accessing the place where symbols are eternally present. This place is called by some physicists the Platonic heaven and is derived from Plato's discovery of the perfect forms.

The Heaven of Pure Symbols

Wallis, Lilly, and Oughtred introduced Newton to a tradition which has since become commonplace among modern scientists. Wallis and Newton discovered the power of mathematics by exploring the consequences of symbolic relationships. They believed that pure symbols arose from the mind of God, existed before the world began, and would endure long after the world had passed into oblivion.

Newton wrote down his explanation of this idea in the *Principia*:

> The most beautiful system of the sun, planets, and comets, could only proceed from the counsel and dominion of an

---

13 http://plato.stanford.edu/entries/newton-principia/
14 Rouse Ball, W W. A Short Account of the History of Mathematics. New York: Dover Press, 1908.

intelligent and powerful being. And if the fixed stars are the centres of like systems, these, being formed by the like wise counsel, must be all subject to the dominion of one; especially since the light of the fixed stars is of the same nature with the light of the sun, and from every system light passes into all the other systems; and lest the systems of fixed stars should, by their gravity, fall on each other, he hath placed those systems at immense distances from one another.

This being governs all things, not as the soul of the world, but as Lord over all; and on account of his dominion he is wont to be called the Lord God or Universal Ruler, for God is a relative word, and has a respect to servants; and Deity is the dominion of God not over his own body, as those imagine who fancy God to be the soul of the world, but over servants. The Supreme Being is eternal, infinite, absolutely perfect, omnipotent and omniscient. ... We know him only by his most wise and excellent contrivances of things and final causes.[15]

Implicit in this eternal world view is the idea that for a mathematical theorem to be discovered it must already exist before any human thinks about it. I have previously mentioned that this idea of a transcendental world of absolute symbolic forms was proposed by the Greek philosopher Plato.

Plato believed that we have genuine knowledge of truth, goodness, and beauty as well as of equality, even though we perceive only imperfect instances in the real world. Things of this sort he called Platonic Forms, abstract entities that exist independently of the sensible world. Ordinary objects are imperfect and changeable, but they faintly copy the perfect and immutable Forms. Many of the Platonic shapes, such as the square, the equilateral triangle, the circle, the pentangle, and the heptangle appear in the Masonic set of symbols.

Plato claimed that all souls have knowledge of these supra-sensible realities, that they cannot possibly have obtained through any bodily experience. He believed this knowledge must be something that our souls learned prior to birth. This implies that Platonic symbols have an independent and eternal existence. It is this vision of Platonic perfection which drives all physicists and is at the heart of many systems of scientific research which were developed in the twentieth century.

Roger Penrose, a committed scientific Platonist, writes about this idea:

The Platonic viewpoint is an immensely valuable one. It tells us to be careful to distinguish the precise mathematical entities from the approximations that we see around us in the world of physical things. Moreover, it provides us with the blueprint according to which modern science has proceeded. Scientists will put forward models of the world — or, rather, of certain aspects of the world — and these models may be tested against previous observation and against the results of carefully designed experiment.

If the model itself is to be assigned any kind of 'existence', then this existence is located within the Platonic world of mathematical forms. Of course, one might take a contrary viewpoint: namely that the model is itself to have existence only within our various minds, rather than to take Plato's world to be in any sense absolute and 'real.' Yet, there is something important to be gained in regarding

---

15 Newton. Principia ([1725] 1934), p. 370.

mathematical structures as having a reality of their own. For our individual minds are notoriously imprecise, unreliable, and inconsistent in their judgments. The precision, reliability, and consistency that are required by our scientific theories demand something beyond any one of our individual (untrustworthy) minds. In mathematics, we find a far greater robustness than can be located in any particular mind. Does this not point to something outside ourselves, with a reality that lies beyond what each individual can achieve?[16]

The Platonist philosophy of eternal and perfect symbols which underlies the scientific method of answering questions about reality gives rise to the term "Re-search", As a scientist, when Penrose conducts Re-search he is repeating a search,

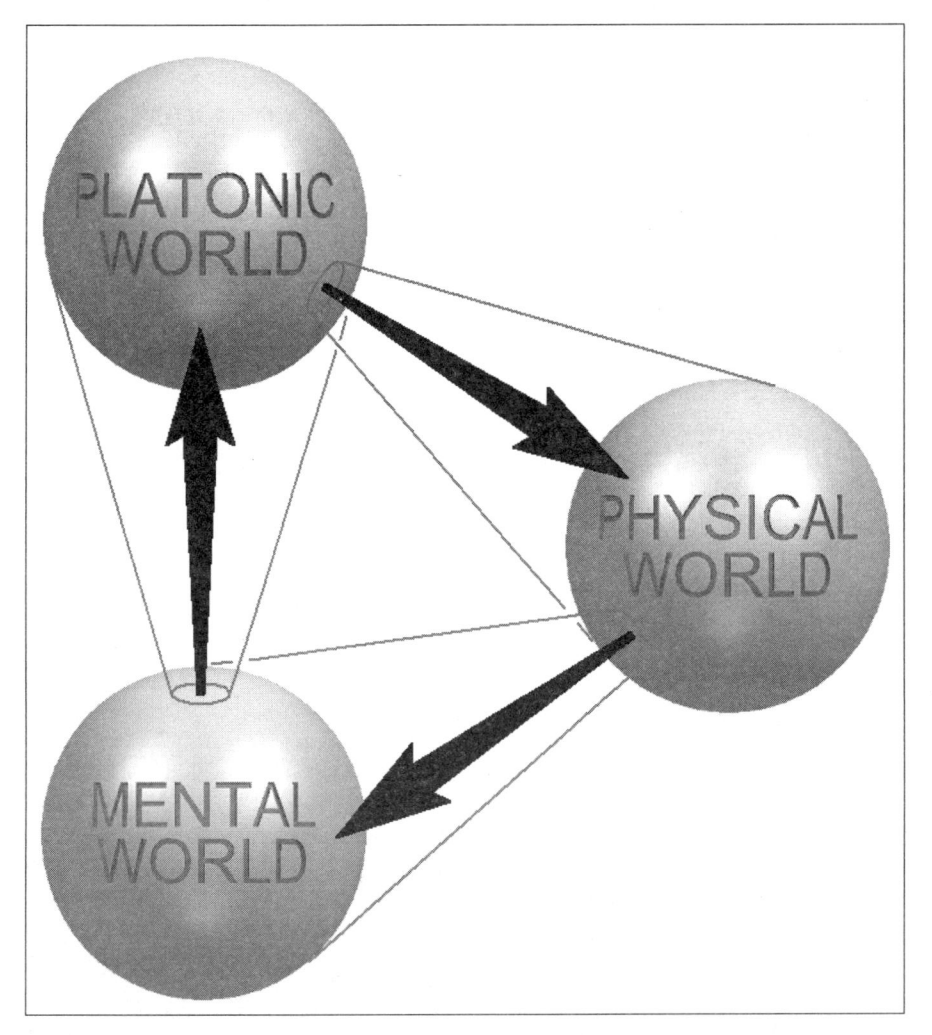

16 Penrose, R. The Road to Reality. London: Vintage Books, 2004.

which any individual could repeat independently, to discover a truth about the symbolic nature of reality which can be found by anyone prepared to interact with the Platonic symbols.

This concept of Re-search was formalised during World War II, when scientists working for the Allies, in particular Leo Szilard and Albert Einstein in the U.S.[17] and Niels Bohr in the U.K., realised that a weapon of immense destructive power already existed within the realms of symbolic Platonic Truth. The implication of this thought was that a frightful weapon was sitting, waiting to co-operate with first bold searcher to discover it and let it help them to win the war. That searcher could be on either side, as basic work on nuclear instability had been carried out by Heisenberg but ignored by Hitler. In the U.K., work on material preparation for a ballistic-impact uranium bomb was already well under way at the Nobel explosive works in Porthmadog, North Wales, under the secret patronage of the MAUD committee.[18] But it was a real fear, shared by Albert Einstein and Niels Bohr, that this fearsome weapon was sitting, unprotected, in the heaven of the Platonic symbols just waiting to be accessed and used.

Szilard and Einstein wrote to President Roosevelt urging him to devote all the U.S.'s scientific talent to searching for this atom bomb. They warned that the consequences of Hitler getting to it first would be catastrophic.[19] Roosevelt, himself a Freemason, took their warning seriously and set up the Manhattan Project. It brought together the organisational and logistic skills of General Leslie Groves and the inspired scientific leadership of Dr. J Robert Oppenheimer in the remote desert site of Los Alamos. The result was two symbolic discoveries, two different types of atom bomb, one based on uranium (Little Boy) and one based on a previously unknown Platonic element, plutonium (Fat Boy). Both bombs worked and were deployed over Japanese cities. Nobody now questions the idea that there are symbolic scientific entities just waiting in the Platonic heaven to be discovered by explorers who know how to reach those realms. The atomic bomb is harrowing proof of this.

[17] See DeGroot, G. The Bomb: A Life. London: Jonathon Cape, 2004.

[18] See Zimmerman, D. Top Secret Exchange – The Tizard Mission and the Scientific War, Montreal: McGill-Queen's University Press, 1996.

[19] See DeGroot, G. The Bomb: A Life. London: Jonathon Cape, 2004.

Chapter 7:

The Secret Symbol of Political Stability

The Pillars that Inspired Republicanism

Without the inspirational Masonic symbol of the two pillars, no truly democratic government would have either emerged or succeeded. The symbol of the two pillars has inculcated political stability in the minds of the people who view it, from the earliest times down to today.

It is no coincidence that this iconic picture of George Washington, the first President of the United States of America, shows him standing in front of one pair of pillars and between another pair.

This pattern of pillars is echoed by the 1's on the front of a dollar bill.

Each pair of 1's represents a pair of pillars. The upper pair is conjoined by the United States of America and George Washington is between the lower pair. Even the symbol of the dollar currency was written as an "S" with two pillars inscribed on top of it. Many current computer fonts now show the dollar symbol as "$" but even this simplified font shows an "S" split into two equal and opposite halves, a less blatant form of the two pillars. The parallel lines of the two pillars imply stability.

This symbol of two equal and opposite

pillars has influenced three of the world's enduring democratic societies. It appeared as the symbol of England's first elected ruler, Oliver Cromwell, Member of Parliament for Huntingdon and Lord Protector of the Commonwealth of Great Britain.

Just as George Washington was depicted a hundred years later, Cromwell stands between two pillars.

The fundamental statement of the aims of the French Revolution, the "Declaration of the Rights of Man and of the Citizen", states that the rights of man are universal: valid at all times and in every place.

What does this symbol represent and why has it figured so strongly in these iconic images from three of the most important democracies of western civilisation?

To understand its meaning, we need to look at its history. And fortunately its history is well documented. It is one of the key symbols which have been preserved, studied, and applied by Freemasons. It represents one of the most important ideas behind the emergence of democracy.

The concept behind the symbol is that there are two powerful forces which rule a state, and if either of them is too dominant the state will become unbalanced and tyrannical. Both pillars must work together for a society to be stable. Let us return to the symbol's beginnings in Freemasonry, in fifteenth-century Aberdeen.

The Pillars that Formed Freemasonry

We saw early Masonic versions of this symbol on the Kirkwall Scroll, dating from around 1480, and it was in two different forms.

The first version shows the two pillars separate and standing apart, as they appear in the foreground of the image of George Washington and in the image of Oliver Cromwell.

The other form of this image to be found on the Kirkwall Scroll shows the two pillars conjoined by a keystone.

These two versions of the pillar symbol were being used in Masonic rituals 200 years before Oliver Cromwell claimed it as an icon to support his political aims.

We can see the same symbols appearing in Masonic images, dating from the time of the French Revolution and the American War of Independence, preserved in a Masonic Lodge in Yorkshire. Here is the conjoined version.

And here are the separate versions.

The Secret Symbol of Political Stability

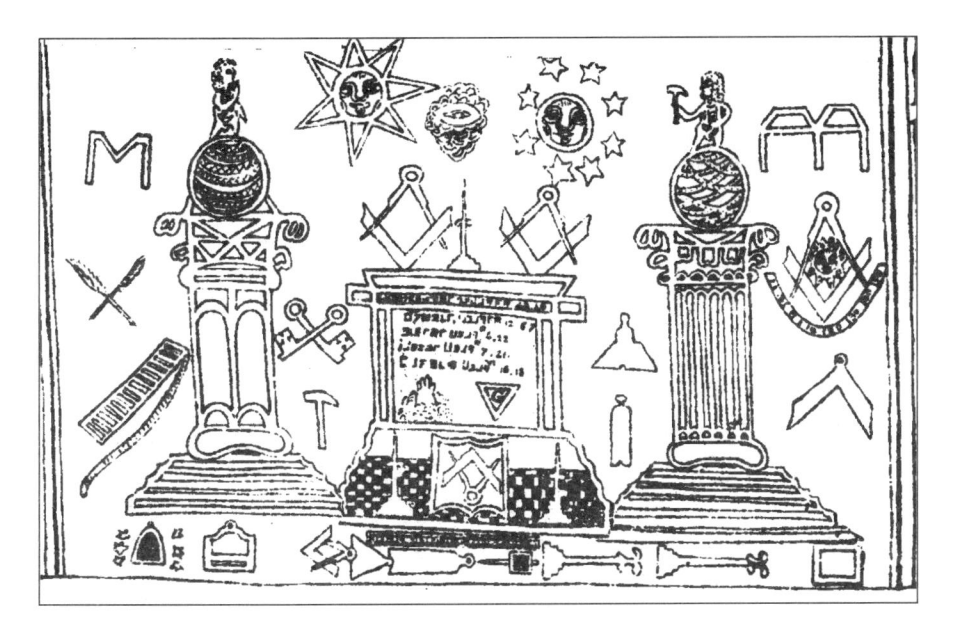

The Symbols that Taught George Washington

George Washington knew about the Masonic meaning of the symbol of the two pillars because both forms were embroidered on the apron he wore to attend Masonic meetings.

Washington was introduced to Freemasonry by a Yorkshire Freemason, Lord Fairfax. Young George got his first job as a surveyor working for Fairfax, who was a major landowner in Virginia. The Fairfax family were active patrons of the Masonic Grand Lodge of York, and were familiar with the Old Yorkshire Masonic symbols shown above. They also took a great interest in the local Masonic Lodges of Virginia, and when George Washington was old enough, encouraged him to join.

He was initiated into Fredericksburg Lodge No. 4 on Saturday, 4 November 1752. He became a Fellowcraft Mason on the first Saturday of March 1753, and on Saturday, 4 August 1753, the Fredericksburg Lodge made him a Master Mason. In 1779, he was offered the Office of General Grand Master Mason of the United States, but declined it because of his military commitments.

A French Freemason, the Marquis de Lafayette, joined George Washington's army in 1777 and became his close friend. In 1784, he presented Bro. Washington with a gift, embroidered by his wife. It was a Masonic apron which Washington wore with enormous pride.[1] Here is proof that Washington was fully aware of the power of the symbol of the two pillars. Lafayette chose the symbols on the apron to inspire Washington in the difficult tasks which lay ahead in the growing dispute over British rule of its American colonies.

Here is Washington's favourite Masonic Apron, showing both types of pillar symbol, the import of which he had learned from his early Masonic patrons and his Masonic training.

But what had Freemasonry taught Washington about this symbol?

The Masonic Meaning of the Two Pillars

Freemasonry teaches that the symbol of the two pillars has two conjoined meanings, each of which is illuminated by a ritual recitation of a traditional myth.

The first meaning is expressed through the names given to the two pillars which stood outside the Temple of Solomon. The left-hand pillar is associated with the power of the king. The ritual says:

Boaz was the name of the left-hand pillar which stood at the porchway or entrance of King Solomon's Temple. It was named after the great grandfather of David who was a Prince and Ruler in Israel and represents the force of temporal power as expressed through the actions of the king.

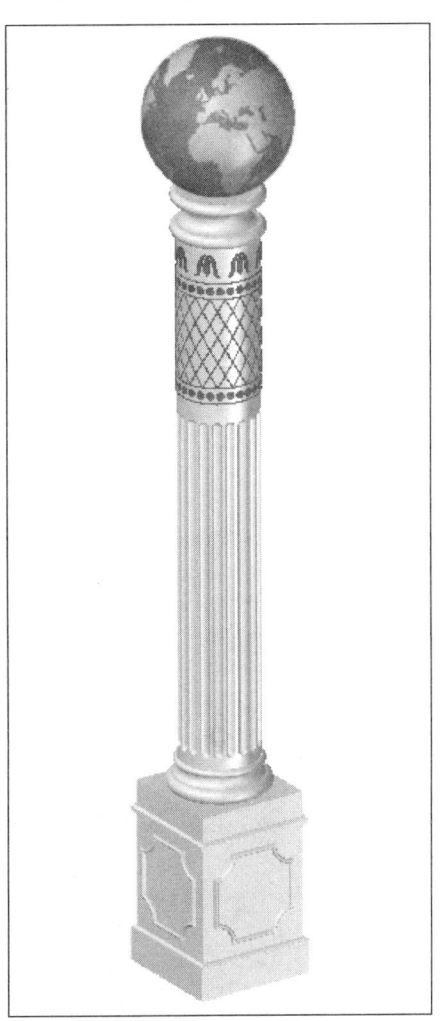

---

1   This apron was presented to the Grand Lodge of Pennsylvania by the Washington Benevolent Society on 3 July 1829, and can be seen in the Grand Lodge Museum at the Masonic Temple in Philadelphia.

The right-hand pillar is associated with the power of the priest. The ritual says:

> Jachin was the name of the right-hand pillar that stood at the entrance or porchway of King Solomon's Temple. It was named after the Great High Priest who officiated at the dedication of the Temple. It represents the power of the priest and the benevolent force of religion.

But when the two pillars are brought together, they take on an additional layer of meaning. They can be symbolically linked by a keystone, a lintel, or by the Royal Arch of the Heavens, but when conjoined the ritual says of them:

> The two great Pillars which were placed at the Porch or Entrance of King Solomon's Temple have a separate and conjoint significance. The former denotes "strength", the latter "to establish", and when conjoined "stability", for God hath said "In strength will I establish My word in this Mine house that it will stand fast forever."

The two pillars represent two forces which act on society. These are the secular force of the king, who rules, protects the people, and governs the land, and the spiritual force of the priest guiding the people's religious and spiritual life. The double pillar symbol represents the great power for stability which flows from these two forces when they work together. If either becomes too powerful, society lurches into either religious or secular despotism, neither of which is desirable.

This same symbol appears in a slightly different form in a myth told about the Patriarch Enoch.

Masonic ritual tells this story of Enoch:

Enoch, the son of Jared, was the sixth in descent from Adam. Filled with the love and fear of God, he strove to lead men in the way of honour and duty. In a vision, the Deity appeared to him in the visible shape of a pure golden triangle, and said to him, "Enoch, thou hast longed to know my true name: arise and follow me, and thou shalt know it."

Enoch, accepting his vision as an inspiration, journeyed in search of the mountain he had seen in his dream, until, weary of the search, he stopped in the land of Canaan, then already populous with the descendants of Adam, and there employed workmen; and with the help of his son Methuselah, he excavated nine apartments, one above the other, and each roofed with an arch, as he had seen in his dream, the lowest being hewn out of the solid rock. In the crown of each arch he left a narrow aperture, closed with a square stone, and over the upper one he built a modest temple, roofless and of huge unhewn stones, to the Great Architect of the Universe.

Upon a triangular plate of gold, inlaid with many precious gems, he engraved the ineffable name of God, and sank the plate into one face of a cube of agate.

None knew of the deposit of the precious treasure; and, that it might remain undiscovered, and survive the Flood, which it was known to Enoch would soon overwhelm the world in one vast sea of mire, he covered the aperture, and the stone that closed it and the great ring of iron used to raise the stone, with the granite pavement of his primitive temple.

Then, fearing that all knowledge of the arts and sciences would be lost in the universal flood, he built two great columns upon a high hill—one of brass, to resist water, and one of granite, to resist fire. On the granite column was written a description of the subterranean apartments; on the one of brass, the rudiments of the arts and sciences.

The Masonic myth continues to say that one of the pillars was found by the Jews and the other by the Egyptians. It claims that an elite group of Freemasons was created to protect the Jewish pillar and its teachings, and the secret meaning of the pillars is said only to survive within Freemasonry. This knowledge is displayed in Masonic Lodges as two free-standing pillars.

The Pillars that Established Ancient Egypt

Ancient Egyptian society lasted for 4,000 years. Its longevity and prosperity grew around the power of the symbol of the two pillars, which became the base on which the dynasties of the pharaohs were founded and sustained.

The River Nile in Egypt supported small, isolated groups of nomadic hunters from about 30,000 BCE onwards, as *Homo sapiens* spread out of Africa. Farming-related symbols began to appear and spread westwards from Anatolian villages. The symbols of counting and writing took root as the proto-Egyptians developed proto-kingdoms and created boundaries which they protected against intruding hunter-gatherers. In this tense environment, the symbol of the two pillars became increasingly important. It was a symbol of co-operation and it engendered a realisation in its observers that unity was more effective than aggression. The lozenge and spiral symbols of farming had developed from patterns of shadows cast by two pillars.

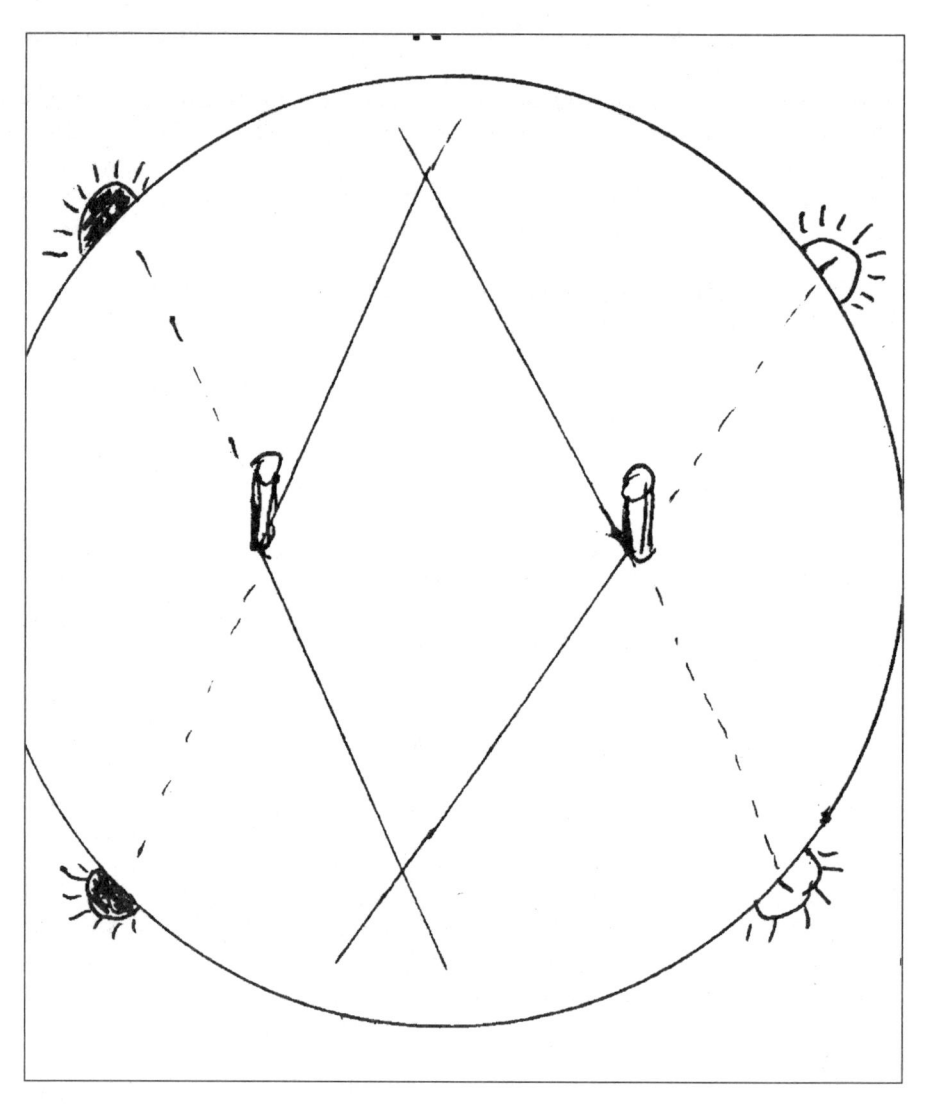

Farming villages turned into towns and then into cities, and these monolithic pillars became a strong emotive symbol. This symbol helped create groups of harmonious communities which gradually coalesced into two kingdoms known as Upper and Lower Egypt. By 3100 BCE they had become a combined kingdom. In many ways, Upper and Lower Egypt remained separate kingdoms, although they were conjoined by a single divine and absolute ruler. A pillar symbol stood at the centre of each kingdom. To explain the myths behind the pillars, we must go back to the early symbolic history of Egypt.

The rulers of Egypt began as kings, with priests assisting them in their relationships with the gods, but they grew into pharaohs, who were half-god, half-king, and who ruled by the divine right of their godly parentage. Each king was a part-divine "son of god", and when he died he joined his forefathers to become a full god.

The sky goddess Nut had five children, the eldest of whom was Osiris. Symbolically, Nut was the sky and her arms and legs were pillars which held up the heavens. She touched the land at the four cardinal points of the horizon. One of her legs was planted in Heliopolis and was the great pillar of Lower Egypt. Her other leg stood in Upper Egypt at the city of Nekheb. But the actual ground of the two Egypts was the province of Geb, the god of the earth, from whose clay humanity was formed. Geb was the lover of Nut and their union gave birth to the first king of the Two Lands of Egypt.

The children of Nut and Geb were part sky and part land. The people of the Two Lands believed Osiris, their eldest son, had become their first king. He was part man and part god. Osiris married his sister Isis, who was also part woman and part goddess, establishing a tradition that would be followed by future kings of Egypt.

Osiris ruled wisely, but his brother Set became jealous of his success and murdered him in the night, while the darkness hid that act from their mother's sight. Set cut Osiris into pieces which he threw into the Nile. When light returned, Isis was distraught, as Osiris had not produced an heir. So, with the aid of Nut's oversight, Isis located the pieces of Osiris's body and reassembled them. She called on her father Geb to breathe a last short moment of life into the human part of her husband. As Osiris's reassembled body quivered with a brief flash of life, she lowered herself onto his phallus and took his seed into her. While Osiris quivered with ecstasy, his mother reached down and took him in her hands. Then she stood upright, her legs planted firmly in the centre of each kingdom, and lifted him to the stars where she made him the ruler of the kingdom of the dead.

Isis gave birth to a son named Horus, who became the next king of the Two Lands. He challenged Set to battle. Horus won the fight, but his eye was gouged out. His grandmother, the goddess Nut, whose pillar legs straddled the Two Lands, took his eye and cradled it in her hands in the sky above his combined kingdoms. So Horus's single, all-seeing eye floated above the two pillars which joined his kingdoms. Nothing was hidden from his sight. From that time on, the pharaoh was believed to be the earthly incarnation of Horus until his death, when he too would be lifted by Nut to the stars.

The twin pillars of Heliopolis and Nekheb reminded the people of the presence of the goddess Nut and her role in supporting the pharaoh. Her legs, planted firmly in each major city, linked the earthly half-god pharaoh to his future destiny as a full-god in the starry sky. And this symbolism reminded the pharaoh's subjects of his overarching power and his all-seeing eye.

These symbolic pillars were important to each of the countries, even though they shared a single king. Lower Egypt was larger and more prosperous but the security, stability, and wealth of Egypt arose from both states working together. The two pillars linked and unified the two lands and the people believed that as long as both were intact their conjoined kingdom would prosper.

The civilisation of Egypt did prosper and the symbol of the two pillars was displayed outside their temples so that the people were reminded of the divine source of wealth and power. The king would pass between the legs of the sky goddess as he entered the temple and remind his people of his divine right to rule.

But how did this symbolism come to pass into the symbolic teachings of Freemasonry? To answer that question we need to look more closely at the mythical Grand Masters of Freemasonry at the time of the construction of King Solomon's Temple. And a key player in this story was a Phoenician king, famed for his building skills: Hiram, King of Tyre.

The Pillars and the Concubines

The Phoenicians occupied a narrow strip on the eastern coast of the Mediterranean about 200 miles long. It penetrated inland by only five to fifteen miles to the mountains of Lebanon. They did not have a unified state but formed a group of city-kingdoms. Around 1800 BCE, the Egyptians invaded and took control for around 400 years. Then the raids of the Hittites, against Egypt, gave the Phoenician cities an opportunity to rebel and by 1100 BCE the Phoenicians were again independent. But the Egyptian political symbol of the two pillars had taken root in the Temple of Tyre, the richest of the Phoenician cities.

After breaking free of the Egyptians, the Phoenicians continued to build temples with a porchway or entrance flanked by two pillars, in similar style to those in Egypt. King Hiram's city of Tyre had just such a temple, with two pillars at its entrance long before King Solomon built one.

Hiram was an extremely successful king and a builder of historic proportions. At the beginning of his reign the main port of Tyre stood on the mainland, but this builder king realised that an island lying six hundred metres from the shore would form a highly defensible stronghold and provide a fully integrated docking system for his fleet. The King of Tyre was a superb engineer. He was far better suited than King Solomon to be an early Grand Master of Freemasonry and his important place in Masonic ritual was well earned. But how much was he helped by the power of the two pillars?

In 1923, a French expedition discovered the stone coffin of Hiram, King of Tyre. It contained a Phoenician inscription around the edge of the lid, written in the linear alphabet.[2] It told the story of a king who was the earthly representative of a goddess and, through his congress with her, became a god himself. The inscription claims he was the lover of Baalat, the powerful Phoenician goddess whose symbol of two pillars marked the entrance to her temple.

The Phoenicians of Tyre worshipped a trinity of gods consisting of El, the father god, his wife Baalat and their son Baal. El was the mightiest of the three. He would see and punish all evil deeds. His only failing was his infidelity to his wife, Baalat. He was fond of impregnating any human female who took his fancy and to do so he would disguise himself as a passing stranger. In order to make sure El could satisfy his desires all Phoenician woman had a religious duty to make themselves sexually available to passing strangers around the spring and autumn equinoxes. They would sit between the symbolic pillars at the front of Baalat's temples and offer themselves for money.

It was the rule that they must charge the strangers for sex and donate the money to Baalat, the long-suffering wife of El and the mother of Baal. While El had his wicked way with all the women of the lands he ruled, the women charged him for his pleasure and gave the money to placate his deceived wife. She in turn took their human king as her lover, using the body of a priestess as her proxy, and made the king a god. So all were satisfied, and passing strangers looking for a bit of fun knew to look between the two pillars for women keen to carry out their duty of religious fornication.

Baalat was widely worshipped in Tyre, where her two pillars stood before the entrance of the Temple Hiram built in her honour. She took Hiram, King of Tyre and Grand Master of Freemasonry, as her lover, as she did every Canaanite king, and made him into a living but mortal god.

---

2   Hackwell, W John. Signs, Letters, Words: Archaeology Discovers Writing. New York: Charles Scribner's Sons, 1987

Hiram was not just a king; he was the consort and lover of the goddess whose symbol was the two pillars. When Hiram was asked by Solomon to design and build a Temple for the God of the Jews in Jerusalem, what could be more natural than to suggest that it should have two pillars at its entrance?

This living god of Tyre, whose power came from the symbolic pillars of the goddess who was his lover, built the Temple for the God of the Jews in Jerusalem. And he provided the craftsmen to build the two great pillars which stood at the porchway or entrance to King Solomon's Temple.

The Pillars that Influenced the English Civil War

By the mid-seventeenth century, the symbol of the two pillars was firmly embedded in the ritual teaching of Freemasonry. I mentioned earlier how Oliver Cromwell used this symbol to rally support for his cause, but the symbol was also used by his opponents.

In this seventeenth-century illustration, shown below, you can see the kingly and priestly pillars being used to try to bolster the right to rule of an anointed king. But this is not a king of Israel; it is a king of England. James VI of Scotland was an enthusiastic Mason, having become a member of the Lodge of Scoon and Perth in 1601, and was well known for introducing Masonic Symbolism and rituals into his court.[3] His son, King Charles I, tried to use the Masonic pillar symbol, but made a critical change in the keystone. The king is shown in the role of guarantor of the good behaviour of both pillars. By identifying himself as the keystone that locks them together, Charles took on the role that God filled for Solomon and David. Charles was making a symbolic statement that he ruled both Church and State by Divine Right. It would also prove his undoing and cause his beheading.

In this engraving of Charles I, he hovers in god-like dominance above the conjoined pillars. The left-hand pillar is labelled "The Church" and is surmounted by the figure of Truth. The right-hand pillar is labelled "The State" and is surmounted by the figure of Justice. The two pillars are linked by the sharing of a Masonic handshake. Charles wanted a monarchical despotism where the temporal power of the king brooked no spiritual challenge and no democratic restraint. His misuse of this symbol reveals that he saw himself in the role of an absolute arbiter with no need for God to ensure fair play. Charles was corrupting the Freemason symbol that had been passed to him. But the symbol had greater resources than Charles realised and it fought back in supporting his chief opponent. This was Cromwell, who is depicted standing between the pillars and beneath the dove of blessing, symbolising God as the keystone conjoining the pillars and balancing the forces of disruption. This symbol carried the day with the common people.

---

3   Lomas, R. The Invisible College. London: Transworld, 2009.

The Pillars that Support the U.S. Presidents

For the symbol of the two pillars to work its hidden influence on the mute right hemisphere of the human brain, it must be kept before the eyes of the people. We have seen it used in banknotes, currency symbols, iconic images, and stone carvings.

George Washington used the iconic image of himself standing amidst the pairs of pillars and also placed the symbol in the written representation of the currency, but he also made sure that it could reinforce the position of the president. To ensure that the symbol's emotional impact would continue to work in the new republic, two sets of pillars were built into the entrance of the White House in Washington, D.C. when he approved James Hoban's design.

The two outer pillars, linked by the triangular arch pointing to the heavens, are the pillars of balance and stability, while the inner ones represent the pillars of knowledge.

When a U.S. president stands before this symbolic entrance, the symbols continue to work their magic by creating a mood of emotional stability and confidence. The portico of the White House symbolises the separation of church and state. Each remains separate and strong. Each is able to limit the excesses of the other. But because neither can become powerful enough to become despotic, freedom is maintained and society prospers.

The Pillars that Reconciled Britain and America

Freemasons have long recognised that the symbol of the two pillars works to stabilise societies. Here is an instance of how Masons used two pillars, which had stood outside the Temple of Heleopolis in Ancient Egypt for 4,000 years to help reconcile Britain and the United States after the War of Independence.

Heliopolis was one of the largest cities in Ancient Egypt, and the home of one of the binding pillars of the Two Lands. At its centre stood a massive temple known as the Great House. It was built around 2000 BCE with two pillars at its entrance. Around 13 BCE the Roman Emperor Augustus moved those pillars to Alexandria and reconstructed them. There they stayed until 1301 CE when one fell on its side, and the other slipped sideways during an earthquake. They were never properly reset and remained uncared for until 1878 CE. That year, both fallen pillars were procured by British and American Freemasons. The two pillars, which had once represented the unity of the two lands of ancient Egypt, were shipped away for a new role, to bind two other states together.

Bro. Dr. Erasmus Wilson paid £10,000 to carry one pillar from Egypt and erect it in London. It was placed on a specially designed cigar-shaped container ship, named the *Cleopatra*, arriving in July, 1878. It was established with a public Masonic ceremony conducted by Bro. Wilson on 12 September 1878. [4]

---

4   Close to Embankment Underground station.

In New York, Bro. William Hulbert persuaded Bro. William J Vanderbilt to pay for the other pillar's transport to America. Its carriage was overseen by Bro. Henry H Gorringe of Anglo-Saxon Lodge No. 137 of New York City. And it went onboard the steamship *Dessoug*, arriving in New York in 1880. Grand Master Mason of the State of New York, the Most Worshipful Jesse B. Anthony, presided as the obelisk was set in place with full Masonic ceremony on 2 October 1880, in Graywacke Knoll, Central Park. Over 9,000 Masons, in full Masonic regalia, paraded up Fifth Avenue from 14th Street to 82nd Street and over 50,000 spectators lined the parade route. The benediction was presented by the Grand Chaplain of New York Masons, the Right Worshipful Louis C Gerstein.

In this way the Brethren of the two oldest Masonic-inspired nations in the world reinstated an ancient symbol of stability to bind them together again.

Part Two

A Practical Introduction to Masonic Symbology

This section contains a popular introduction to the ancient Masonic teaching about symbology, starting with the symbols which took humanity from hunter-gathering to farming, right down to the symbols of democratic government and the search for new frontiers.

The method of teaching is to reveal the symbol, either as part of the Lodge decoration, by wearing it as badge or token, or by drawing it on a Tracing Board.

As a Mason is shown the symbol, ritual statements are made about it that help him understand its purpose and become sensitised to its emotional power.

The aim of this part of the book is to illustrate the symbols alongside the ritual statements as they have been traditionally taught to Freemasons for the last 500 years.

The ritual poetry that sensitises each Candidate to the power of the symbol follows each image.

I have also added a personal view on how I interpret the symbol. This is not intended to be a guide to how others should use and view the meaning of the symbol. As I have made clear, it is often extremely difficult to capture the full import of the symbol within the precise meaning of words. The personal view at the end of each ritual definition should be simply taken as a rough guide to the way the symbol speaks to me. It may have a different meaning for you. Neither of us is right and neither is wrong.

Chapter 8

Symbols of the First Degree

When each symbol is introduced to a new Freemason, a series of poetic ritual statements are made about the purpose and function of each symbol so that the Brother may learn how to apply the emotional import of the symbol to his own soul. The ritual description of the symbol is memorised and repeated whilst the Brother looks at the image.

The Square

The Square is to try, and adjust rectangular corners of buildings, and assist in bringing rude matter into due form. It teaches us to regulate our lives and actions according to the Masonic line and rule, and to harmonise our conduct in this life, so as to render us acceptable to that Divine Being from whom all goodness springs, and to whom we must give an account of all our actions.

It is by the assistance of the Square that rude matter is brought into due form. It is by the Square that animosities are made to subside should any unfortunately arise among the Brethren, that the business of Masonry may be conducted with harmony and decorum.

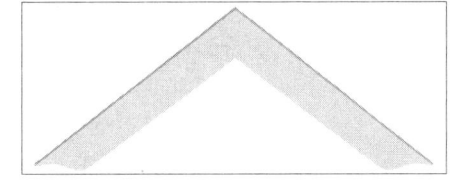

Thus the Square teaches morality and how to regulate our actions.

A Personal View

The Square is a symbol which measures accuracy of a right angle. Two squares make up a triangle and four squares from the angle subsumed by the centre of a circle. It is one of the perfect Platonic shapes and can be made up using sticks of three, four, and five units. The task of a Mason is to shape the roughhewn stone of his/her soul into a smooth and perfect cube. The cube is the three dimensional representation of the soul in all its aspects. These are symbolised by the four squares at the centre of a circle making up the emotions, intellect, spirit, and soul for the Master Mason all in forming the fourth part of the complete circle of the complete Mason.

The Craft Square is an approximation of a triangle with its apex downwards and base upwards, which is a very ancient symbol of the mind or intellect of man and is known as the Water Triangle.

The Level

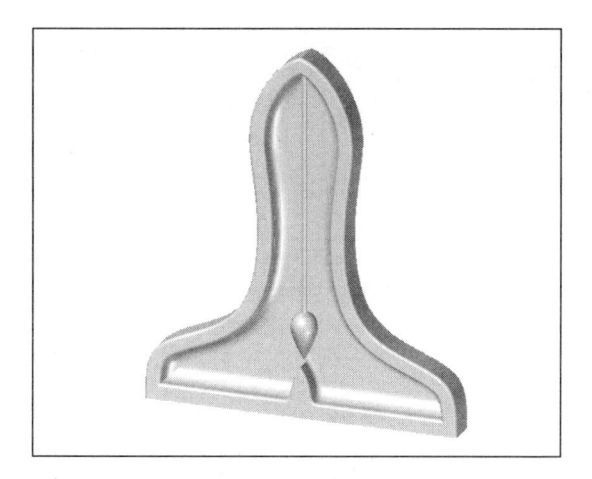

The Level is to lay levels, and prove horizontals.

The Level demonstrates that we are all sprung from the same stock, partakers of the same nature, and sharers in the same hope; and although distinctions among men are necessary to preserve subordination, yet ought no eminence of situation make us forget that we are Brothers; for he who is placed on the lowest spoke of fortune's wheel is equally entitled to our regard; as a time will come and the wisest of us knows not how soon when all distinctions, save those of goodness and virtue, shall cease, and Death, the grand leveller of all human greatness, reduce us to the same state.

The Level being an emblem of equality, points out the equal measures the Senior Warden is bound to pursue in conjunction with the Master in the well ruling and governing of the Lodge.

The Level teaches equality.

A Personal View

The Level is a working tool given to the Mason to help bring into balance and equality of application the senses, the emotions and the mind so that all play an equal part in the interaction of the soul with the mystery of the centre. The floor of the Lodge, as shown in the First Degree Tracing Board is a level expanse of alternating black and white squares. These represent the good and the bad experiences we meet with in our daily lives. Our task, if we are to learn Wisdom, is to rise above this dualism. We must readjust our consciousness to a level of outlook which sees beyond them; and learn to become master of our lower nature and bodily tendencies, to stand detached from the inevitable fluctuations of fortune and emotion to which they are subject, and to regard the ups and downs, the whites and blacks, of life as being of equal educative value to us.

The Plumb Rule

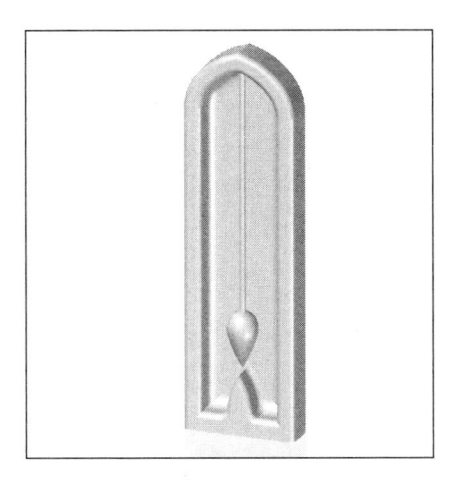

The Plumb Rule is to try, and adjust uprights, whilst fixing them on their proper bases.

The infallible Plumb Rule, which, like Jacob's ladder, connects Heaven and Earth, is the criterion of rectitude and truth. It teaches us to walk justly and uprightly before God and man; neither turning to the right nor left from the paths of virtue. Not to be an enthusiast, persecutor, or slanderer of religion; neither bending towards avarice, injustice, malice, revenge, nor the envy and contempt of mankind, but giving up every selfish propensity which might injure others. To steer the bark of this life over the seas of passion, without quitting the helm of rectitude, is the highest perfection to which human nature can attain, and as the builder raises his column by the level and perpendicular, so ought every Mason to conduct himself towards this world; to observe a due medium between avarice and profusion; to hold the scales of justice with equal poise; to make his passions and prejudices coincide with the just line of his conduct; and in all his pursuits to have Eternity in view.

The Plumb Rule teaches justness and uprightness of life and actions.

A Personal View

The Plumb Rule is a symbol of the silver cord which extends from the mystical centre to the soul of the individual Mason. It always forms a right angle with the level chord to the circumference where the Brethren dwell in darkness as they await the rising of the bright morning star and the coming of the light of wisdom. It is the means by which a Mason can determine the direction of the centre, even as its mystery remains as darkness visible.

All Squares, Levels, and Perpendiculars are true and proper signs to know a Mason by; you are therefore expected to stand perfectly erect, your feet formed in a Square; your body being thus considered an emblem of your mind.

The Square, Level, and Plumb Rule are called movable jewels because they are worn by the Master and his Wardens, and are transferable to their successors on nights of Installation.

The Altar

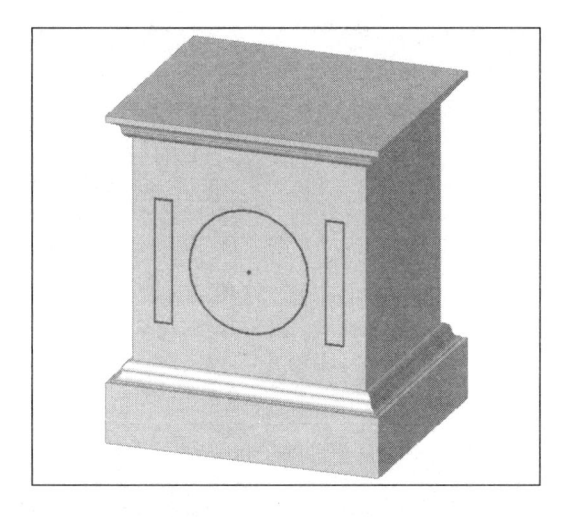

The Altar is a double cube, worked from a rough ashlar into a perfect six-sided form. It is a symbol of how your mind will be when made perfect in all its parts. The concealed underside resting on the Earth stands for the hidden submerged depths of your subconscious. The four sides facing the four quarters of the Lodge signify your human elementary nature brought into a balance as a harmonious four-square foundation stone for a spiritual building.

The upper side is exposed to the light of the bright morning star. On its surface rest the three great lights of Masonry. This is the reverse of the concealed underside and represents the consciousness of a purified personality turning away from mundane interests and facing towards the source of light. From the Altar a ladder of innumerable steps leads to the firmament and thence to infinity.

You must be an altar made from earth, the builder of it, the offering upon it, the priest who serves it, then you must ascend the great spiritual ladder to achieve union with the centre beyond the heavens.

A Personal View

The Altar represents the Mason's personality when "made perfect in all its parts". It is a double cube with a six-sided form. Its concealed underside stands for the hidden, submerged depths of the unconscious mind. The four sides facing the quarters of the Lodge symbolise the human soul moulded into a balanced, harmonious four-square foundation for loftier work. On the exposed upperside rest the three great emblematic lights. It represents the consciousness of the purified personality turned towards the heights in aspiration for union with the source of light.

The Volume of the Sacred Law

I would first recommend to your most serious contemplation the Volume of the Sacred Law, charging you to consider it as the unerring standard of truth and justice, and to regulate your actions by the Divine precepts it contains. Therein you will be taught the important duties you owe to God, to your neighbour, and to yourself.

To God, by never mentioning His Name but with that awe and reverence which are due from the creature to his Creator; by imploring His aid on all your lawful undertakings; and by looking up to Him, in every emergency, for comfort and support.

To your neighbour, by acting with him upon the square; by rendering him every kind of office, which justice or mercy may require; by relieving his distresses and soothing his afflictions; and by doing to him as, in similar cases, you would wish he should do to you.

And to yourself, by such prudent and well regulated course of discipline that may best conduce to the preservation of your corporeal and mental faculties in their fullest energy; thereby enabling you to exert the talents wherewith God has blessed you; as well as to His glory as to the welfare of your fellow creatures.

A Personal View

The Volume of the Sacred Law (VSL) represents the Mason's own view of the order which underlies the nature of the universe. The actual volume considered to hold this truth will vary according to the beliefs of the individual Mason. Symbolically as the volume is opened a Christian will see the bible as his VSL, a Jew will see it as the Torah, a Muslim will see it as the Koran and a physicist will see it as the *Principicia Mathematica*. Sometimes a Brother will ask for his particular volume to be opened alongside a Lodge Bible. More often the individual views the particular book which is opened as a symbol of the inner truth which is contained in his own volume. The written Word is the emblem and external expression of the unwritten Eternal Word, the Logos or Substantial Wisdom out of which every living soul has emanated and which, therefore, is the ground or base of human life.

The Compasses

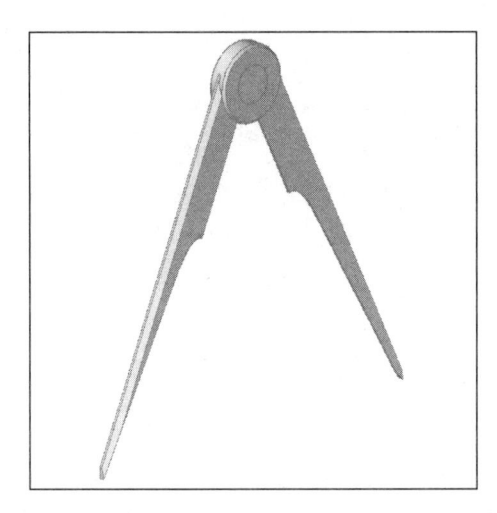

The Compasses are to keep us in due bounds with all mankind, particularly our Brethren in Freemasonry.

The Compasses belong to the Master in particular, being the chief instrument made use of in the formation of architectural plans and designs, and is peculiarly appropriated to the Master, as an emblem of his dignity; he being the Chief, Head, and Governor of the Lodge.

Compasses and Square, when united, regulate our lives and actions.

> ### A Personal View
>
> The Compasses are a symbol of the functional energy of the spirit. This fiery energy is the spirit of a Mason (a force for good or evil according to how it is shaped) and is shown as the shape known as the Fire Triangle (a triangle with its apex upward and base downward), which is how the Compasses are placed when the Lodge is open. There is an interaction between the Square and Compasses
>
> In the First Degree the points of the Compasses are hidden by the Square. In the Second Degree, one point is disclosed. In the Third both are exhibited. The implication is that as the Candidate progresses, the inertia and negativity of the soul become increasingly transmuted and superseded by the positive energy and activity of the spirit. The Fire Triangle gradually assumes preponderance over the Water Triangle, signifying that the developing Mason becomes a more vividly living and spiritually conscious being.

The Sun

The Sun is to rule the day.

Our Lodge is situated due East and West, because all places of Divine worship, as well as Masons' regular, well-formed, constituted Lodges, are, or ought to be, so situated; for the Sun, the Glory of the Lord, rises in the East and sets in the West.

The Sun rises in the East, gains its meridian lustre in the South, and sets in the West; likewise to light Brethren to, at, and from labour.

The Sun enlightens the Earth, and by its benign influence dispenses its blessings to mankind in general. The Sun's white light is invisible till passed through a prism that decomposes it into seven constituent colours, of which three are primaries. When the spiritual light of the centre falls upon the prism of the human spirit, its sevenfold properties begin to manifest, and of these there are three primaries. Masonry calls them Wisdom, Strength, and Beauty.

As the Sacred Laws are the centre of the whole universe and control it, so the Sun is the centre and life-giver of our solar system and controls and feeds with life the planets circling round it, just as at the secret centre of individual human life exists a vital, immortal principle: the soul.

A Personal View

The Masonic Sun symbolises the Mason's soul, that large spiritual area in each of us that is not subject to time and space but lives in the daylight beyond the dark prison-house of the mundane personality. The deathless soul is the permanent incorruptible principle in every human being. The solar body endures but the present character, the dominant tendencies, of each of us is the net product of all our former activities; we are today what we have made ourselves in the past, and we may be assured that our future destiny is being moulded by our present conduct and thought.

The Moon and Stars

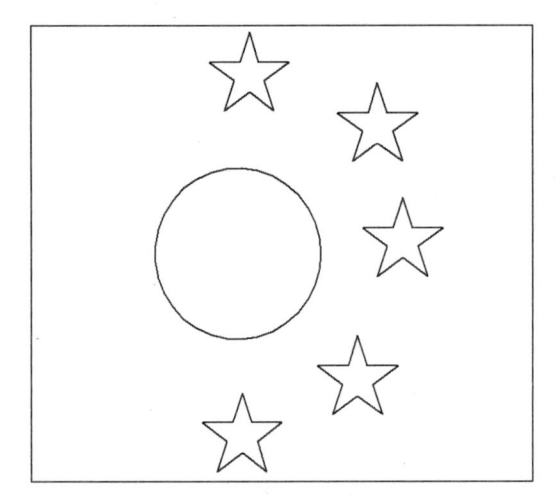

The Moon is to govern the night. The Universe is the Temple of the Deity whom we serve. The Heavens He has stretched forth as a canopy; the Earth He has planted as a footstool; He crowns His Temple with Stars as with a diadem, and with his hand He extends the power and glory. The Sun and Moon are messengers of His will, and all His law is concord.

The Moon is a satellite moving with and illumining the Earth, so in us the reasoning mind is a satellite moving with and enlightening the body, but it has no light in itself and shines only by reflection from the superior solar luminary.

Those two grand luminaries, the Sun and Moon, were created one to rule the day, and the other to govern the night. They were ordained for signs and for seasons, for days and years. Besides the Sun and Moon, the Great Architect was pleased to bespangle the ethereal concave with a multitude of stars, that man, who He intended to make, might contemplate thereon, and justly admire the majesty and glory of His creator.

A Personal View

The Moon, surrounded by the Stars, symbolises the natural reason or lower carnal mind, which Masons share in common with all intelligent creatures. It symbolises our reasoning or intellectual faculties, which (as the Moon reflects the light of the Sun) should reflect the light coming from the higher spiritual faculty and transmit it into our daily actions. In the personal heavens of a Mason metaphysical forces operate. In the make-up of each of us there exists a field of various forces, determining our individual temperaments and tendencies and influencing our future. To those forces have also been given the names of sun, moon and planets, and the science of their interaction and outworking was the ancient science of astrology, which is one of the liberal arts and sciences recommended to the study of every Mason and the pursuit of which belongs in particular to the Fellow Craft stage.

The North East Corner

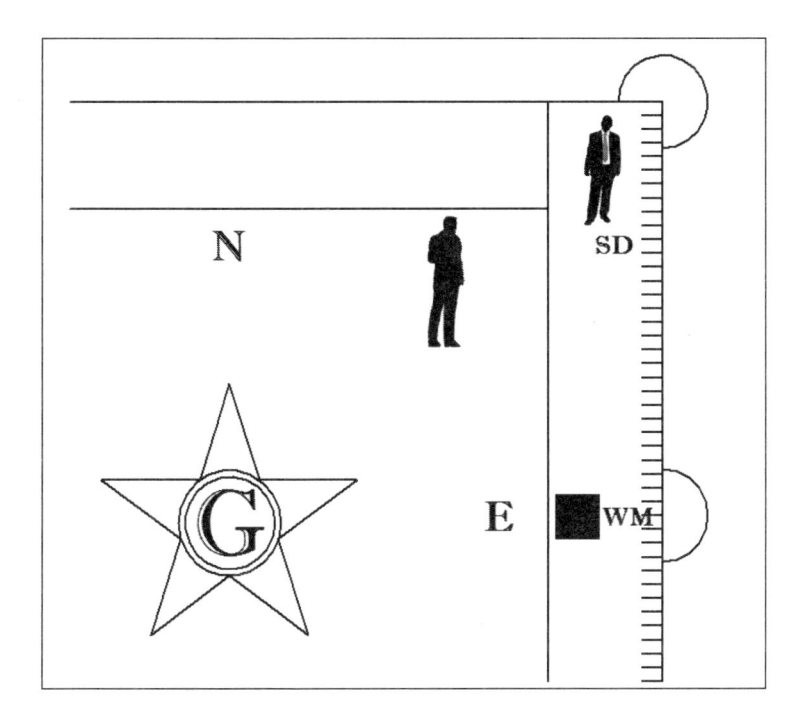

At the erection of all stately and superb edifices, it is customary to lay the first, or foundation stone, in the North East corner of the building. You, being newly admitted into Freemasonry, are placed in the North East corner of the Lodge figuratively to represent that stone, and, from the foundation laid this evening, may you raise a superstructure, perfect in all its parts, and honourable to the builder.

A Personal View

The Sun is in the North East corner of the Tracing Board, and it is in the North East corner of the Lodge that the newly made Mason is placed as a foundation where he is enjoined to build a perfect superstructure. The soul, or solar body, is the superstructure referred to and it is built up from our personality in the physical world, which serves as its foundation stone. Whatever we do or think in our physical body builds something fresh into our soul, either strengthening or weakening it, clarifying or clouding it. So a Mason aspires to a state when all his thoughts, words, and actions may ascend pure and unpolluted into his solar body, since that is the permanent receptacle where all our activities are gathered up and preserved.

The Glory at the Centre

When our Ancient Brethren were in the Middle Chamber of the Temple, their attention was peculiarly drawn to certain Hebrew characters, which are now depicted in a Fellow Craft's Lodge by the letter G in the centre of a blazing star. The letter G denotes God, the Grand Geometrician of the Universe; to whom we must all submit; and whom we ought humbly to adore.

Let us remember, wherever we are, whatever we do, He is with us. His all-seeing eye ever beholds us, and whilst we continue to act as faithful Fellow Crafts may we never forget to serve him with fervency and zeal.

A Personal View

In the First Degree Tracing Board the chequered pavement and the firmament represent a Mason's physical and mental faculties, but in the East is a symbol which transcends both. It is the spiritual essence that is the ultimate root of a Mason's being and affiliates him with the Centre. This ultimate Spirit is beyond words and the grasp of the language as it has no form. In the board it is only suggested as a blazing "Star in the East", and by a formless blinding effulgence suffusing the East and outshining the light of the sun, moon and stars, which are but subordinate luminaries and instruments to its supreme light.

This Centre is the supreme spiritual essence in us. The Glory at the Centre is the goal of all mystical attainment in Masonry, being the union of our individual consciousness with the shared consciousness of the universe.

The Left-Hand Pillar

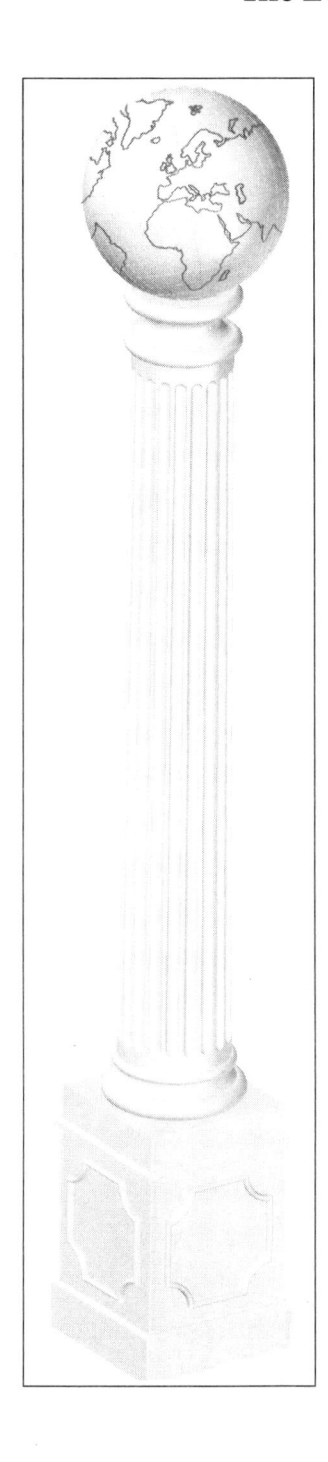

Boaz was the name of the Left-Hand Pillar which stood at the porchway or entrance of King Solomon's Temple. It was named after the Great Grandfather of David who was a Prince and Ruler in Israel and represents the force of temporal power as expressed by the rule of the king.

A Personal View

The Left-Hand Pillar which stood before Solomon's Temple signifies the power of a king or prince to rule over his people. It is one of two pillars which form what can be called "pairs of opposites." The chequered floor shows that everything in life is dual and can only be known by contrasting it to its opposite. The two in combination produce a metaphysical third which is a synthesis of perfect balance. Thus we have good and evil; light and darkness; active and passive; positive and negative; yes and no; outside and inside. Neither is complete without the other; taken together they form stability, as morning and evening unite to form the complete day.

The first pillar is the temporal power of an earthly ruler but it alone is not enough to ensure stability. For that we need another pillar whose symbol we meet elsewhere in the Craft.

The Master of the Lodge

The Master represents the Eternal Spirit of Wisdom from above. He is throned in the East that through him that Spirit may flow into every part of the Lodge. For as the Lodge is the image of the soul of man, so is he the image of the Divine Spirit which quickens that soul. He is the head and directing intellect of the assembled Brethren.

The Master is distinguished by the Square, turned downward, that is the representative of the Great Architect. He may shape into the Divine likeness all below him who have been entrusted to his care, whether in his Lodge or in his own being, of which the Lodge is a symbol.

A Personal View

The Master of the Lodge symbolises the eternal spirit of wisdom. He sits on a throne in the East symbolizing the rising of the sun to bring light and wisdom to his Brethren. The Lodge is a model of the soul of a Mason, and the Master is the head and directing intellect of the assembled Brethren, and hence the soul of the Mason. Without the light and wisdom in his spirit, the soul of a Mason is darkness and his body of flesh worthless. Until the soul and body are brought together in harmony, the spirit cannot grow and flourish. The Great Architect has joined these three together and appointed the spirit as a wise master-builder, symbolised by the Master of the Lodge to rule over soul and body, and from these imperfect corruptible materials a Mason will learn how to shape himself to become a Living Stone in the immortal Temple of Humanity.

The Sun is to rule the day, the Moon to govern the night, and the Master to rule and direct his Lodge.

The 24-inch Gauge

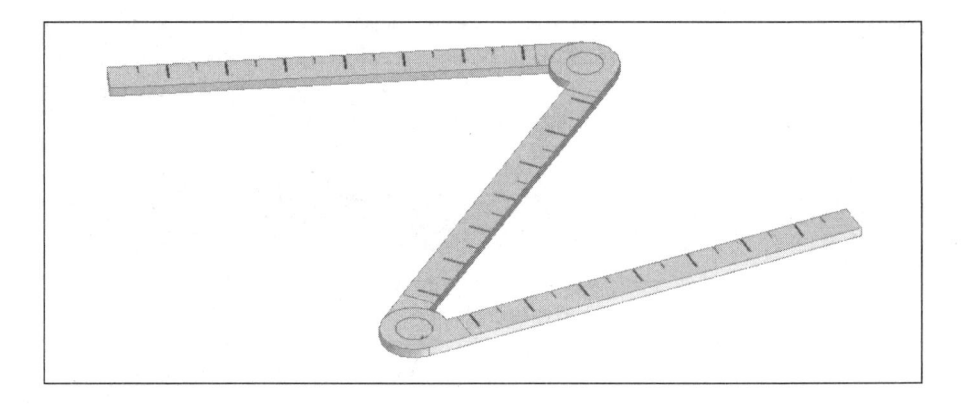

A working tool of an Entered Apprentice Freemason is the 24-inch Gauge. It is to measure our work. But as we are speculative Masons we apply this tool to our morals. In this sense, the 24-inch Gauge represents the 24 hours of the day, part to be spent in prayer to Almighty God, part in labour and refreshment, and part in serving a Friend or Brother in time of need.

A Personal View

The 24-inch gauge is a spiritual tool to help a Mason balance his daily time between three duties, not necessarily involving equal amounts of time, but each of equal value. This ancient practice of the Craft is something modern jargon calls establishing a work/life balance.

The three important things to make time for are your spiritual tranquillity, to ensure you are at peace with yourself and have time to think and reflect; your material pursuits and the care of your person, and family, to ensure that you put enough effort into work to keep yourself and your dependants; and your altruistic responsibility to those less happily placed than yourself, the work of charity, which should always be done by stealth as it is done for the benefit of the recipient not for the aggrandisement of the donor.

The Common Gavel

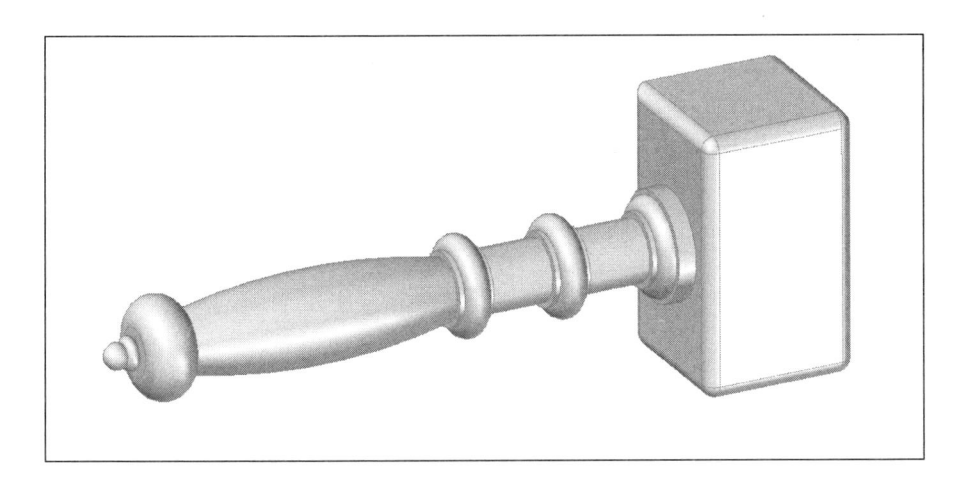

A working tool of an Entered Apprentice Freemason is the common Gavel, which is used to knock off all superfluous knobs and excrescences. But as we are Free and Accepted Masons we apply this tool to our morals. In this sense, the common Gavel represents the force of conscience, which should keep down all vain and unbecoming thoughts which might obtrude during any of the aforementioned periods, so that our words and actions may ascend unpolluted to the throne of grace.

A Personal View

The Master's Gavel controls the Lodge and its knocks create order and obedience within the Lodge which is itself a symbol of the Mason's soul. A Mason learns that his body and his soul are level ground upon which he is to build an altar in the shape of his own spiritual life. He should allow no debasing habit of thought or conduct to defile this work. As an apprentice the Mason is given the common wooden Gavel to help him smooth the rough ashlar of his imperfect soul and shape it to become the perfect symbol of the cubical altar which stands at the centre of his own consciousness. The common Gavel is a symbol of the force of conscience, and by learning to use it skillfully you learn to control your anger and intolerance.

The Chisel

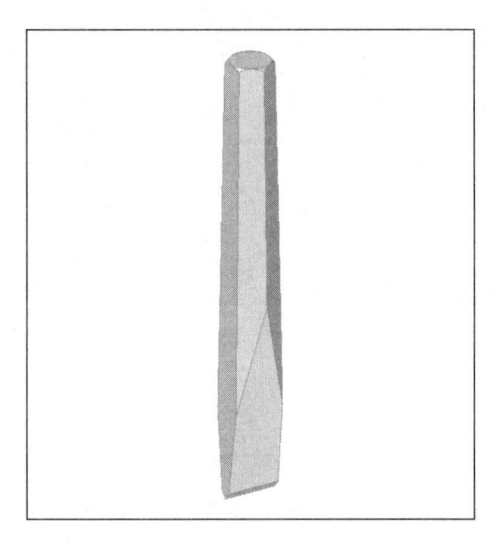

A working tool of an Entered Apprentice Freemason is the Chisel, which is used to smooth and prepare the stone, and render it fit for the hands of the more expert workman. But as we are Free and Accepted, or Speculative Masons, we apply these tools to our morals. In this sense, the Chisel points out to us the advantages of education, by which means alone we are rendered fit members of regularly organised society.

A Personal View

The Chisel is a symbol of education, as when it is driven by the force of the common Gavel, it is able to chip away the rough exterior of a freshly quarried stone and reveal the perfect cube hidden within. Education shapes a Mason's intellect, develops and expands a Mason's mind, broadens his perspective and makes him a more civilised human being. The discipline of study and learning is a good habit to acquire and as Masons we are all encouraged to make a daily step in Masonic knowledge.

The Form of the Lodge

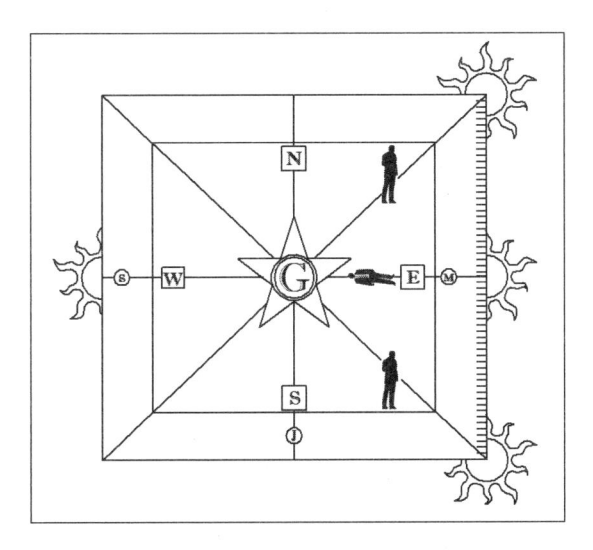

The Form of the Lodge is a parallelopipedon in length from East to West, in breadth between North and South, in depth from the surface of the earth to the centre, and even as high as the Heavens. A Freemason's Lodge is described of this vast extent to show the universality of the science; likewise, that a Mason's charity should know no bounds save those of prudence.

A Personal View

Throughout the rituals and lectures, references to the Lodge are not to the building in which we meet. That building is but a symbol itself. The real Lodge is our own individual personalities, and if we interpret our symbols in this light of this we find it reveals a new aspect of our Craft: that when we talk of a building we are referring to the spirit of a Mason.

This means that each Mason is a Lodge. Just as a Masonic Lodge is an assembly of Brethren met to reflect on the mysteries of the Craft, so each human consciousness is a composite structure of various properties and faculties put by our mind for the harmonious interaction and working out the purpose of life. Everything in Masonry is symbolic of mankind, its human constitution and spiritual evolution. Your first entry into a Lodge is symbolical of your first entry into the science of knowing yourself.

The four sides of the Lodge have a further significance. The East of the Lodge represents spirituality. The West represents normal rational understanding. Midway between these East and West extremes is the South, the meeting-place of the spiritual intuition and the rational understanding, symbolising abstract intellectuality and knowledge. The North is the side of ignorance, accessible by the lowest mode of perception, our physical sensations.

Thus the four sides of the Lodge make up four possible ways of gaining knowledge about yourself.

The Pillar of Wisdom

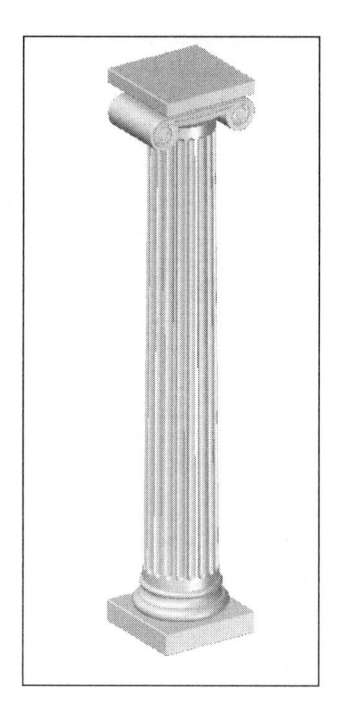

The column's capital is adorned with volutes, and its cornice has dentils. The famous Temple of Diana at Ephesus (which took over 200 years to build) was composed of the Ionic Order. Both elegance and ingenuity were displayed in the invention of this column. It is modelled after a beautiful young woman, echoing her elegant shape and flowing hair.

It is also known as the Pillar of Wisdom. For Wisdom is to contrive, and Wisdom is to conduct us in all our undertakings. The Universe is the Temple of the Deity whom we serve and Wisdom is the first pillar of His throne.

A Personal View

The Ionic Pillar is a symbol which is placed in the East of the Lodge. From its summit flows forth the fountain of Wisdom, dividing itself into active and passive properties, to indicate that in the up-building of the soul the right hand of action must be balanced by the left hand of understanding, and that the mind and heart must labour equally and aspire together. The elegant symmetrical shape of the pillar incorporates this duality in its form. The Pillar of Wisdom is in the care of the Master of the Lodge to inspire him to strive to adjust and harmonise the different elements of his Lodge that they may be as Brethren dwelling together in unity, in one house.

The Pillar of Strength

This Doric column has no ornament except mouldings on the base or capital. Its frieze is distinguished by triglyphs and metopes, and its cornice by mutules. Being the most ancient of all the Orders, it retains more of the primitive-hut style in its form than any of the rest. The triglyphs in the frieze represent the ends of the joists, and the mutules in its cornice represent the rafters.

The composition of this Order is both grand and noble; being formed after the model of a muscular, full-grown man; delicate ornaments are repugnant to its characteristic solidity. It therefore succeeds best in the regularity of its proportions; and is principally used in warlike structures where strength and a noble simplicity are required.

It is also known as the Pillar of Strength. For Strength is to support us under all our difficulties. The Universe is the Temple of the Deity whom we serve and Strength is the second pillar of His throne.

A Personal View

The Doric Pillar is placed in the West of the Lodge. Its strength and plainness symbolise the enduring substance of the soul. It stands upright as before the Lodge is opened, symbolising the strength needed to face the hardships and threats of the world. But once the Lodge is open it is lowered as the corporate mind of the open Lodge no longer needs its protection. As the sun sets in the West to close the day, so the Senior Warden lowers the pillar of strength to close the Lodge. As the pillar is lowered, the Brethren remember the splendour which has shone upon it and reflect that the soul grows to perfection, yet looks forward to that time when it shall rise beyond duality and change, and pass into the enduring unity of the Centre.

The Pillar of Beauty

The capital of this column is adorned with two rows of leaves and eight volutes which sustain the abacus. This Order is chiefly used in stately structures.

Calimachus was inspired to create the capital of this column from the following remarkable circumstance. Accidentally passing the tomb of a young lady, he saw a basket of toys which had been left there by her nurse, covered with a tile, and placed over an Acanthus root; as the leaves grew up, they encompassed the basket, till they overgrew the tile, met with an obstruction, and bent downwards; Calimachus set about imitating the figure; the base of the capital represented the basket, the abacus the tile; and the volutes the bending leaves.

It is also known as the Pillar of Beauty. For Beauty is to adorn the inward man. The Universe is the Temple of the Deity whom we serve and Beauty is the third pillar of His throne; for Beauty shines through the whole of creation in symmetry and order.

A Personal View

The Corinthian Pillar of Beauty is placed in the South of the Lodge. It is a symbol of an upright soul whose ascending sides have been fluted into beauty by the chisel of education, and at whose summit intelligence breaks forth into the leafage and tendrils of Wisdom.

When the Lodge is opened the Junior Warden raises it in token that with the light of the Centre is now visible within the open Lodge. But when the Lodge closes and the superior Light become as darkness visible, the Pillar of Beauty is raised as a symbol that during the hours of darkness, Strength and Wisdom will prevail and govern the outward actions of the Brethren.

The Celestial Canopy

The Heavens He has stretched forth as a canopy; the Earth He has planted as a footstool; He crowns His Temple with stars as with a diadem and with His hand He extends the power and glory. The Sun and Moon are messengers of His will, and all His law is concord.

A Personal View

The Celestial Canopy of the Lodge, painted on the ceiling, symbolises the ethereal nature of a Mason. The chequered floor and the Celestial Canopy are the reverse and the opposite pole of each other. The Mason's ethereal nature is tenuous and invisible, like the subtle fragrance of a flower. Its existence is not physically demonstrable, but a Candidate enters the Craft with the acknowledged desire of seeking to cast light upon the nature of his own being. The Order assists him in his search for that light by teachings and symbols that have been devised by wise and competent instructors. The Mason who yields to the discipline of the Order does more than improve his morals and character. He builds an inner ethereal body to match the beauty of the Celestial Canopy.

Jacob's Ladder

Rebecca, the beloved wife of Isaac, knowing by Divine inspiration that a peculiar blessing was vested in the soul of her husband, was desirous to obtain it for her favorite son Jacob. But by birthright, it belonged to Esau, her first-born. Jacob had no sooner fraudulently obtained his father's blessing, than he was obliged to flee from the wrath of his brother, who in a moment of rage and disappointment had threatened to kill him. He journeyed towards Padanaram, in the land of Mesopotamia. Weary and benighted in the desert, he lay down to rest, taking the Earth for his bed, a stone for his pillow, and the Canopy of Heaven for a covering. In a vision, he saw a Ladder, the top of which reached to the Heavens, and the Angels of the Lord ascending and descending thereon. It was then the Almighty entered into a solemn covenant with Jacob, that if he would abide by His laws, and keep His commandments, He would not only bring him again to his father's house in peace and prosperity, but would make of his seed a great and mighty people.

This ladder had many staves or rounds, which point out as many moral virtues, but the three principal ones are Faith, Hope, and Charity.

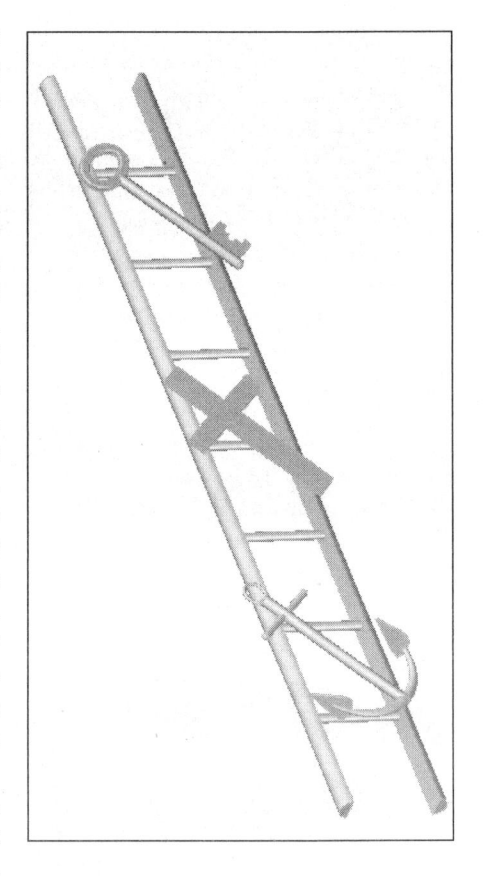

A Personal View

The symbol of Jacob's Ladder rests on the Volume of the Sacred Law and extends to the Bright Morning Star, rising in the East. It represents the lower and physical part of a Mason that is animal and earthy, and stands upon the Earth. From this base our spirit reaches to the Celestial Canopy. These two parts of a Mason's nature are in perpetual conflict, the spiritual and the carnal at war with each other. The Master Mason has learned to bring about a perfect balance between them and to establish himself in strength so that his own soul stands firm against weakness and temptation.

Faith

Faith is the foundation of justice, the bond of amity, and the chief support of civil society. We live and walk by Faith. By it we have a continual acknowledgment of a Supreme Being. By Faith we have access to the Throne of grace, are justified, accepted, and finally received. A true and sincere Faith is the evidence of things not seen, but the substance of those hoped for. It will bring us to those blessed mansions, where we shall be eternally happy with God the Great Architect of the Universe.

A Personal View

Faith symbolises the possibility of attaining Masonic enlightenment. The Masonic path from West to East is not easy to tread. The spiral steps to the Middle Chamber are steep and call for fortitude and a steadfast sense of purpose. But for all that effort, as the climber mounts, in faith of reaching the light of the Centre, broad vistas open out. Wisdom descends upon the faithful Mason as a sanctifying and increasing brightness. A Mason is strengthened by a Power mightier than any individual and as the hoodwink falls away through the Gate Beautiful he can see the land of far distances. Faith in attaining this vista sustains the Mason on his journey.

Hope

Hope is the anchor of the soul, both sure and steadfast. We must rely on the Almighty to animate our endeavours, and teach us to fix our desires within the limits of His most blessed promises. So shall success attend us. If we believe a thing impossible, our despondency may render it so, but he who perseveres in a just cause will ultimately overcome all difficulties.

A Personal View

One of the patron saints of Masonry (St. John) teaches, "He who hath this hope in him purifieth himself, even as the Master whom he is seeking is pure."

The essence of the Masonic philosophy is that all Masons are searching for something in their own nature which they have lost. With proper instruction and by their own patience and industry they hope to find if. This missing knowledge is symbolised by the Lost Word, and the hope offered by Masonry is that it can be found, by the application of the Masonic Art.

Hope symbolises our persistent desire for the rediscovery of that within ourselves which is lost.

Symbols of the First Degree

Charity

Lovely in itself, it is the brightest ornament which adorns our Masonic profession. It is the best test and surest proof of the sincerity of our religion. Benevolence, rendered by Heaven-born Charity, is an honour to the nation whence it springs, is nourished, and cherished. Happy is the man who has sown in his breast the seeds of benevolence; he envies not his neighbour, he believes not a tale reported to his prejudice, he forgives the injuries of men, and endeavours to blot them from his recollection. Then, Brethren, let us remember that we are Free and Accepted Masons; ever ready to listen to him who craves our assistance; and from him who is in want let us not withhold a liberal hand. So shall a heartfelt satisfaction reward our labours, and the produce of love and Charity will most assuredly follow.

A Personal View

An illumined Masonic Candidate is said to attain what is known in the East as the state of *Samadhi*. It also known as universal or cosmic consciousness. When it is experienced it transcends all sense of personal individualisation, time and space. When a Mason enters this state of mind the bliss and peace surpass all temporal understanding. The Mason has risen to an exalted state where there is resolution in blissful concord with the Eternal. Once this has been experienced, the Mason is in conscious sympathy and identity of feeling with all that lives and feels. This takes the form of universal Charity and limitless love which is the corollary of perceiving the unity of the cosmos. As an Apprentice, the Mason was told that this attainment of illumination was the summit of the Mason's profession. Once reaching it he sees that there is a universe within him as well as without him. He microcosmically sums up and contains all that manifested to his temporal intelligence as the vast spatial universe around him so how can he fail to practise Charity to his fellow beings?

The Mosaic Pavement

The Mosaic Pavement is the beautiful flooring of a Freemason's Lodge, by reason of its being variegated and chequered. This points out the diversity of objects which decorate and adorn all of creation.

Our days are variegated and chequered by unpredictable events, both good and evil. This is why our Lodge is furnished with Mosaic work, to point out the uncertainty of all things here on Earth. Today we may travel in prosperity, while tomorrow we may totter on the uneven path of weakness, temptation, and adversity. Then while such emblems are before us, we are morally instructed not to boast of anything but to give heed to our ways, to walk uprightly and with humility before God; for though some are born to more elevated situations than others, yet, when in the grave, we are all on the level, death destroying all distinctions. While our feet tread on this Mosaic work, let our ideas recur to the original whence we copy; let us, as good men and Masons, act as the dictates of reason prompt us: to practise charity, maintain harmony, and endeavour to live in unity and brotherly love.

A Personal View

When the ritual says "The square pavement is for the High Priest to walk upon", it is not merely the Jewish High Priest of centuries ago that is referred to. It is a symbol for each individual member of the Craft.

Every Mason should aspire to become the High Priest of his own personal temple and to make of it a place where he may meet the Great Architect of the Universe to become aware of the plan of the cosmos.

Every living being, whether a Mason or not, in this dualistic world walks upon the square pavement of mingled good and evil. The Mosaic Pavement is a symbol of a philosophical truth. For the Mason to be master of his fate he must walk upon these opposites in the sense of transcending and dominating them. He must learn to trample upon his lower sensual nature and keep it under his subjection and control. He must be able to rise above the motley of good and evil, to be indifferent to the ups and downs of fortune swaying his thoughts and actions. The Mason is trying to develop his innate spiritual potencies and that is impossible so long as he is overruled by material tendencies and the fluctuating emotions of pleasure and pain that they invoke. By rising above them a Mason gains serenity and mental equilibrium under all circumstances. In this way a Mason walks upon the chequered ground work of existence and the conflicting tendencies of his material nature.

The Blazing Star

The Blazing Star is the Glory in the Centre and refers us to the Sun, which enlightens the Earth, and by its benign influence dispenses its blessings to mankind.

A Personal View

The Blazing Star is another name for the symbol of the Sun. The Sun in turn is a symbol of the great potential which is inherent in the hidden centre of the Candidate's soul. A Mason is taught that there is a mysterious centre to his being which is at first but as darkness visible. As he progresses into his own interior he reaches the Blazing Star or Glory at his own Centre. By this awe inspiring light he simultaneously knows himself and the Great Architect and realises his unity with the Cosmic Plan and the "points of fellowship" between him and the Plan. From this awful and sublime experience, his initiated soul is brought back to its bodily encasement and reunited to the companions of its former toils. He resumes his temporal life with conscious realisation of his place in the cosmos. Only then is he entitled to the name of Master Mason. The secrets of Freemasonry and of Initiation are concerned with this process of introversion of the soul to its own Centre and the vision of the Blazing Star which symbolises awareness of the mysterious nature of the Centre.

The Indented or Tessellated Border

The Indented or Tessellated Border refers us to the planets, which in their various revolutions form a beautiful border or skirtwork round that grand luminary, the Sun. In the same way, this border forms a skirtwork round a Freemason's Lodge.

A Personal View

The Brethren of a Masonic Lodge are placed in different and unequal degrees of perception upon the chequerwork floor of life, but the Tessellated Border, with its tassels at each corner, encloses all alike — wise and foolish, learned and uninformed. It is a symbol of the unifying nature of Lodge membership. The skirtwork symbolises a border of common Providence and from the mutual interplay of the light and darkness in all Masons comes the realisation that Wisdom will at last be justified and we need not complain of her processes, which although they may work out to a beneficent conclusion may temporarily involve sharp and painful contrasts. The Tessellated Border shows that the corporate spirit of the Lodge enfolds and supports the individual Brethren.

Symbols of the First Degree

The Tracing Board

The Tracing Board is for the Master to lay lines and draw designs on, the better to enable the Brethren to carry on the intended structure with regularity and propriety. The Volume of the Sacred Law may justly be deemed the spiritual Tracing Board of the Great Architect of the Universe, in which are laid down such Divine laws and moral plans, that were we conversant therein, and adherent thereto, would bring us to an ethereal mansion not made with hands, eternal in the Heavens.

A Personal View

In ancient times the symbols of the Degree were drawn on the floor of the Lodge by the Right Worshipful Master using chalk and charcoal. During the ceremony the Candidate walked the steps of the Degree above the symbols which illuminated the knowledge being imparted. At the end of the ceremony the Candidate would mop away the symbols to hide them from the eyes of the profane. In recent years this freshly drawn set of symbols has been largely replaced by artistic images of the symbols in the context of the Degree. From studying the Tracing Boards a Mason can draw aside the veils of allegory that shroud the teachings of the Craft.

The Craft sometimes calls itself the Sons of the Widow. In this name the symbol of Freemasonry as a mystical and beloved Mother is invoked. Within the Tracing Board the Craft stands draped with dark and forbidding veils of the mourning widow. As we lift those veils, we reveal behind them the presence of something of deepening wonder and ever-increasing beauty, something that will make of us and our Craft greater than we yet are.

The Rough Ashlar

The Entered Apprentice works, marks, and indents on the Rough Ashlar. It is a stone, rough and unhewn as taken from the quarry, until, by the industry and ingenuity of the workman, it is modelled, wrought into due form, and rendered fit for the intended structure. This represents man in his infant or primitive state, rough and unpolished as that stone, until by the kind care and attention of his parent or guardians, in giving him a liberal and virtuous education, his mind becomes cultivated, and he is thereby rendered a fit member of civilised society.

A Personal View

A Mason who desires to rise to the heights of his own being must first crush his own lower nature and inclinations. He must perfect his conduct, by struggles against his own natural propensities. His base material nature is symbolised by the Rough Ashlar, as it is dragged from the clay of the quarry. The Candidate is given spiritual tools to work the Rough Ashlar of his own nature into the perfect cube of enlightened soul. And the cube itself contains a secret, for unfolded, it denotes and takes the form of the cross made up of four right angles or squares.

The Perfect Ashlar

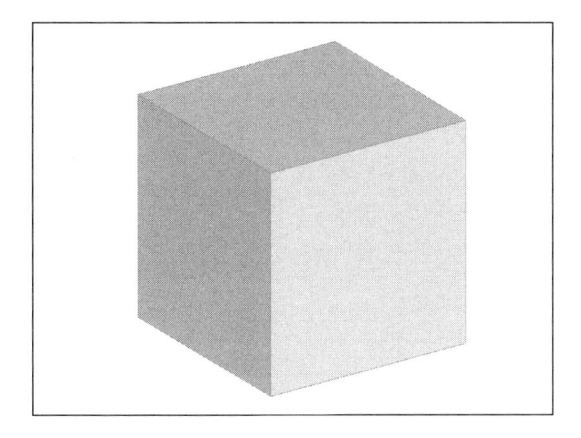

The Perfect Ashlar is for the experienced craftsman to try, and adjust his jewels on. The Perfect Ashlar is a stone of a true die or square, fit only to be tried by the Square and Compasses. This represents man in the decline of years, after a regular well-spent life in acts of piety and virtue. He can only be tried and approved by the Square of God's Word and the Compass of his own self-convincing conscience.

A Personal View

To attain the state of spiritual development signified by the Perfect Ashlar (which is the work involved in the Masonic Second Degree), the Mason's soul and body must be brought into a balanced relationship before passing through a crucial regenerative experience known as the cross or transition from natural to supranatural life.

The cross as a philosophical symbol long pre-dates Christianity. It is significant in Freemasonry as a symbol of the four primordial elements (Fire, Water, Air, Earth) brought together into a state of balanced union. All newly made Masons have too much or too little of one or other of them in their composition, and to restore the inner elements of the body, mind, spirit, and soul to balance and harmony with ourselves is the life-problem we all share.

The cross of the unfolded Perfect Ashlar is a conspicuous symbol of the human soul. Our ego is bound by the cross of the four material elements which it must subdue into balance and harmony. As the ritual says, we must "make all our passions and prejudices coincide with the strict line of virtue and in every pursuit to have eternity in view".

The Perfect Ashlar symbolises the state of balance and harmony which is the goal of every Fellowcraft Freemason.

The Point Within a Circle

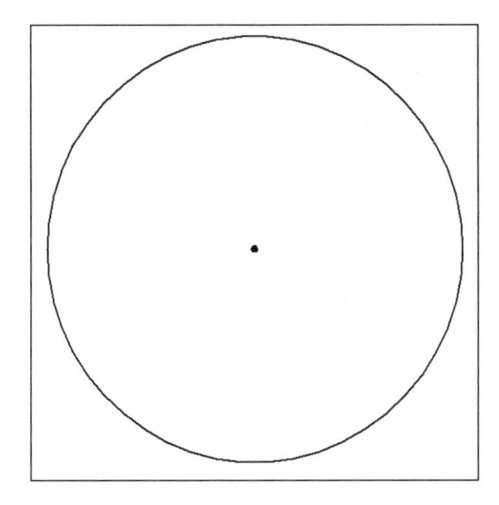

In all regular, well-formed, constituted Lodges, there is a point within a circle round which the Brethren cannot err. This circle is bounded between North and South by two grand parallel lines, one representing Moses and the other King Solomon. On the upper part of this circle rests the Volume of the Sacred Law, supporting Jacob's ladder, the top of which reaches to the heavens. In going round this circle, we must necessarily touch on both those parallel lines and likewise on the Sacred Volume, and whilst a Mason keeps himself thus circumscribed, he cannot err.

A Personal View

A dormant but vital principle exists as the central point of the circle of a Mason's individuality. As the outward universe is an externalised projection of the Great Architect, so is the outward individual Mason the externalisation of an inherent Divine spark which through personal self-will and desire has become dislocated and has shut off the Mason's consciousness. To recover contact with that central Divine Principle is the purpose of Freemasonry. Once a Mason ceases to be simply a rationalised animal and becomes privy to mysteries of the Centre, he recovers the lost and genuine secrets of his own being. The Mason who reaches that point lives from the Centre for it is the end, object and goal of his Masonic existence.

A Mason who has found, and lives from, the Divine Centre of his being — that point from which a Master Mason cannot err — possesses wisdom and powers beyond the imagination of the uninitiated world.

Chalk, Charcoal, and Clay

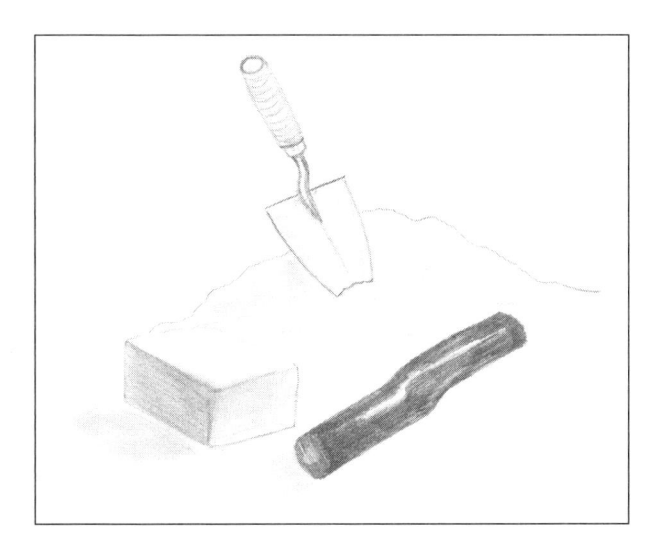

Chalk is an ancient deposit, pure in its whiteness and abundant. It is an emblem of Masonic secret wisdom, which is an ancient doctrine revealed and deposited from heavenly sources for the uplift of man. It is free to whoever seeks it, and as such it cannot fail to leave a mark upon his mind. Charcoal, an emblem of fervent heat, meant Masonic doctrine must become burned into the fabric of our being, mingled with our personal "Clay" and inscribed on the fleshy tablets of the heart. Just as with chalk and charcoal, the Tracing Board was personally imprinted upon the earthy flooring of the Lodge.

A Personal View

These materials, white Chalk, black Charcoal and malleable Clay, symbolise truth, understanding and growth. Nothing is more free than chalk; its slightest touch leaves a trace. Nothing is more fervent than charcoal; for when properly lighted no metal can resist its force. Nothing is more zealous and adaptable than clay, our mother Earth; who is continually labouring for our support. From clay we came, and to clay we must all return.

Chalk is abundantly free to the service of man and leaves a mark on whatever it touches. This symbolises that secret Masonic wisdom, which is an ancient doctrine revealed and deposited from the mystical centre for the spiritual uplift of all Masons. Its whiteness symbolises the purity of Truth in its teaching and its nature shows how easily it adheres to those who seek it out.

The Lewis

If you wished to give your son a Masonic name, you would call him Lewis, which denotes "strength" and is depicted in our Lodges by certain pieces of metal dovetailed into a stone, forming a cramp; and when in combination with some of the mechanical powers, such as a system of pulleys, it enables the Operative Mason to raise great weights to certain heights with little encumbrance, and to fix them on their proper bases.

A Lewis, being the son of a Mason, has a duty to his aged parents to bear the heat and burden of the day, which they by reason of their age ought to be exempt from; he is to assist them in time of need, and thereby render the close of their days happy and comfortable. And his privilege for so doing is that of being made a Mason before any other person, however dignified.

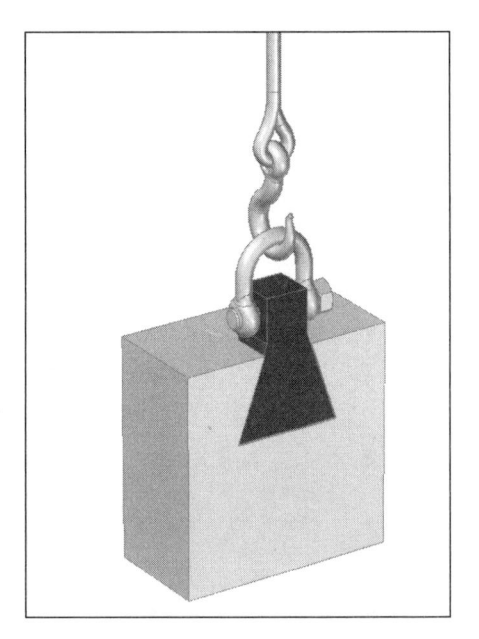

A Personal View

The name "Lewis" is traditionally associated with the Craft. It is the name given to the son of a Mason. But the symbol of the Lewis as associated with light is also said to be a device which "when properly dovetailed into a stone forms a clamp, enabling Masons to lift great weights with little inconvenience whilst fixing them on their proper bases".

Symbolically this refers to the fact that when the Divine Light is brought forward from a Mason's submerged depths and dovetailed into his soul he becomes able easily to grapple with difficulties, problems and "weights" of all kind. It also symbolises a Mason's moral judgment which teaches him to judge real values and "fix them on their proper bases".

Symbols of the First Degree

The Square and Compasses, Both Points Covered

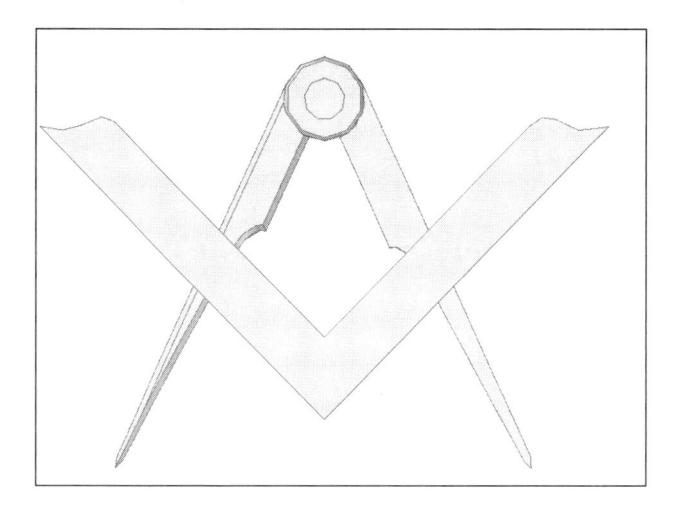

Your progress in Masonry is marked by the position of the Square and Compasses. When you are made an Entered Apprentice both points are hidden. This is the distinguishing badge of an Entered Apprentice.

A Personal View

Masonically, we speak of the Great Architect of the Universe, and the cosmos as the Cosmic Temple being built in accordance with the Divine Plan and measured out with the help of the Divine Compasses and Square. This idea, which is the basis of Masonic doctrine and philosophy, is the first secret revealed to every Candidate. He is shown the square and compasses immediately after having his hoodwink removed. As he is yet but an Apprentice, the points of the Compasses are hidden beneath the Square, as he is not yet prepared to take part in the application of the Divine Plan. But as a Mason, it is now his duty to co-operate with the Great Architect in executing His plan and erecting the Great Cosmic Temple. The Square, which covers the Compasses, symbolises the spiritual tool he will need to master in order to shape his soul into a perfect cube.

Chapter 9

Symbols of the Second Degree

The Square and Compasses, One Point Covered

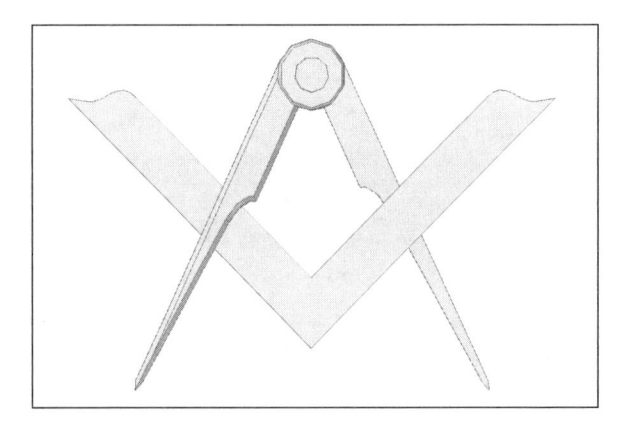

Permit me to call your attention to the position of the Square and Compasses. When you were made an Entered Apprentice both points of the Compasses were hid from your view, showing that you were newly admitted.

Now you are a Fellow of the Craft and one point is exposed, proving that you are midway in Freemasonry, superior to an Entered Apprentice but inferior to what I trust you will hereafter attain.

A Personal View

As a Mason progresses through his degrees, darkness is gradually being dissolved by light. In the degree of the Fellow Craft one point of the Great Architect's Compasses is brought into sight to overlay the Square of human activity in shaping his soul. Having been initiated into the mystic and cosmic principles of the Square and Compasses, the Mason sees that they rest on the unshakeable basis of the Divine Plan. The change in the visibility of the points of the Compasses reflect the Fellow Craft's midway position in the Craft. He can now discern, in both them and himself the ongoing conflict of darkness and light. As the points of Compasses emerge from darkness they symbolise that light always conquers in the end. This evolving symbol is preparing him to expect difficulties in endeavouring to focus bring his understanding, as symbolised by the points of the Compasses rising fully into the light.

The Right-Hand Pillar

Jachin was the name of the Right-Hand Pillar which stood at the entrance or porchway of King Solomon's Temple. It was named after the Great High Priest who officiated at the dedication of the Temple. It represents the power of the priest and the benevolent force of religion.

A Personal View

Just as the Left-Hand Pillar was named for king and ruler and symbolised force of secular power in society, so the Right-Hand Pillar is named for a high priest. It symbolises the power and force of religion in the life of society. Wise activity (Boaz) must be balanced with an equally wise passivity (Jachin) if a Mason is to become established in strength and stand firm and spiritually consolidated.

This is not work to be hurried; those who build temples of humanity must build slowly and let nothing be done in excess, and need to consider but the force of temporal and spiritual power.

The Two Pillars at the Entrance to King Solomon's Temple

The pillar on the left of the porch of King Solomon's Temple was called Boaz, and that on the right Jachin.

Each of the two pillars was seventeen cubits and a half high and their circumference was twelve cubits. They were four cubits in diameter and were cast hollow the better to serve as archives to Masonry, for therein were deposited the constitutional rolls. The thickness of the outer rim or shell was four inches and they were made of molten brass, cast in the plain of Jordan, in the clay ground between Succoth and Zeredathah where King Solomon ordered those and all his holy vessels to be cast. The casting was superintended by Hiram Abif.

A Personal View

All matter is composed of positive and negative forces in perfect balance and contains objects that would disintegrate and disappear if they did not stand firm in perfect balance.

The two pillars symbolise that perfect integrity of body and soul which is essential to achieving spiritual perfection.

In ancient philosophy all created things were made from fire and water, fire being their spiritual and water their material element. The two pillars represent these universal properties. In this symbolism the path to true wisdom is an entrance between fire on the right hand and deep water on the left. It is so narrow that a Mason must go through it alone. This narrow path of true initiation is symbolised as we enter the Cosmic Temple between the symbolic pillars. For as the ritual tells us, "The former denotes strength, the latter to establish, and when conjoined stability, for God said "In strength will I establish My word in this Mine house that it will stand fast forever."

The Chapiters

Each pillar was adorned with a Chapiter. The height of each Chapiter was five cubits and they were enriched with Net-work, Lily-work, and Pomegranates.

A Personal View

There are additional layers of symbolism to the two pillars which stood at the entrance to King Solomon's Temple. The Chapiters were formed hollow when they were cast from molten brass on the plain of Jordan, in the clay ground between Succoth and Zeredathah. This work of casting was superintended by the Master Architect Hiram Abif and he cast then hollow in order to serve as a repository of archives of Masonry, which were deposited within them. To mark the fact they contained the hidden secrets of Masonry, the Chapiters were decorated with suitable symbols

The Net-work

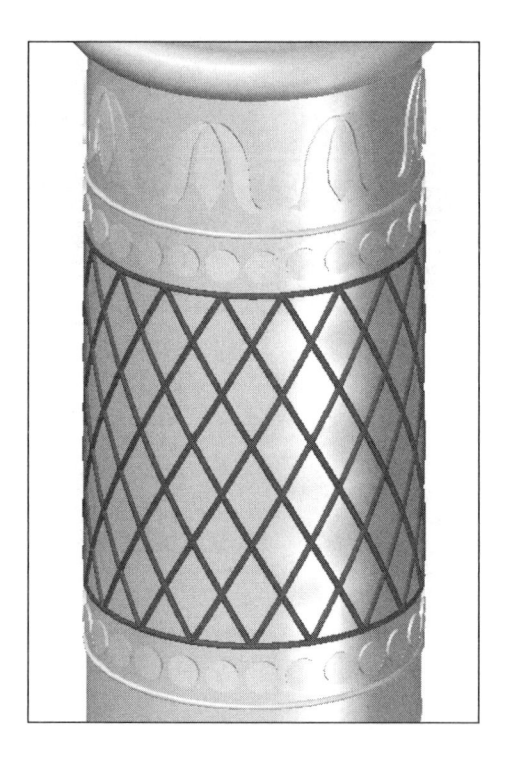

Net-work, from the connection of its meshes, represents unity.

A Personal View

The ritual tells us that the heads of the two pillars were enriched with Net-work. Net-work by the unity and interconnected nature of its meshes symbolises the unity and brotherhood of Masonry Universal. The Net-work was the final work which was done before the pillars were considered to be finished. In this symbolism the Brethren are told that the work on the Temple of Humanity will not be complete until all people can honour one another as Brethren. The hidden records contain the Divine Plan of how this was to be achieved.

Symbols of the Second Degree

The Lily-work

Lily-work, from its whiteness, represents peace.

A Personal View

The Lily-work which adorns the Chapiters is a symbol of purity and peace. Its whiteness speaks of light and truth, whilst the lily is the flower of peace. The lily is a traditional symbol of divinity, purity, and abundance. It signifies a love most complete in perfection, charity, and benediction. It surrounds each of the two pillars as the brotherly love of the Tessellated Border surrounds the Lodge.

The Pomegranates

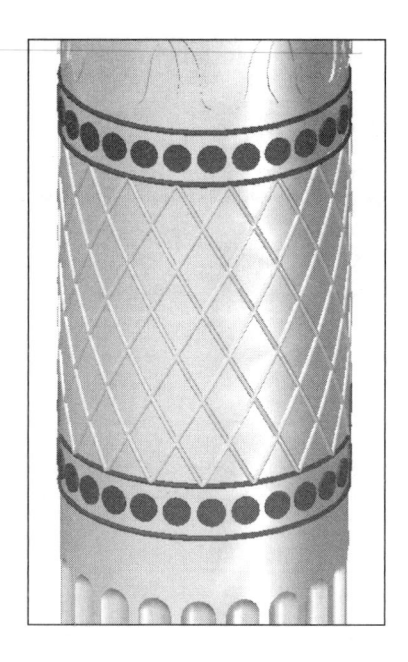

Pomegranates, from the exuberance of their seed, represent plenty. There were two rows of Pomegranates on each Chapter, one hundred in each row.

A Personal View

The Pomegranate was a highly esteemed symbol by the nations of antiquity. The fruit, because of the exuberance of its seed, was known as a symbol which denoted wealth, abundance or plenty.

Masons are told that the skirt of Aaron's robe was decorated with golden bells and pomegranates, and the pomegranate also adorned the golden candelabra within the Temple.

There were two rows, each of one hundred pomegranates, on each Chapter to symbolise the wealth and richness of knowledge which the secret archives of Freemasonry contained.

The Globes

The pillars were further adorned with two spherical balls on which were delineated maps of the Celestial and Terrestrial Globes, pointing out that Masonry is a universal science.

A Personal View

The Chapiters of the two pillars were also decorated with two spherical balls. The pillar of Boaz had a Terrestrial Globe and the pillar of Jachin a Celestial Globe. These symbolise the power of the king over the lands of the earth and the power of the priest of the heavenly realms. These Celestial and Terrestrial Globes are echoed in the pillars of the Senior and Junior Warden. When the Lodge is open the Senior Warden's Celestial Globe is raised, whilst the Junior Warden's Terrestrial Globe is lowered to show that the Lodge is working on the spiritual rather than the temporal level.

The Middle Chamber

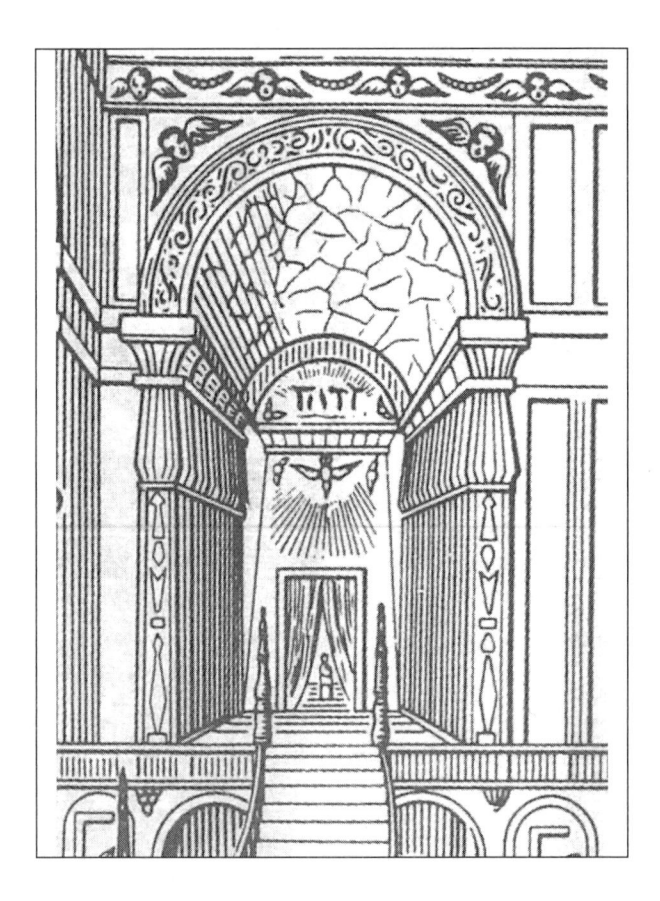

Our ancient Brethren went to receive their wages in the Middle Chamber of King Solomon's Temple. They got there by the porch or entrance on the south side, arriving at the foot of the winding staircase, which led to the Middle Chamber.

A Personal View

The Middle Chamber is a symbol of the human mind. It stands midway between things material and things spiritual. It is represented as an intermediate holy place which the Mason must pass through before that ultimate holy of holies; the fire of the spirit is reached. It is a Middle Chamber so that the Mason is led to follow a gradual ascent from the material to the spiritual. This symbolism is why we ascend to progressively higher levels by symbolically opening up from one Degree to another and exposing in each level the appropriate Tracing Board. But we must not forget that each "opening" implies an uplift of mind and heart to a higher level of contemplation than in the lower Degree.

The Spiral Staircase

When the Brethren approached the Winding Staircase, their ascent was opposed by the Junior Warden. He demanded of them the Pass Grip and Pass Word. Only those who could give it correctly were allowed to proceed.

They then passed up the Winding Staircase consisting of three, five, seven, or more steps — three to rule a Lodge, five to hold a Lodge, and seven or more to make it perfect. The three steps represent the Right Worshipful Master and his two Wardens; the five steps represent the Right Worshipful Master, two Wardens, and two Fellow Crafts; the seven steps represent two Entered Apprentices added to the former number.

Three rule a Lodge because at the building of King Solomon's Temple there were three Grand Masters who held sway: Solomon, King of Israel; Hiram, King of Tyre; and Hiram Abif. Seven or more make it perfect because it took King Solomon seven years and upwards in building and dedicating the Temple at Jerusalem to God's service; the seven steps also represent the seven liberal arts and sciences (Grammar, Rhetoric, Logic, Arithmetic, Geometry, Music, and Astronomy). After our ancient Brethren had gained the summit of the Winding Staircase, they arrived at the door of the Middle Chamber, which they found open but properly guarded by the ancient Senior Warden, who demanded of them the sign, token, and word of a Fellow Craft. After giving these convincing proofs, they were allowed to pass. They then passed into the Middle Chamber to receive their wages, which they did without scruple or diffidence. When they were in the Middle Chamber, their attention was drawn to certain Hebrew characters, which are now depicted in a Fellow Craft Lodge by the letter G, which denotes the Grand Geometrician of the Universe, to whom we must all submit.

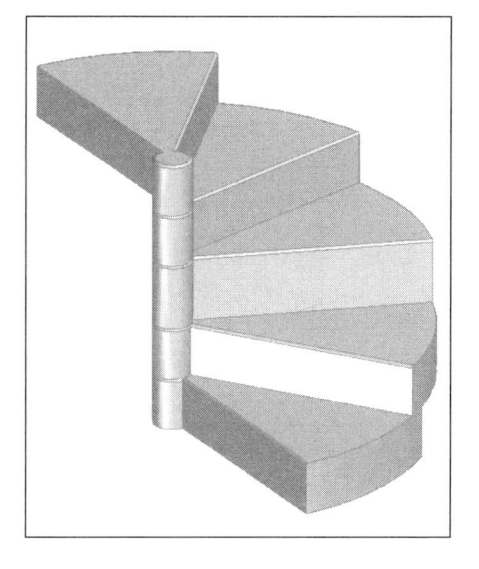

A Personal View

When the Candidate for Fellow Craft first enters the Lodge he traces a square path during which he visits each of its four sides, and symbolic methods of gaining knowledge, in turn. But then he is directed to mount spirally, by a series of winding steps. The level steps have given way to a spiral ascent. This symbolises that the Candidate is ready to leave the level of the sense-world and rise to the supra-sensual. As he ascends the Winding Staircase the Candidate is mentally leaves the outer world behind and rises into an inner spiritual world. Symbolically as he climbs the spiral stairway his mind ascends to the source of light. To explore these new regions and learn their many secrets and mysteries are his duty as a Fellow Craft.

The Wages

Our ancient Brethren received their wages, without scruple or diffidence, in the Middle Chamber of the Temple. They received them without scruple, well knowing they were justly entitled to them. When they were in the Middle Chamber their attention was particularly arrested by certain Hebrew characters, which are now depicted in a Fellow Craft Lodge by the letter G, which denotes the Grand Geometrician of the Universe, to whom we must all submit, and whom we ought most cheerfully to obey.

A Personal View

The Rough Ashlar can only be squared and perfected by chipping and polishing. The Mason learns that difficulty, adversity and persecution serve a useful purpose. These hardships are his wages and he must learn to accept them "without scruple and without diffidence, knowing that he is justly entitled to them, and from the confidence he has in the integrity of his Employer".

When a Mason sets his feet upon the path towards the light of the East; when he seeks to pass between the pillars and enter deeper knowledge; when he mounts the Winding Staircase to the heights, he makes a break with his past and puts his old methods of life behind him. He detaches himself from the interests he previously prized, in favour of something better. He will find himself moved between states of light and joy, and periods of darkness and dismay. He will doubt the path he has set himself upon. Experiences of this constitute the "wages", and they are wages which he must learn 'to accept without complaining, "without scruple or diffidence". The fact they are being paid is evidence of spiritual progress. If you remain stagnated in your old unregenerate life you are spiritually asleep. But as you awake from your torpor you set up adverse energies. These experiences are salutary lessons in wisdom and are conducive to that stability of soul which you will need in higher Degrees.

An Ear of Corn near a Pool of Water

An ear of corn near a pool of water denotes plenty. This symbol dates from the time that an army of Ephraimites crossed the river Jordan in a hostile manner against Jephtha, the renowned Gileaditish general. The Ephraimites had always been considered a clamorous and turbulent people. Jephtha tried to appease them but failed. So he gathered his army and fought the Ephraimites until they retreated. To render his victory decisive, he sent detachments of his army to secure the passages of the River Jordan, over which he knew the insurgents would flee. He gave strict orders to his guards, saying that if an Ephraimite fugitive came that way, he should immediately be slain; but if he prevaricated, or said nay, a test Word was to be put to him to pronounce. If the fugitive could not pronounce it properly, it would cost him his life. King Solomon afterwards caused this test Word to be adopted as a Pass Word in a Fellow Craft's Lodge, to prevent any unqualified person from ascending the Winding Staircase, which led to the Middle Chamber of the Temple.

A Personal View

In the Second Degree Ceremony the Apprentice is given an ear of corn as he leaves the Lodge to be properly prepared to be passed to the Degree of a Fellow Craft. This ear of corn is a symbol of the growth of the Apprentice. When he was first admitted as a dry, unnourished seed he was planted in the good level earth of the North East corner of the Lodge. He has been nurtured by careful watering from a calm, wise pool of wisdom that is the corporate soul of the Lodge and has now flowered in a head of seed. The Pass Word that describes the ear of corn incorporates the sound of a gentle breeze, symbolising the breath of divine knowledge which is blown from the Centre into the developing mind of the new Fellow Craft. As his head of seed sways lightly in the breeze of understanding so the Mason grows in awareness of the Centre.

The Five Noble Orders of Architecture

The five Masons needed to hold a Lodge are represented by the Five Noble Orders of Architecture, which are the Tuscan, Doric, Ionic, Corinthian, and Composite.

The race of mankind, in full possession of wild and savage liberty, hid themselves in thickets of the wood, or in dens and caverns of the Earth. In those poor recesses and gloomy solitudes, Masonry found them, and the Grand Geometrician of the Universe, pitying their forlorn situation, instructed them to build houses for their defence and comfort. The first efforts were small, and the structure simple and rude; no more than a number of trees leaning together at the top, in the form of a cone, interwoven with twigs, and plastered with mud to exclude the air.

In this early period, we may suppose each desirous to render his own habitation more convenient than his neighbour's, by improving on what had already been done. This led them to consider the inconveniences of the round sort of habitation, and to build others, more spacious and convenient, of the square form, by placing trunks of trees perpendicularly in the ground to form the sides, filling the interstices between them with the branches, closely woven, and covered with clay. Horizontal beams were then placed on the upright trunks, which being strongly joined at the angles, kept the sides firm. The roof of the building was composed of joists, on which were laid several beds of reeds, leaves, and clay.

These ancient builders invented methods to make their huts more lasting and handsome, as well as convenient. They took off the bark and other unevenness from the trunks of the trees that formed the sides; raised them above the earth and humidity, on stones; and covered each of them with a flat stone or tile to keep off the rain. The spaces between the ends of the joists they closed with clay or some other substance, and the ends of the joists they covered with boards, cut in the manner of triglyphs. The form of the roof was likewise altered; because of its flatness, it was unfit to throw off the rain that fell in abundance during the winter seasons. So they raised it in the middle, giving it the form of a gable roof by placing rafters on the joists to support the clay, and other materials, that composed the covering.

From these simple forms, the Orders of Architecture began. Buildings of wood were set aside, and men began to erect solid and stately edifices of stone. Soon, these primitive huts grew into the first Temples. These were improved to such a degree of perfection on different models, that each was by way of eminence denominated an "Order".

Of the Orders, three are of Greek origin, and are called Grecian Orders. They are distinguished by the names Doric, Ionic, and Corinthian, and exhibit three distinct characters of composition suggested by the diversity of form in the human frame. The other two are of Italian origin, and are called Roman Orders; they are distinguished by the names Tuscan and Composite.

The Tuscan Order is the simplest and most solid. It is placed first in the list of the five Orders of Architecture on account of its plainness. The base of its column has few mouldings. It has been compared to a sturdy labourer dressed in homely apparel.

The Doric is the first of the Grecian Orders, and is placed second in the list of the five Orders of Architecture. Its column has no ornament except mouldings on either base or capital. Its frieze is distinguished by triglyphs and metopes, and its cornice by mutules. Being the most ancient of all the orders, it retains more of the primitive-hut style in its form than any of the rest. The composition of this Order is both grand and noble, being formed after the model of a muscular, full-grown man; delicate ornaments are repugnant to its characteristic solidity. It is principally used in warlike structures where strength and a noble simplicity are required.

At this era, their buildings, although admirably calculated for strength and convenience, wanted something in grace and elegance, which a continual observation of the softer sex supplied; for the eye that is charmed with symmetry must be conscious of woman's elegance and beauty. This gave rise to the Ionic Order. Its capital is adorned with volutes, and its cornice has dentils. The famous Temple of Diana at Ephesus (which took more than 200 years to build), was composed of this Order. Both elegance and ingenuity were displayed in the invention of this column. It is formed after the model of a beautiful young woman.

A new capital was invented at Corinth by Calimachus, which gave rise to the Corinthian, deemed the richest of the Orders. The capital of its column is adorned with two rows of leaves, and eight volutes which sustain the abacus. This Order is chiefly used in stately and superb structures.

The final Order is the Composite, so named from being composed of parts of the other Orders. Its capital is adorned with the two rows of leaves of the Corinthian, the volutes of the Ionic, and has the quarter-round of the Tuscan and Doric Orders. Its cornice has dentils or simple modillions. This Order is chiefly used in structures where strength, elegance, and beauty are displayed.

A Personal View

The Five Noble Orders of Architecture show how a Mason can develop and enhance all aspects of his character. The Tuscan pillar shows the virtue of personal effort which must be applied to the work of developing the wisdom of the soul. It represents persistence. The Doric represents the strength needed to bring about change within your soul and the virtue of working for the good of society. The Ionic pillar shows the need to appreciate and create beauty within the world. The Corinthian pillar shows how wisdom, strength, and beauty may be combined to produce a soul which is stately and impressive. The Composite pillar shows how all the teachings of the Craft must be brought together to form a structure (meaning a soul) which can display strength, wisdom, and beauty according to the aspect it is viewed from.

Chapter 10:

Symbols of the Third Degree

The Square and Compasses, Both Points Revealed

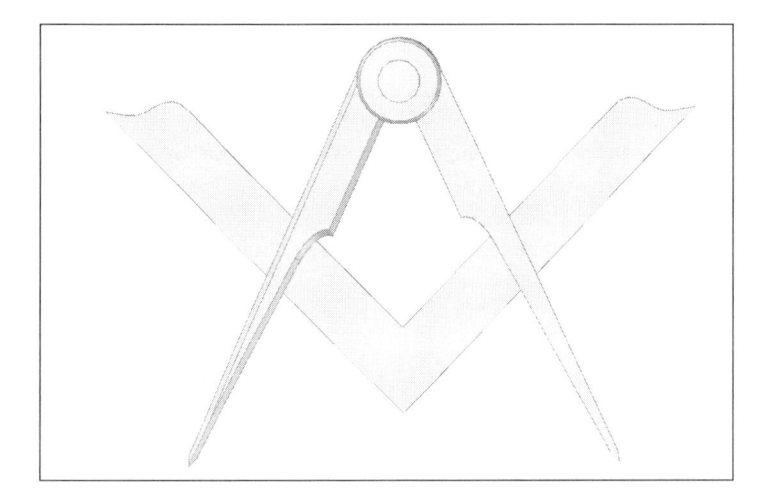

Let me call your attention to the position of the Square and Compasses; when you were made an Entered Apprentice both points were hidden, and in the Second Degree one was disclosed. Now you are a Master Mason and the whole is exhibited, implying that you are now at liberty to work with both those points in order to render the circle of your Masonic duties complete.

A Personal View

When a Candidate becomes a Master Mason the position of the Square and Compasses is changed to reveal both points of the Compass and the separated Square. Now the Master Mason has faced the ultimate trial of the Third Degree he has shown that he understands that honour, loyalty and self-sacrifice can be more important than life itself. In gaining this knowledge he has extended the scope of his soul's understanding. The Square shows how he has laboured to shape his soul into a perfect cube, which can be tried and proved on any corner by the freely separated Square, while the Compasses are now free to help him find the mystical centre, which is that point equidistant from the circumference and marks the spot from which, once found, no Mason can possibly err.

The Open Grave

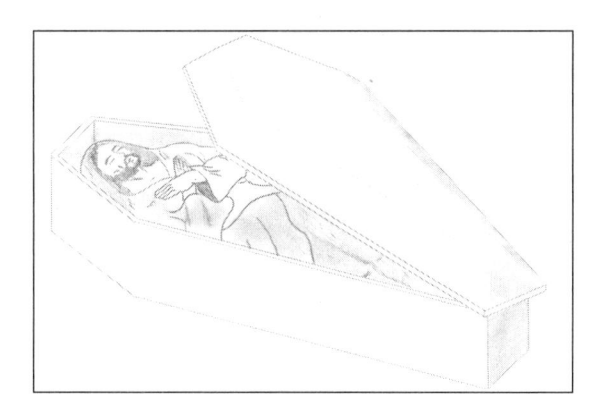

Let me now beg you to observe that the light of a Master Mason is darkness visible, serving only to express that gloom which rests on the prospect of futurity; it is that mysterious veil which the eye of human reason cannot penetrate, unless assisted by that light which is from above; yet, even by this glimmering ray, you may perceive that you stand on the very brink of the grave into which you have just figuratively descended, and which, when this transitory life shall have passed away, will again receive you into its cold bosom.

A Personal View

At the centre of every Mason's soul is buried an immortal principle, a vital spark that links him to the Divine Centre. It is never extinguished, no matter how evil or imperfect his life may be.

The lost light for which all Masons search is buried at the centre of ourselves. You can reach upwards or downwards from the centre of your own body — i.e., 3 feet between North and South and as far as you can reach outwards from the centre of your body — i.e., 3 feet between West and East — and 5 feet or more perpendicular — which is the height of typical Masons. These are the symbolic indications by which the ritual describes the grave of Hiram Abiff at the centre of every Mason who represents him.

This symbolism guides a Mason to the knowledge that initiation has as its purpose revealing union between the individual soul and the Mystery of the Centre.

This union is symbolised by the familiar conjunction of the Square and the Compasses. The Square is the emblem of the soul; the Compasses of the spirit which dwells in that soul. As we have seen, the Mason first sees the points of the Compasses concealed behind the Square, and, as he progresses, their points emerge from that concealment until both rise above the Square. This symbolises a progressive subordination of the soul and the corresponding release of the inner spirit into the personal consciousness of the mind. In this way a Mason can work with both points of the Compasses to become an efficient builder of his spirit and so render the circle of his own being complete as he attains conscious alliance with his true self.

The Perfect Cube

We can change from a rough ashlar to a perfect cube, and be carried from natural darkness into supernatural light. Just as the outer body can be opened for surgical investigation, so the Lodge can be opened so we can understand the mechanism and purpose of our inner self. The spirit indwells the mind, just as the mind suffuses the body; but only in the mind, once it is rectified, purified and worked, from the rough ashlar to the perfect cube, can the Centre be brought to life and consciousness.

A Personal View

When a man first joins a Lodge his soul is thought of as a rough stone freshly hacked from the living rock of the quarries. It has a coarse and crude aspect, yet within it there is a perfect cube of polished stone. The Mason is given tools to work on his soul and is encouraged to make daily progress in shaping himself into a perfected state. He is urged to control his base feelings so that his soul may become more regular in shape; he is urged to develop his mind that he might acquire the polish of a liberal education; and, above all, he is urged to behave honestly and fairly, to treat all society in a square and honest way, until he becomes a perfect square in all his aspects, so his soul assumes the shape of a perfect square and all three dimensions.

The Porch

The Porch stands before the entrance to the Sanctum Sanctorum.

A Personal View

The porchway of the Temple symbolises an opening into an inner supranatural awareness to be found in the central sanctuary. To reach it we must labour to ascend the Winding Stairway, by gradually building our body and mind as we adapt to a sublime degree of consciousness. We feed on the elements of consecration which were used to establish the Lodge that is now a Temple of Living Stones.

Our growing mind requires sustenance to build it. Symbolically the elements which consecrate the Temple feed our mind as we enter progress towards the inner sanctum. The ears of corn fashion its structural form. Wine vitalises and stimulates it and strengthens its intellect, to deepen our inner vision. Oil is a lubricant enabling its parts to run smoothly and without friction as it develops.

The Dormer

The Dormer was the window that gave light to the Sanctum Sanctorum.

A Personal View

The Dormer is a window set high in the Eastern aspect of the Temple where the rays of the rising sun shine on the dawn of the vernal equinox when day and night are in perfect balance. Only when the sun rises due East can its rays shine through the Dormer and illuminate the Sanctum Sanctorum, or inner sacred space. In Freemasonry whenever the ritual refers to a Temple it is a symbol of the soul of a Mason. At certain times of the year, in the season of balance between light and dark, a ray of spiritual truth shines directly from the eternal East, and if the building has been built well, and the Dormer has been correctly aligned, the golden streaks of the dawn light will shine as a beam of truth to illuminate the as yet still dark centre of the Freemason's soul so that he may know the glory of Truth deep within himself.

The Square Pavement

The Square Pavement is for the High Priest to walk on, meaning that every Mason, as high priest of the temple of his own body, must walk upon the ever-changing occurrences of existence. He must stand superior to them, remaining stable, serene, and detached amid events which elate or deject those whose affections are still focused upon the transient and unreal. He must not try to pick out a timorous and pleasant way over the white squares only, but with confidence and fortitude must tread the black ones also, perceiving good and evil, pleasure and pain, birth and death, adversity and prosperity, and all the other opposites signified by the parti-coloured squares, as but alternating aspects of a single process and as of equal value to his own growth.

A Personal View

The chequered floor of the Lodge is a major symbol built into the Lodge furniture. The ritual tells us "The Square Pavement is for the High Priest to walk upon".

It is not merely ancient High Priests who are referred to, but each individual Freemason. Every Mason must learn to become the High Priest of his own personal temple and to make of it a place where he and the Great Architect may meet.

Every Mason walks upon a Square Pavement of mingled good and evil in every action of his life. The floor-cloth is a symbol of this elementary philosophical truth. But the Mason who aspires to be master of his fate must walk upon these opposites and so transcend and overcome them. He must trample on his lower sensual nature and keep it in subjection. He must become indifferent to the ups and downs of fortune. The Mason strives to develop his innate spiritual potencies, and this is not possible whilst he is overruled by fluctuating emotions of pleasure and pain. By attaining serenity and mental equilibrium under all circumstances a Mason truly "walks upon" the chequered groundwork of existence and the conflicting tendencies of his more material nature.

The Scurret

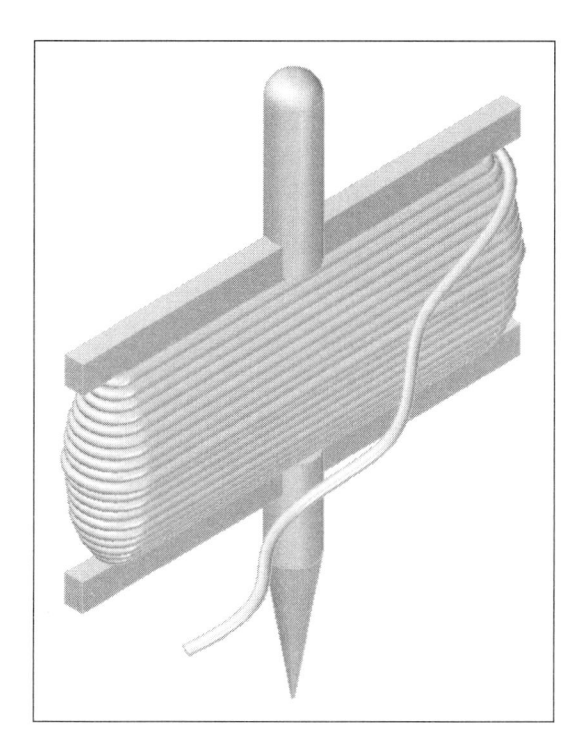

The Scurret is an implement which acts on a centre pin. A line is drawn to mark out ground for the foundation of the intended structure. But as we are not all Operative Masons, but rather Free and Accepted, or Speculative, we apply this tool to our morals. In this sense, the Scurret points out that straight and undeviating line of conduct laid down for our pursuit in the Volume of the Sacred Law.

A Personal View

The Scurret symbolises the way to find the centre. When placed accurately at the centre it marks out the circumference where every point is equidistant from the centre. Only by finding the centre can the Mason come to understand its mystery. Whilst reflecting on the role of the Scurret he reflects on how he can find the centre point of the circle of his being and so "delineates the building" i.e. his soul, so that he can place the centre pin, and draw a true line to mark out ground for the foundation of the intended structure.

The Pencil

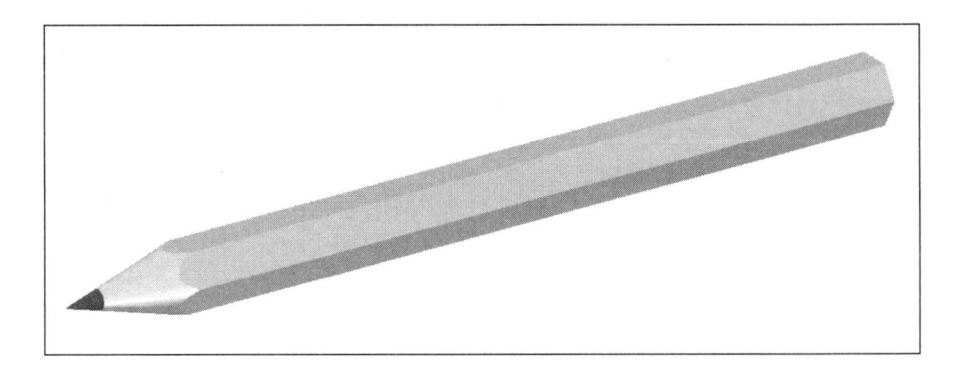

With the Pencil the skilful artist delineates the building in a draft or plan, for the instruction and guidance of the workmen. But as we are not all Operative Masons, but rather Free and Accepted, or Speculative, we apply this tool to our morals. In this sense the Pencil teaches us that our words and actions are observed and recorded by the Almighty Architect, to whom we must give an account of our conduct through life.

A Personal View

The Pencil symbolises the recording of old scores due by the Mason to his fellowmen and old wrongs righted. The wages of past bad behaviour are recorded upon his subconsciousness by a Pencil that observes and there records all our thoughts, words and actions. The philosophical Candidate receives those wages "without scruple or diffidence", knowing himself to be justly entitled to them and is glad to purge himself of old offences. We are all debtors to someone or other for our present position in life, and must repay what we owe to humanity. The Pencil not only records our past, it draws up the plans for a better future.

The Compasses

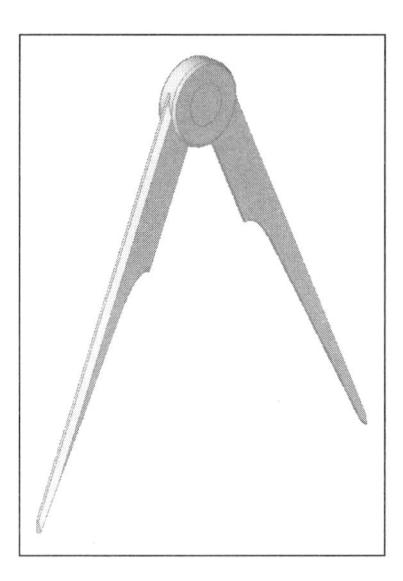

The Compasses enable the skilful artist, with accuracy and precision, to ascertain and determine the limits and proportions of a building. But as we are not all Operative Masons, but rather Free and Accepted, or Speculative, we apply this tool to our morals.

In this sense the Compasses remind us of the unerring and impartial justice of the Almighty Architect, who having defined for our instruction the limits of good and evil will reward or punish, as we have obeyed or disregarded His Divine commands.

A Personal View

The compasses, which rest upon the Volume of the Sacred Law represent the Divine Principle issuing forth from Great Architect to manifest cosmically, and in the individual, so that each may function and be understood in accordance with the laws which govern the Universe.

The Compasses symbolise the range of a discerning mind and its ability to measure a Mason's spirit. Along with the Square of bodily form, which is used to try and prove the soul, the Compasses delineate the due shape of a living stone fit to be used in the Cosmic Temple.

The Sprig of Acacia

The Sprig of Acacia marks the grave of a Master Mason. It came about after the murder of Hiram Abif. Twelve craftsmen who had originally joined in the conspiracy came before King Solomon one day and made a voluntary confession of all they knew. His fears being naturally increased for the safety of Hiram Abif, he then selected fifteen trusty Fellow Crafts and ordered them to make diligent search after the person of our Master to ascertain if he were yet alive, or had suffered death. A stated day having been appointed for their return to Jerusalem, they formed themselves into three Fellow Craft's Lodges, and departed from the three entrances of the Temple. Many days were spent in fruitless search; indeed, one class returned without having made any discovery of importance. But the second Lodge was more fortunate. One evening, after having suffered the greatest privations and personal fatigues, one of the Brethren who was resting caught hold of a shrub that grew near, which, to his surprise, came easily out of the ground; on a closer examination, he found that the earth had been recently disturbed; he therefore hailed his companions, and with their united endeavours reopened the grave and there found the body of our Master very indecently interred. They covered it again with all respect and reverence, and to distinguish the spot, stuck a Sprig of Acacia at the head of the grave; they then hastened to Jerusalem to impart the terrible news to King Solomon.

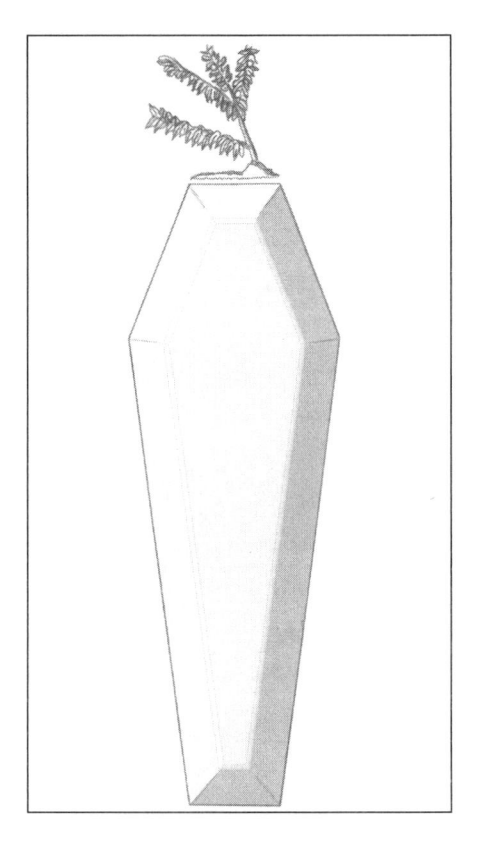

A Personal View

The ritual and the Tracing Boards tell us that a Sprig of Acacia marked the grave of the murdered architect. It is loosely planted and off-centre.

The grave symbolises the Mason's soul. The Sprig of Acacia typifies the divine germ planted in that soil. When that Sprig of Acacia blooms at the head of his soul's sepulchre, the Mason will understand the mystery of the death of Hiram, and the mystery of spiritual consciousness. How perception of the Divine Centre opens up human intelligence to the Universal and Omniscient Mind of the Great Architect. The Sprig of Acacia, which stands for the eternal spirit of man, is symbolically planted at the head of the grave since it is our supreme life-principle from which all our subordinate faculties issue.

The Emblems of Mortality

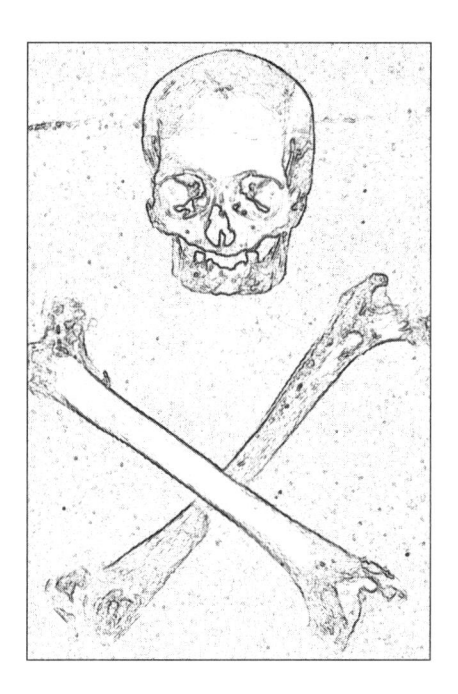

Let the emblems of mortality which lie before you, lead you to contemplate on your inevitable destiny, and guide your reflections to that most interesting of all human studies, the knowledge of yourself. Be careful to perform your allotted task while it is yet day; continue to listen to the voice of nature, which bears witness, that even in this perishable frame resides a vital and immortal principle, which inspires a holy confidence that the Lord of Life will enable us to trample the King of Terrors beneath our feet, and lift our eyes to that Bright Morning Star, whose rising brings peace and salvation to the faithful and obedient of the human race.

A Personal View

There is an important moment in the ritual of the Third Degree when darkness suddenly gives way to bewildering light. By that light which comes from the rising of the Bright Morning Star, the newly made Master Mason gazes for the first time upon the remains of his own past and is shown the emblems of his own mortality. The mystical Sprig of Acacia has bloomed at the head of his grave, nourished by his purified mind and soul.

In Masonic ceremony this is when the Mason attains knowledge of his true self. His expansion of consciousness and wisdom has become part of his new character and his spiritual evolution is complete. He now returns to the "companions of his former toil" to help the rest of humanity reach his level of spiritual awareness.

The Bright Morning Star

Be careful to perform your allotted task while it is yet day; listen to the voice of nature which bears witness that, even in this perishable frame there resides a vital and immortal principle, which inspires a holy confidence, that the Lord of Life will enable us to trample the King of Terrors beneath our feet, and lift our eyes to that Bright Morning Star whose rising brings peace and tranquillity to the faithful and obedient of the human race.

A Personal View

The "star in the East" or five-pointed "morning star" symbolises the ultimate core of our being, beyond time and space.

To become a real Initiate a Mason has to experience the passage through the "divine dark", the unstable psychic region, to find the light of that distant "Bright Morning Star". Its rays promise he will endure the last and greatest trial to the end and emerge triumphant.

The symbolism of death is not the physical death of the body but mystical death of the ego. Only when the Craft has taught the Mason's ego how to die does his spirit obtain freedom. A Master Mason has died that death, and experienced the transformation it involves. He has no dread of death, for he has already been to the other side of it, has seen what lies beyond, and knows it to be the inevitable complement to life, an incident of existence like falling to sleep when tired. He has balanced his pillars and become "established in strength". He lives from the Centre and the Centre lives in him. He enters upon his new life with the light of his own Morning Star to guide him.

Chapter 11

General Symbols of the Wider Craft

The Equilateral Triangle

Three mythical characters, two Hirams and a Solomon, combine to symbolise a three-fold creativity. Wisdom (represented by Solomon, King of Israel) has the vision to create. Strength and resources, personified by Hiram, King of Tyre, project the world of Nature as the material out of which the creative idea is to take shape in the creature. Architectonic and geometrical power finally moulds that idea into the beauty of objective form. Hiram Abif personifies this third aspect of creative energy. He represents the Cosmic Builder; the Great Architect by whom all things are made.

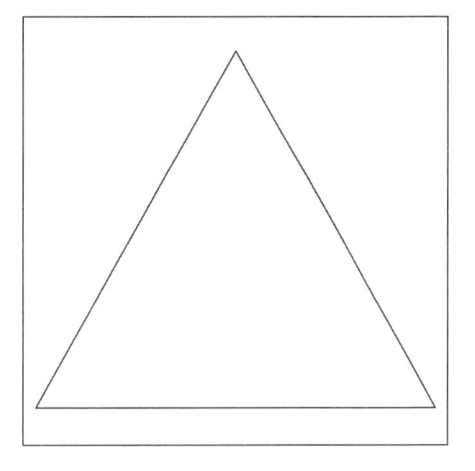

A Personal View

An Equilateral Triangle, sometimes shown with a point at its centre, is a symbol of the Great Architect. A golden version of this symbol is worn by Companions of the Holy Royal Arch Order. The twofold significance of this triangle is that it represents the spiritual, mental and physical parts of the Mason brought into perfect balance around the life-principle of the centre and also the threefold nature of the Great Architect's Plan. The very large, exemplified by relativity, the very small, exemplified by quantum mechanics and the human scale, represented by Newtonian mechanics. All three explain part of the mystery of the Centre, yet none alone able to explain the totality of the Cosmic Law.

A Mason uses the Equilateral Triangle to signify that he is striving to bring his threefold nature — senses, reason, and spiritual intellectuality — into balance, symmetry and unity. This symbol acknowledges that the veil of finite existence has been drawn apart to allow him to see the light of the Bright Morning Star rising in the East of his personal Lodge.

The Double Triangle (The Seal of Solomon)

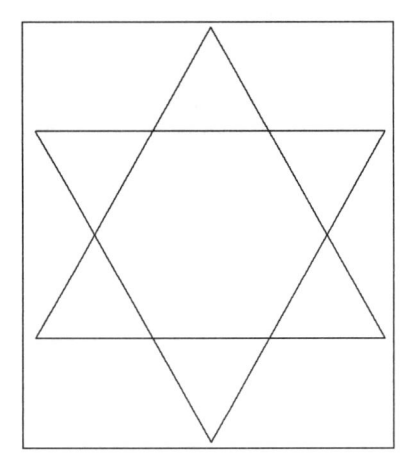

Two interlaced equilateral triangles, one with its base to the sky and its point towards the earth, and the other with its base on the Earth and its point to the sky, is known as the Seal of Solomon. The triangles have similar symbolic meanings to the two pillars. The upward-facing triangle represents the king, with his power based on the Earth and looking to heaven for guidance from the Great Architect. The other triangle, with its base in the heavens and its point reaching down to Earth, represents the power of the priest who draws his spiritual authority from the heavens and uses it to guide the actions of men on Earth. In a Royal Arch Chapter, seven lights are placed in the angles and centre of this Double Triangle. Three represent Wisdom, Truth, and Justice; and the other three Truth, Concord, and Peace, The whole, including the light at the centre, represents the beauty and harmony which is visible in all the works of nature, where nothing is wanting nor anything superfluous.

A Personal View

The Seal of Solomon is a symbol which builds on the union of the Two Pillars of Boaz and Jachin. Through that symbol the Candidate is taught to see that two opposite but complementary principles exist within himself. Both Boaz (spirit) and Jachin (matter) are present in him. For spirit to be effective it needs a body to express itself. For matter to become perfected it must be suffused by spirit. To be "established in strength and stand firm forever" implies the perfect balance and harmony of these two opposites.

This same basic Masonic truth is expressed in the United Square and Compasses and in the symbol of the interlaced triangles known as King Solomon's Seal.

The interlaced triangles of lights surrounding the central altar in the Degree of the Holy Royal Arch of Jerusalem symbolise the union of the Mason's perceptive faculty with the object of his contemplation; the blending of the human consciousness with the Cosmic Law of the Centre.

The Triple Tau

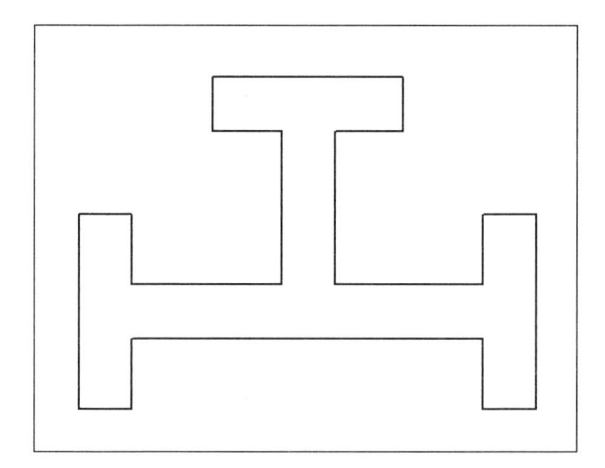

The Triple Tau is the symbol of a Royal Arch Mason. It signifies Hiram of Tyre, or Hiram Abif. It also signifies the Temple of Jerusalem, and is used in the Royal Arch by the wearer to reveal himself as a servant of the true God. The Triple Tau therefore may aptly recall to our minds our constant duty to offer worship to the Great Elohim; the Most High: the Everlasting: the Almighty God.

A Personal View

The Tau cross in the shape of the letter T is a symbol which describes the regular steps a Freemason takes as he learns the secrets of the centre. When three of these symbols are combined together in the form of a Triple Tau the ritual says they symbolise "a place where a precious thing is concealed". This is the knowledge of the Centre which is now held by the Mason who has now taken the first three regular steps in Freemasonry and holds the knowledge of each of the three steps.

The symbol has two right angles at each of the exterior lines and two at the union of the centre. This is eight right angles in all, corresponding to two triangles, which makes it a cryptic representation of the Seal of Solomon. The Royal Arch ritual says the symbol contains a given number of right angles which "represent the five regular platonic bodies".

When worn by a Master Mason, the Triple Tau indicates that he is able to govern that Lodge which is within himself, as he has passed through the three degrees of purifying and self-perfecting, and has squared, levelled, and harmonised the triple nature of his body, soul, and spirit.

The Triangle within a Circle

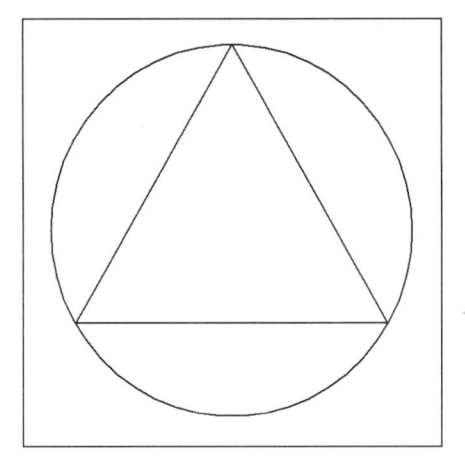

The Circle is an emblem of eternity having neither beginning nor end, and fitly reminds us of the purity, wisdom, and glory of the Omnipotent, which is without beginning or end. The Triangle is a symbol of divine union, and an emblem of the mysterious Triune, equally representing the attributes of Deity, and His Triune essence. The Triangle within the Circle represents the great and awful name of God, the sacred, mysterious, and ineffable Tetragrammaton (the Hebrew name for the God of Israel).

A Personal View

Freemasonry is a system of religious philosophy that provides us with a doctrine of the universe and of our place in it. It has two purposes.

Its first purpose is to show that man has fallen away from a mysterious Centre to the circumference. But that we may regain that Centre by finding it in ourselves, for, since Great Architect is as a circle whose centre is everywhere, it follows that a Divine Centre, a "vital and immortal principle", exists within ourselves.

Its second purpose is to teach the way that Centre may be found within ourselves, and this is embodied in the discipline and ordeals delineated in the three degrees.

The Equilateral Triangle is a symbol of the Great Architect, and the circle is a symbol of the Mason. The Triangle within the Circle reminds all Masons that the path to the Centre is within themselves.

The Keystone

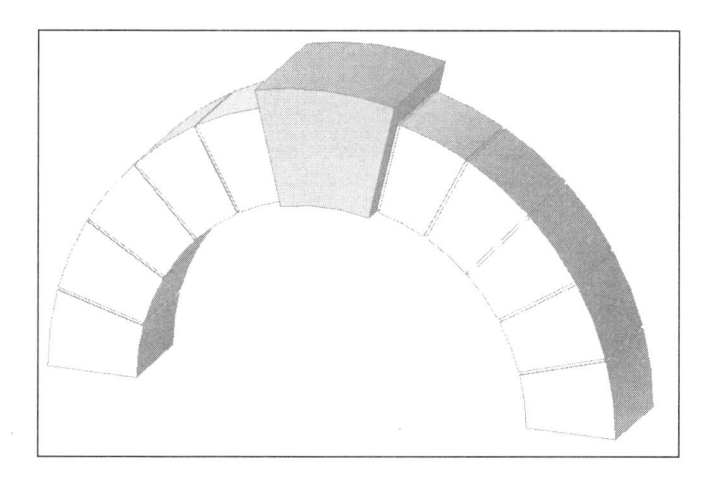

At the building of King Solomon's Temple, the curious keystone, containing many valuable coins and the ten letters in precious stone work which Hiram Abif took so much pain to complete, was lost, supposed to have been taken away by some of the workmen. A reward was offered by King Solomon for the speedy finding or making of another to fit the place. An ingenious Entered Apprentice made one and fixed it in the vacancy in the arch, which, being known to some of the Fellow Crafts, they conceived it a disgrace to the Order to let an inferior degree bear the palm of honour. In the heat of jealousy, they took it and threw it into the Brook Kedron, adjacent to the Temple. A reward was also offered for the finding of this second stone. The Brother who had made it, together with two other Entered Apprentices, went in pursuit of it; and when they had found it, they received equally among them the last reward, and with it the degree of a Fellow Craft. The Brother who made it received the first reward to his own share for his ingenuity, and had the honour with his two Companions to fix it the second time in the arch.

A Personal View

The Keystone is that essential part of an arch which binds together the two sides into a strong and coherent whole. Without the presence of this vital stone the arch is weak and flimsy. It is not strong enough even to support its own weight until the Keystone is put in place. The Keystone can be overlooked as it is not a regular shaped stone. For Masons who are used to creating rectangular blocks it can appear to be misshaped and may be rejected because it is not square and does not fit in. But this is an illusion. It is perfectly shaped for its job when placed in the correct position and can support the entire weight of a building. A newly made Mason may appear odd and malformed, ill-suited and clumsy, but once he has found his place and developed his strengths, he becomes a valuable support for himself and his Brethren.

The Vault

David intended to build a temple to God, but bequeathed the enterprise to Solomon, his son, and Solomon selected a place near Jerusalem. Finding the remains of Enoch's temple there, and supposing them to be the ruins of a heathen temple, he selected Mount Moriah for the site of his Temple to the true God. Under this Temple he built a secret vault, the approach to which was through eight other vaults, all underground, and to which a long and narrow passage led beneath the king's palace. In the ninth vault, he held his private conferences with King Hiram of Tyre and Hiram Abif.

A Personal View

The ritual tells us that the lost word of Freemasonry was first given to Enoch and hidden in a secret vault. That vault was found when Solomon's Temple was built on the same spot, was the word was re-hidden by King Solomon in that secret vault which remained under his Temple. It was found and restored to Freemasonry when Zerubbabel rebuilt the Temple and can only be spoken by three Royal Arch Masons acting together.

The vault symbolises the divine spark which is deep within the Mason's soul which enables him to recognise the light of the Centre. Symbolically the Mason stands in the presence of the stone vault or dense matrix out of which his finer being has emerged and of his own heavens the Bright Morning Star rises to bathe him in the light of knowledge. The *Fiat Lux* transforms his character from chaos and unconsciousness into a form perfect and lucid as it becomes a co-conscious vehicle with the Divine Plan.

The Uncompleted Temple

The death of Hiram the Chief Architect threw the workmen of the Temple of King Solomon into great confusion; and for a time the construction of the building was delayed, for the want of essential plans and an expert director of the work. The period of mourning having expired, King Solomon, upon consultation, appointed five Superintendents — one for each of the five Departments of Architecture — and under their supervision the building progressed. The work of completing the Temple thus became the purpose of Freemasonry.

> ### A Personal View
>
> Freemasonry does not deal with the material building-work of any outward structure, but with the disordered temple of the human soul. Its rituals symbolise something deep and personal: the shaping of the Mason's soul from the rough ashlar into the perfect cube.
>
> The Craft Degrees are solemn instructions in the preparation for that work. But the work of the Craft is not complete until the Master Mason ventures into the dark vault of his inner being during the ritual of the Holy Royal Arch. The Craft work remains unfinished without the attainment of the Royal Arch. The Master Mason who has not yet been exalted to the Royal Arch is thus symbolised as an unfinished temple.

The Pillars, Circle, and Centre

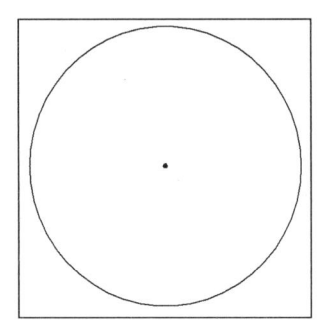

The Circle is that of Infinity whose centre is everywhere and circumference nowhere. You are Infinity shrunk and compressed to a point, but a point from which it is possible for you to expand consciously to Infinite Being. Your personal temporal self is but a separated individualised point in the ocean of the Universal Spirit encompassing you. By renouncing your personal self you will transcend it, and, losing the sense of separateness, grow into conscious union with the one indivisible Life which comprehends all.

The parallel lines bounding the Circle declare that this one indivisible Life is everywhere characterised by two opposite aspects bound together in perpetual equilibrium: spirit and matter; the formless and the formal; freedom and necessity; inflexible justice and boundless mercy. These are parallels permeating the universe on all planes, characterizing every part of it, present in every atom. But they are held together in eternal balance at one neutral central point where these opposites blend into unity. That point in yourself is the Centre. To find this, you must follow a middle way, a straight and narrow path, turning neither to the right nor the left, and in every pursuit having the Eternal Unity in view.

A Personal View

The Pillars, Circle, and Centre symbolise the whole purpose of the Craft. By this Centre we hope to regain the secrets of our lost nature. As the Laws of the Great Architect are at the centre of the whole universe and control it, as the sun is the centre and life-giver of our solar system and controls and feeds with life the planets circling round it, so at the secret Centre of each individual human life exists a vital, immortal principle, the spirit and the spiritual will.

This is the faculty, by using which (when we have found it) we can never err. It is a point within the circle of our own nature and, living as we do in this physical world, the circle of our existence is bounded by two grand parallel lines; "one representing Moses; the other King Solomon", that is to say, law and wisdom; the divine laws regulating the universe on the one hand; the divine wisdom on the other. The Mason who keeps himself thus circumscribed cannot err.

Chapter 12

The Tracing Boards

When a Freemason's Lodge is opened the Tracing Board of the Degree is displayed to the Brethren. Each Tracing Board is a visual summary of the main objects of study of the Degree concerned. By looking at the Tracing Board a Brother is immediately reminded of the main elements of the Degree and what it sets out to teach.

Tracing Boards also serve as a focus for aiding the understanding of the lessons learnt whilst working the degree. It was an inspired decision by Bro. John Hogg to include images of the Tracing Board in the ritual book, so that a Brother learning the words of the ritual could also absorb the emotional impact of the symbolism by seeing a pictorial story board.

By publishing the Tracing Boards of each Degree, John Hogg, under his pen name of A Lewis, made it possible for Masons to learn the lessons of each Degree in the traditional manner. They could now learn to recite the words whilst having the symbols of the Degree in view. This harked back to the traditional teaching that the symbols of the Degree to be conferred would be drawn on the floor of the Lodge and later erased by the Candidate. Over time these temporary drawings were replaced with permanent painted boards.

After each ceremony has taught a Candidate about each of the individual symbols and provided training to sensitise him to their import, the symbols are combined into a composite image, called a Tracing Board.

The main points of each of the four main Tracing Boards are below. These are personal views, as a full understanding of the symbolism can only be gained by using the images to act as a focus of your private meditation on the meaning of each part of the Masonic teaching.

Tracing Boards can be used in two ways.

First, a Tracing Board shows how the symbols can be combined to provide greater insight into the issues being considered.

Secondly, it provides a focus for Masonic reflection where the Candidate is drawn to consider what message the combination of symbols can impart.

The method of teaching is to reveal the Tracing Board and then give a ritual explanation of its Masonic meaning.

There are four traditional boards which lead towards a full understanding of the final mystic symbol; known as the Centre — the point from which no Mason can err.

A Personal View of the First Degree Tracing Board

The First Degree Tracing Board is a set of symbols to focus your thoughts and guide your meditation. At first sight it seems to be a casual collection of the emblems found in every Masonic Lodge. But as your Masonic insight develops, order and purpose emerge from it. You begin to see that it is a diagram of the material, mental, and spiritual elements in us all. These are shown as the Earth, the intermediate firmament, and the heavens.

The floor represents your physical state, or body. It is your lower or material nature. The sky with its sun, moon, and stars stands for your mind or intellectual nature. But the Blazing Star or Glory in the centre represents your ultimate spiritual core. This Bright Morning Star dominates the centre of the diagram and lights the whole board with its blinding rays.

This board shows the newlymade Mason a vision of the philosophical scope of his Craft. The chequered floor of the Lodge, encompassing both darkness and light, stretches out to meet the distant sky, which in turn is split into day and night. The Sun, in the North East corner, is shown governing the day and illuminating the Rough Ashlar that is shaded by the Pillar of Beauty. The Moon and stars in the North West corner, is shown to govern the night and its rays of knowledge illuminate the Perfect Ashlar which stands before the Pillar of Strength, supported by a Lewis.

On the floor lie the working tools of the officers of a Lodge: the Square, the Level, and the Plumb Rule, illuminated by the Sun at its meridian. In the centre of the Lodge stands the Altar, supporting the three great landmarks of the Square, the Compasses, and the Volume of the Sacred Law. The Altar supports the base of Jacob's Ladder, which reaches towards the rising of the Bright Morning Star in the East, and on the ladder are to be found the seven angelic officers of the Grand Lodge Above, including Faith, Hope, and Charity. On the face of the Altar is the symbol of the Centre, the point from which no Master Mason can err. The Altar is illuminated by the Bright Morning Star and its shadow falls on the Tracing Board showing the Divine Plan, still in darkness, and the working tools of the Installed Master whose job it is to bring it into the light. The working tools of all the Degrees are distributed about these main symbolic landmarks.

To understand this board you need to reflect on the other emblems in the diagram. These are:

1. Some working tools and models casually spread about the floor. The meaning of these is explained in the ordinary Lodge teaching.
2. An emblem consisting of a point within a circle bounded by two parallel lines.
3. An altar, on which rest the three main emblematic lights of Masonry. From this altar a ladder of innumerable steps leads to the firmament and thence to infinity.
4. Three pillars, one Doric, one Ionic, and one Corinthian. Their pedestals are on the Earth and their capitals in the heavens.

The three Pillars represent a trinity of attributes that are born within every Candidate upon whose inner altar celestial light descends. Like the Master and Wardens of a Lodge who always act in concert, so Wisdom, Strength, and Beauty are inseparable. They are a triple cord, not easily broken.

This board maps out a route towards the understanding of the main symbols of the Craft and their links to the realm of transcendental Truth.

A Personal View of the Second Degree Tracing Board

The Second Degree Tracing Board portrays a landscape of open country, through which runs a river, flowing over a weir and making a waterfall, beside which grows a single ear of corn. They are placed on the South side of the board, and from this sunny region a man approaches the porchway. It is protected by an armed guard and allows entrance to a winding stairway. At the top of this spiral stair is a second guard and an upper concealed chamber. Upon the wall overlooking the spiral stair is blazoned in Hebrew the words "Holiness to the Lord".

The purpose of this board is personal. If you want to work the Second Degree you must allow it to speak to your intellect. This Degree is about the higher mental reaches of your nature.

The First Degree taught you to lay the foundation of a new life in the sacred law. You were told to erect a temple purged of the weaknesses of the flesh upon the ground floor of your natural personality. Now with your animal instinct beautified with virtue and adorned by grace of character you are bidden to move upwards, to gain instruction and experience a higher level of your being.

Body, mind, spirit — these are the three storeys of our building, the three degrees of our being, and each has its own secrets and mysteries.

The mysteries of the ground floor, the body, in the First Degree are as nothing compared with those of the mind, which we study in the Second Degree. The mysteries of the mind are hidden in the Middle Chamber. And if you come properly prepared, you can ascend to this chamber and delight in its provisions.

The Second Degree Tracing Board shows the Candidate arriving at the foot of spiral staircase which winds upward to the Inner Chamber where he will receive his wages. He has left the distant city, crossed the stream of flowing water, and the fields full of ears of corn to stand at the porchway or entrance to King Solomon's Temple. There he is challenged by the Junior Warden, who stands before the Temple entrance between the Terrestrial and Celestial pillars of Boaz and Jachin. These pillars respectively denote strength; and to establish, and, when conjoined, stability.

Equilateral lozenges of black adorn the beautiful white pavement of the porchway. The chequered pavement of the upper hallway leads to the dark and mysterious centre of the Temple, which conceals a sacred symbol of the Great Architect of the Universe. The entrance to the Middle Chamber is guarded by the Senior Warden whose duty is to challenge the Fellow Craft, demand the Pass Grip and Pass Word of his Degree and so prove him worthy to receive his wages of intellectual knowledge.

A Personal View of the Third Degree Tracing Board

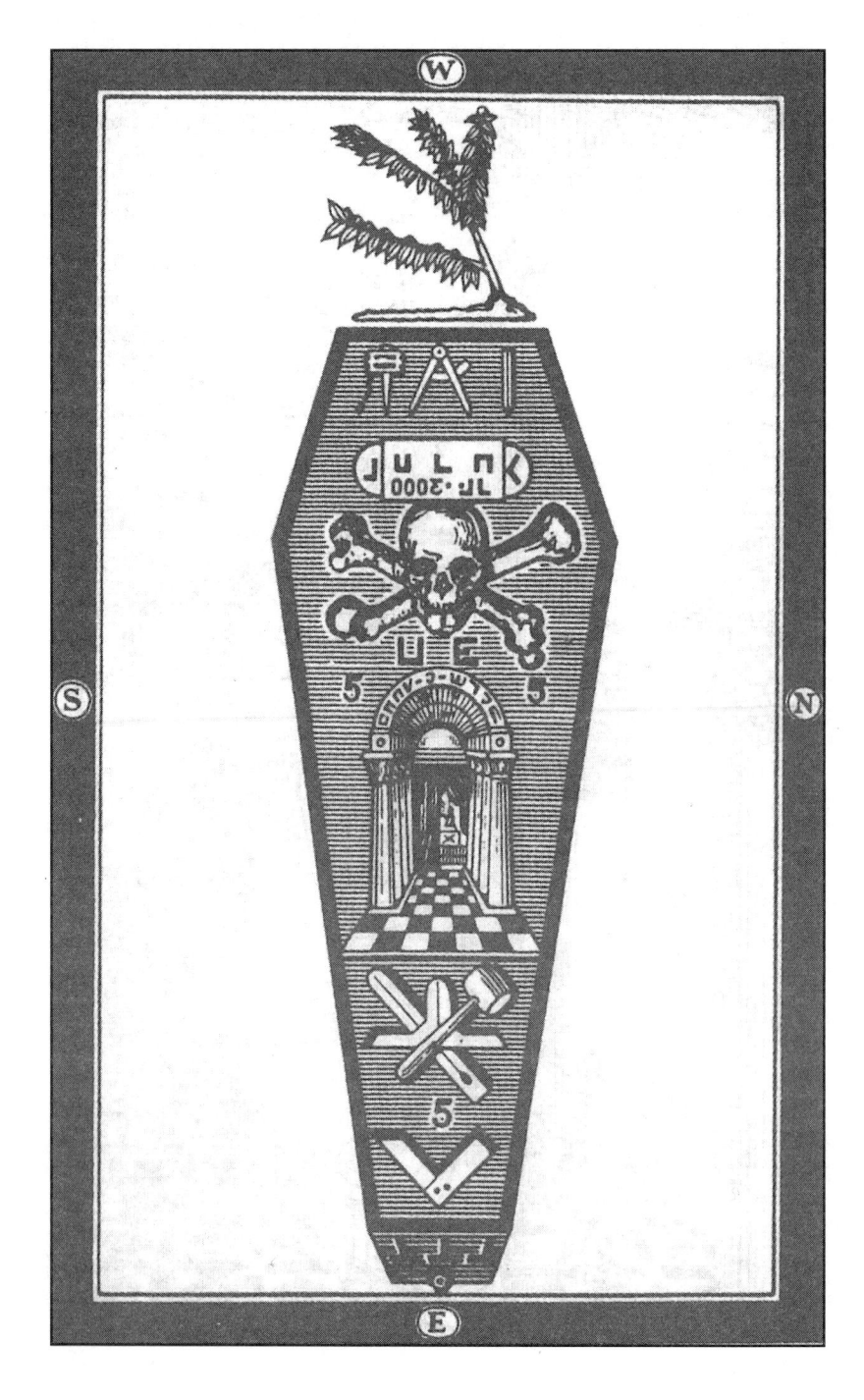

The Third Degree Tracing Board shows the shallow grave in which the mortal remains of our Grand Master, Hiram Abif, were found by the Lodge of Fellow Crafts who were searching for him. They reverently covered him with white cloth, as a badge of innocence, and marked the spot with a sprig of acacia at his head. Around the grave are placed the tools of the Master Mason, which remind us to carry out our allotted tasks while it is yet day and to listen to the voice of nature. Within our perishable frame resides a vital and immortal principle, which inspires a holy confidence, that the Lord of Life will enable us to trample the King of Terrors beneath our feet, and lift our eyes to that Bright Morning Star whose rising brings peace and tranquillity to the faithful and obedient of the human race.

It is a diagram that is capable of several meanings, each one true upon its own level.

Its first and simplest meaning is the quasi-historical one acted out in the ritual. It shows the grave of the murdered Hiram and the tools that killed him. Secondly, it has a cosmic and philosophic meaning. At this level it is a hieroglyph of the spiritual mystery of the origin of evil and death. Thirdly, it has a personal application. It is a symbol of yourself and shows the traditional way of being raised from darkness to light. It is in this personal sense that I will analyse it.

It comprises three main features:

- A tomb and a shroud.
- A sprig of acacia at the head of the grave, not in true alignment with the body interred in it, but planted to one side of it.
- Working tools or implements of destruction scattered around the grave.

The grave, not only depicts the tomb used for the ritual of Initiation, but represents the darkness of your human personality. That physical body is one of darkness and mortality.

A Square, the badge of the Master Mason, is placed on his chest and the Plan, the Scurret, the Compasses, the Pencil, the Level, and the Plumb Rule are arranged on his shroud.

At his feet are the emblems of mortality which will lead a Mason to contemplate his inevitable destiny and guide his reflections into that most interesting and useful of all human studies: the knowledge of himself.

When you advanced to the East in this Degree you signified that you trampled your bodily nature under foot, making it your servant instead of simply giving in to its demands. Into that material body is infused a spirit. It is the psychic principle that elevates your animal nature to become a rational being. In the board the spirit is indicated by a chevron or triangle.

Beyond body and mind, abides the spirit, the higher principle that affiliates you to the Cosmic Centre. This is represented by a sprig of acacia, planted at the head of the grave, symbolising your supreme life-principle, from which all your subordinate faculties issue. This is the Centre, the ultimate core of your being, beyond time and space, and beyond death and evil.

A great irony lies in the fact that the tools that slew the Master and served to bring about his destruction are the same tools which we must use to reconstruct our own fallen temple. The simple truth thus conveyed is that evil is misapplied good, and good transmuted evil. From our errors we may learn wisdom and return to grace by the correct use of that which involved us in disgrace.

The implements point to the means by which we can get back into true alignment with our spiritual principle.

They consist of:

1. The Plumb Rule of uprightness applied to all parts of our being, namely, the senses, the emotions, and the mind.

2. The level of "equality", by which those parts (which in most people are very unequally balanced) must be brought into a condition of harmony and equilibrium.
3. The heavy maul of a strong and resolute purpose which nothing shall deflect from the end in view.

By meditating on the board you can balance your pillars and become established in strength. Having lain in the "tomb of transformation", the grave of the temporal self loses its sting and neither bodily nor mental death can have further victory over you. Having died to your root of egoism, of sorrow, and of personal ambition, every selfish desire at the expense of others, also withers. You learn to know infinity and to live from theCentre.

A Personal View of the Royal Arch Tracing Board

The Tracing Board of the Holy Royal Arch explains the discovery of the secret vault beneath the ruins of King Solomon's Temple by the three sojourners employed by the Sanhedrin of Jerusalem to rebuild the Temple. They lift the Keystone from the archway to give access to the secret chamber which contains the sacred altar and the Lost Word of Masonry.

The shaft of light from the sun falls into the dark vault, which contains the Lost Word carved into the face of the pedestal. The pedestal is set in an Equilateral Triangle, which is the ancient Enochian symbol of the Great Architect.

The chequered pavement represents the uncertainty of life, and the instability of things terrestrial; and the pedestal of pure white marble, in the form of a true double cube, is the perfect emblem of innocence and purity. It is placed within a Circle, which is an emblem of eternity, having neither beginning nor end, and reminds us of the purity, wisdom, and glory of the Omnipotent, who is without beginning or end.

In the background, at the end of the spiral path is the dais of the three Principals of the Sanhedrin: Zerubbabel, Haggia and Joshua. They stand between the pillars of stability and the pillars of knowledge. Behind them is the Eternal City and above it the Rainbow and the Holy Royal Arch of the Heavens.

If you consider that the Temple you are rebuilding is yourself, then the board can help you learn that within the depths of your being there is a vital spark which you need to bring out into the light if you are ever to understand yourself.

A View of the Centre

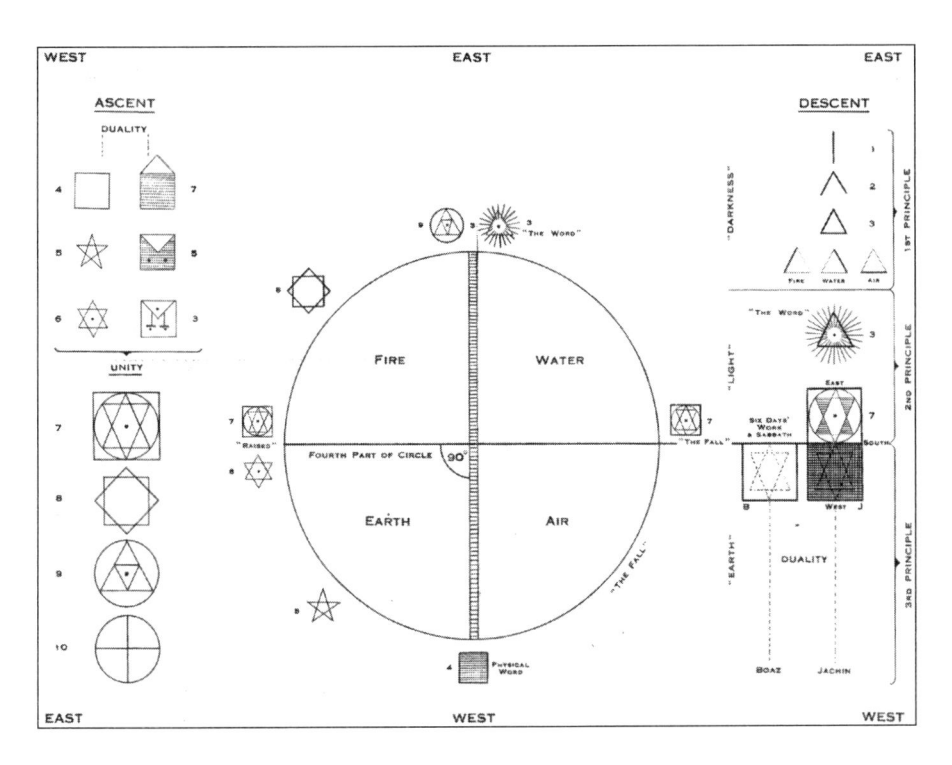

Brother Junior Warden: While contemplating the duties of your office, what have you observed?

A profound symbol, Brother Master.

Brother Senior Warden: Where is this profound symbol to be found?

In the centre of the Lodge, Brother Master.

Brother Junior Warden: How may the Brethren recognise this symbol?

By the letter "G" shining from the centre of a blazing star, Brother Master.

Brother Senior Warden. To what does this symbol refer?

To the Grand Geometrician of the Cosmos, to whom you, I, and all must show respect, Brother Master.

So Brethren, let us remember, wherever we are, whatever we do, the all-seeing eye of the Grand Geometrician of the Cosmos ever sees us, and all actions throughout the universe. May we persevere as faithful Brethen of the Craft and apply geometry with fervency and zeal to reach that point from which no Master Mason can ever err.

The message of this symbol is that the vital spark which connects you with the realms of Eternal Truth is hidden within yourself and that is where you should seek it.

Appendix

The Story of John Hogg and the Birth of the Lewis Masonic Imprint

John Hogg was born in Edinburgh in 1836, just one year before his father James left the employment of printer James Muirhead to whom he had been apprenticed and then worked as a master printer, helping to produce the seventh edition of the *Encyclopaedia Britannica*. With John just a year old, James Hogg became a publisher in his own right, producing his first pamphlet, entitled *The Honest Waterman*. James made a reasonable living by producing a weekly magazine entitled *Hogg's Weekly Instructor*. He continued to produce this for the next 14 years and it ran to 29 volumes.

In 1858, John and his brother James moved to London. They were soon followed by their father (now 52 years of age) and together the family set up a new publishing company called James Hogg & Sons. The new firm began life as an ecclesiastical publisher, getting the Archbishop of Canterbury, the Bishop of Salisbury and the Bishop of Limerick to write uplifting books for the new imprint. The old *Hogg's Weekly Instructor* was reborn as *The Churchman's Family Magazine* and James Hogg Junior created a successful social magazine called *London Society*. For a while the firm did well, and John decided to venture into illustrated books. His first major book was an illustrated edition of *The Pilgrim's Progress* by John Bunyan, which featured drawings by John Absolon, who had previously illustrated a lighted hearted book about the eccentric ways of Oxford dons, entitled *Almae Matres* and written by John under the pen name of Megathym Splene B.A. Oxon.

Over the next decade he produced a further four illustrated books for James Hogg & Sons working with J Absolon and J Franklin as illustrators, and they were moderately successful commercial ventures. However, his father was now well into his sixties and slowing down, and his brother James's society magazine was failing in popularity and losing money for the firm. A study of his publishing history, as recorded in the British Library, shows that John must have been worried about the long-term future of James Hogg & Sons as in 1864 he had printed an illustrated book of Scots poetry entitled *Auld Reekie Musings* under the imprint A Lewis. His choice of pseudonym is interesting as the book was published about the time when the Earl of

Zetland laid the foundation stone of a new extension to Freemasons' Hall in London. Contemporary newspaper reports told how a lewis was used to lift the foundation stone into place in the North East corner of the new building, whilst the great and good of London put on their aprons and regalia to applaud the act. It must have passed through John Hogg's mind that a word which would appeal to Scottish Freemason's might help the sales of his private venture into illustrated poetry. It is, of course, possible, that his father James might have been a Scottish Mason, making John a 'Lewis' (the name used for the son of a Freemason) himself, but I have not been able to find any evidence of James Hogg being a member of any Edinburgh Lodge. Whatever the reason for his choice of imprint name, it was to prove fortuitous as we shall soon see. He used the A Lewis imprint again, early in 1869, to publish an illustrated account of explorer John Tillotson's Arctic expeditions, under the title *Adventures in the Ice*. These two independent books had ensured that John would be able to survive as a publisher, even if the family firm was pulled down by his brother's failing society magazine. But he was certainly on the lookout for new business opportunities as J Hogg & Sons was struggling to keep going.

On the evening of Wednesday 4 August 1869, John Hogg walked the half a mile from his home in York Street, Covent Garden, to Great Queen Street. I wonder how nervous he felt as his stood outside Thomas Sandby's original impressive Hall and admired the recently completed extension in the severely classical style of Frederick Cockerell. He must have felt that the greatly extended Freemasons' Hall showed how popular the Order he was about to join had become. He would have known that HRH Prince Albert Edward, Prince of Wales had recently become a Mason and that he was about to enter the building where the Marquess of Ripon presided as Grand Master. Later that evening he became an Entered Apprentice in Oak Lodge No. 190 on the roll of the United Grand Lodge of England (UGLE). In the following November he was passed to the degree of a Fellow raft and by December he was made a Master Mason. His pleasure in his Masonic preferment must, however, have been tempered by the fact that in the New Year the family firm of James Hogg & Sons went bankrupt. It had not published a new book since the illustrated book of biographical sketches of great English statesmen entitled *The Men at the Helm* in 1863. Its only ongoing source of income was the sales of its two monthly magazines and *London Society*, which had once enjoyed a circulation of 25,000 a month but had been haemorrhaging cash.

However, John's venture into independent publishing under the A Lewis imprint had given him enough private reserves to be able to publish a biography of Bismark, under the imprint John Hogg & Co. But he hedged his bets by also publishing an illustrated edition of *The Revolution and Siege of Paris, with the elections, and entry of the Prussians, in 1870-71* by Percival Brine under his separate and unacknowledged imprint A Lewis. This was successful enough for him to buy out the assets of James Hogg & Sons from its creditors and incorporate its book backlist, without the loss-making magazines, into John Hogg & Co.

John now developed a new venture for A Lewis. He had the idea of publishing a ritual book for the use of Freemasons. Richard Carlile had published his *Manual of Freemasonry* in 1845 which contains all the rituals of the Craft Degree, but Carlile was not a Freemason and had published his book as an exposé. Nevertheless Hogg would have noticed that it was widely used by Freemasons to help them learn their ritual words. But Hogg had a revolutionary idea. He decided that he would publish not just the words but

"EMULATION" WORKING.

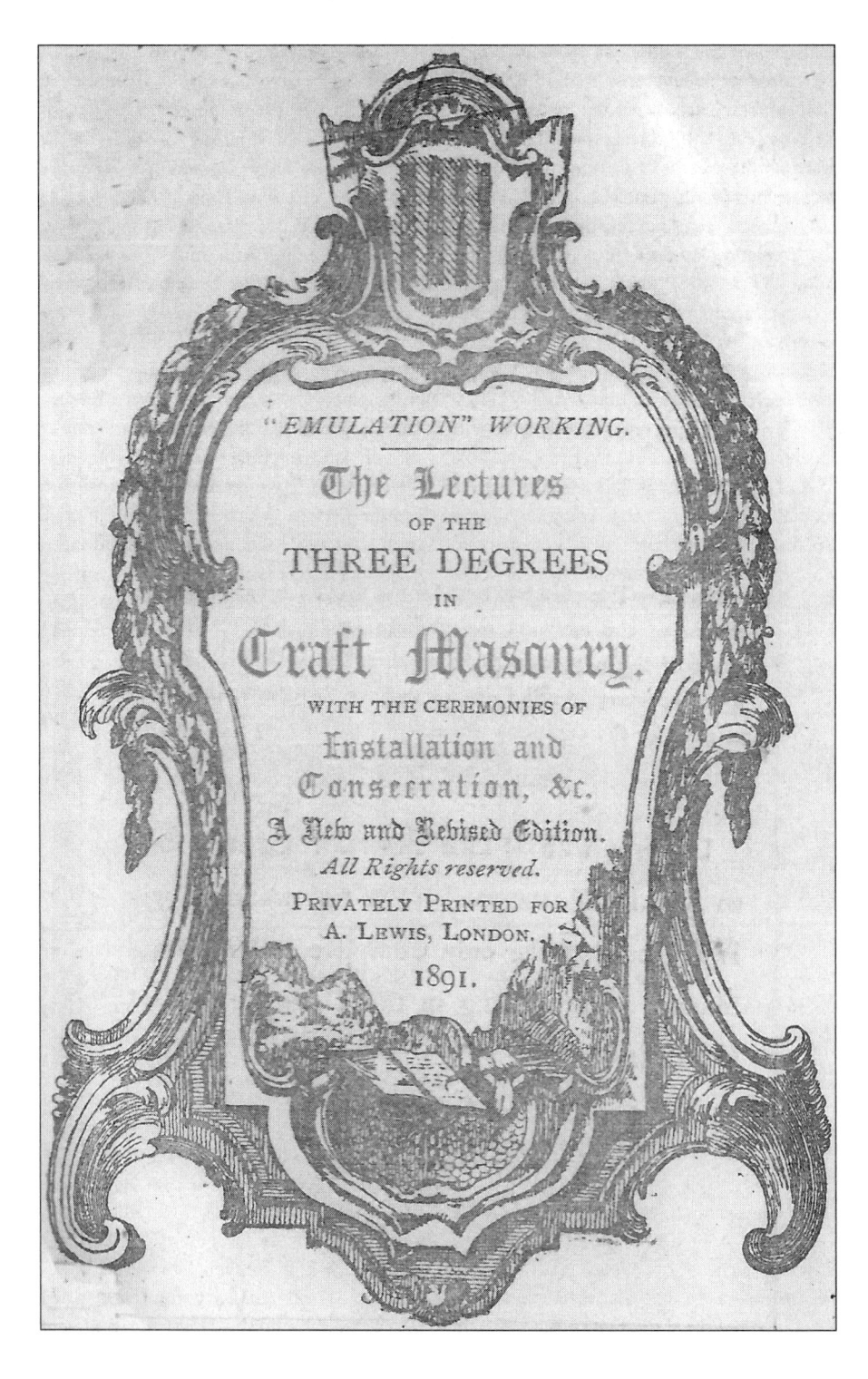

The Lectures
OF THE
THREE DEGREES
IN
Craft Masonry.

WITH THE CEREMONIES OF

Installation and
Consecration, &c.

A New and Revised Edition.

All Rights reserved.

PRIVATELY PRINTED FOR
A. LEWIS, LONDON.

1891.

also illustrations of the Tracing Boards for the Brethren to study as they learned their parts in the ritual. His main concern was how Grand Lodge would react to such a book. He was not prepared to risk personal censure by publishing it under his own name, John Hogg & Co., but instead used his successful little side venture A Lewis. And this was how A Lewis published their first ritual book, complete with illustrations of the Tracing Boards, establishing A Lewis (Masonic Publishers) Ltd, as a publisher of rituals and Tracing Boards.

Over the next 15 years Lewis published a series of Masonic books. Eventually UGLE became reconciled to the need for accurate ritual books and John Hogg went on to publish many Masonic books under the Lewis imprint as well as under the John Hogg & Co. imprint. He also occasionally published non-Masonic books under the Lewis name, the last being *Hand-Reading; or, the Science of Chirology. By an Adept. With illustrations* in 1896. From then on the Lewis imprint only published Masonic books.

John was very successful as a Masonic publisher and when he died in 1909, he left his business to his wife and nephew, his house in Iford Bridge, Christchurch, to Rosabella, his wife, and a legacy of some £28,000 to set up a charity known as The Printing Charity.

Lewis was run by the Hogg family until 1973 when at the grand old age of 109, A Lewis became part of Ian Allan Publishing and its name was changed to Lewis Masonic. Ritual books remain a priority at Lewis Masonic, but the company's focus has grown to embrace all areas of Masonic publishing and the tradition of illustrating Masonic ideas with Masonic symbols, which Bro. John Hogg introduced into British Masonic Publishing, continues.

Acknowledgements

I would like to thank the team at Lewis Masonic: Martin Faulks for proposing the idea and managing the production; Pip Faulks for editing the text. Will Kiestler for his hard work in developing the original concept and sharing his challenging thinking; and Delyth and Alex Jamieson for their help with the illustrations.

I also thank my agents Bill Hamiliton and Charlie Brotherstone of A M Heath Ltd for all their hard work in making sure the project came to fruition.

My brother Masons of the Lodge of Living Stones have helped me study and understand the symbols and been a sounding board for many of my ideas, and I thank them for the regular intellectual stimulation of our Lodge meetings and discussions.

And finally I would like to thank my family for their continuing support of my writing efforts.

About the Author

Dr. Robert Lomas has written several cult classics about Freemasonry and science, including *The Invisible College*, *Freemasonry and the Birth of Modern Science*, *The Man who Invented the Twentieth Century*, *Turning the Hiram Key*, *Turning the Solomon Key*, and *Turning the Templar Key*. His work with co-author Christopher Knight in *The Hiram Key* series was used by novelist Dan Brown to create characters and symbols in his bestsellers *The Da Vinci Code* and *The Lost Symbol*. And some Freemasons believe Lomas is the inspiration for the protagonist, Dr Robert Langdon.

Lomas holds a First Class Honours degree in electronic engineering and a Ph.D. for his research into solid-state physics and crystalline structures. He has established himself as one of the world's leading authorities on the history of science, and lectures on information systems and research methods at Bradford University's world-ranking school of management. He is a popular speaker on the Masonic lecture circuit, has been a regular speaker at the Orkney Science Festival, and is much in demand for live Webcast lectures to Masonic groups around the world.

Bibliography

Arnheim, R. *Visual Thinking*. California: University of California Press, Berkeley, 1969.

Cann R, et al: "L Polymorphic sites and mechanisms of evolution in human mitochondrial DNA," Genetics, p. 106, 479-99, 1984.

Dawkins, R. *The Ancestor's Tale*. London: Wiedenfield and Nicholson. 2005,

DeGroot, *The Bomb a Life*, London: Jonathon Cape, 2004.

Edelman, G M. *Wider Than the Sky: A Revolutionary View of Consciousness*. London: Penguin, 2004.

Edwards, B. *Drawing on the Right Side of the Brain*. London: Fontana/Collins, 1987.

Gimbutas, M. *The Living Goddess*. Los Angeles: University of California Press, 1999.

Gimbutas, M. *The Language of the Goddess*. London: Thames and Hudson, 2001.

Gourlay, K. *Dating the Kirkwall Scroll*. Daily Telegraph. July 2000.

Hackwell, W. J. *Signs, Letters and Words*. New York: Charles Scribner's Sons, 1989.

Jacobs. J. *The Economy of Cities*. London: Pelican, 1968.

Jammer, M. *Einstein and Religion: Physics and Theology*. New Jersey: Princeton University Press, 2004.

Jung, C G. *Man and his Symbols*. London: Aldus, 1964

Logan, G. *Knowth and the Passage Tombs of Ireland*. London: Thames & Hudson, 1986.

Lomas, R and Knight, C. *Uriel's Machine*. London: Arrow, 1999.

Lomas, R. *The Invisible College*. London: Transworld, 2009

Lomas, R. *Turning the Hiram Key*. London: Lewis Masonic, 2005.

Lomas, R. *Turning the Templar Key*. London: Lewis Masonic, 2009.

McGilchrist. *The Master and His Emissary*. Connecticut: Yale University Press, 2009.

Mellaart, J. *Çatalhöyük*. London: Thames & Hudson, 1967.

Mithen, S. *The Prehistory of the Mind*. London: Phoenix, 1996.

Penrose, R. *The Road to Reality*. London: Vintage, 2004.

Plato, *Phaedo* 75b

Renfrew, C and Bahn. P. *Archaeology, Theories, Methods and Practice*. London: Thames & Hudson, 1998.

Renfrew, C. *Bronze Age Migrations in the Aegean*. London: Birchall, 1973.

Rouse Ball, W.W. *A Short Account of the History of Mathematics*. New York: Dover Press, 1908.

Schmandt-Besserat, D. *How Writing Came About*. Houston: University of Texas Press, 1996.

Shreeve, James. *The Neanderthal Enigma*. William Morrow & Co. 1995.

Sykes B. *The Seven Daughters of Eve*. London: Bantam, 2001

Wallis, J. *A Defence of the Royal Society*. London: Private Pamphlet, 1678.

Williams, D L. *The Mind in the Cave*. London: Thames and Hudson, 2004.

Zimmerman, D. *Top Secret Exchange: the Tizard Mission and the Scientific War*. McGill-Queen's Press - MQUP, 1996

Websites (as accessed June 2013)

http://plato.stanford.edu/entries/newton-principia/

http://www.archive.org/details/TheWhetstoneOfWitte

http://www.catalhoyuk.com/archive_reports/1997/ar97_03.html

http://www.isaacnewton.ca/gen_scholium/scholium.htm

http://www.maths.ox.ac.uk/about/history

http://www.maths.tcd.ie/pub/HistMath/People/Newton/RouseBall/RB_Newton.html

http://www-history.mcs.st-andrews.ac.uk/Biographies/Wallis.htm